Jesus an

Jesus and the Scrolls

by
Ken Clayton

This book is a revised and re-titled edition of *Jesus Identified*

Ken Clayton 1992 ©

ISBN: 0 906463 01 7

Typeset and designed by The Word Shop, Bury, Lancs. BL9 0TD
Printed in Great Britain by: BPCC Hazells Ltd
Member of BPCC Ltd
Published by Belvedere Fine Publishing Co., P.O. Box 27,
Wilmslow, Cheshire, England.

Contents

Appreciation

I am grateful to the following publisher for permission to quote from the following book used in the research for *Jesus and the Scrolls*.

The Essene Writings from Qumran by Professor A. Dupont-Sommer. Published by Basil Blackwell of Oxford, OX4 1JF

Dedication

This book is dedicated first to my family – my wife Denise and my children Susan, Robert and Jill.

Second, to Professor Dupont-Sommer without whose book *The Essene Writings from Qumran* I might not have continued my researches.

Third, to the local library service at Handforth, Wilmslow and Stockport whose choice of books was so helpful to me.

CHAPTER ONE

Jesus and Qumrangate

Identify this man:

   He was a Jewish Rabbi.
   He lived approximately 2,000 years ago.
   He claimed to be the Son of God.
   He opposed the Pharisees.
   To avoid their persecution, he hid.
   He was betrayed by a friend.
   He was arrested.
   His followers deserted him.
   This happened at the time of two High Priests.
   He was brought before the High Priest for judgement.
   He was crucified.
   This was at the time of the Passover.
   He returned and appeared to his followers.

If your answer is 'Jesus Christ' then congratulations are in order.

   But not for you.

   They are for the Christian Churches whose determination to conceal the truths about the origins of Christianity have been successful.

   I have been describing a man referred to in the Dead Sea Scrolls as the Teacher of Righteousness. He was a figure highly revered by the Essene sect. He was crucified in 63 BC, 93 years before the supposed death of Jesus in AD 30.

   The Churches know full well that Jesus was the Essene Teacher and that their teachings about the origins of Christianity must be wrong. But they say nothing. The Dead Sea Scrolls were found in 1947 and the years that followed.

However 75 per cent of the translations remain unpublished. Why?

It has been suggested, with good reason, that the translations are being suppressed because they would make it clear, beyond any doubt, that the Christian Jesus was the Essene Teacher. It seems appropriate to coin a word to convey the seriousness of the deception and 'Qumrangate', based on Qumran, the Essene headquarters and 'Watergate' the political scandal that rocked the U.S.A., fits neatly. There is, however, one significant difference, because whereas the Watergate scandal was confined to the U.S.A., the Scroll revelations reach out to all parts of the Christian world.

The wording of one passage from the unpublished Scrolls has been leaked. It bears a striking resemblance to verses in the Gospel according to Luke. Consider the wording of these texts:

Taken from the unpublished Scroll and referring to the Teacher of Righteousness	*Taken from the Gospel according to Luke and referring to Jesus*
He shall be great upon the earth. He shall be called the Son of God and they shall call him the Son of the Most High	He will be great and will be called the Son of the Most High (chapter 1: 32) . . . and will be called holy, the Son of God (chapter 1: 35)

This is just a solitary example from a volume of evidence which links the two men.

There are other facts about the life of Jesus which are being concealed. He was the illegitimate son of Mary Magdalene, his principal betrayer was Peter and he did not die on the cross. Further, when we examine the writings of Paul, there can be no doubt that a writer called Theophilus was the hand behind some of the writing attributed to Paul.

Christianity is a very simple form of Esseneism taken to the gentiles by the resourceful Essenes after their camp at Qumran had been destroyed by Roman soldiers in AD 68. I know it; the Churches know it.

The scale of the deception is enormous. On the one hand, we have a Church which is devoted to truth, honesty and righteousness. On the other hand, we find the same Church exposed as one having knowledge which has been deliberately concealed. In the final chapter, I set out the reasons which, perhaps, have motivated the Church to suppress the publication of the Scrolls. The risks of revealing them were of such proportions that the Church probably feared that when the laity knew the extent of the concealment, the future of Christianity would be at risk. The Church faces turbulent times ahead, quite unprecedented for an organisation which has sailed serenely through 2,000 years with barely a tremor. But it will recover.

The strength of the Church lies not in the archbishops, bishops and their acolytes, but in the laity. Their simple but unassailable belief that there must be a loving creator behind this quite amazing universe will hold the Church together. In the final chapter, I set out what changes there might be to the teaching of the Church. Then, with so little to separate them, perhaps there might come the unexpected reward for 2,000 years of misunderstanding – the unification of the Christian Churches. Co-operation between the Churches leading to a strong and vibrant united Church, which could expand its influence and bring the new Christianity to a wider audience.

The teaching of Jesus – encompassed by the injunction 'Love thy neighbour' – together with a more realistic understanding of our relationship with God might help many more to live happier lives and make a greater contribution to the welfare of their fellow humans.

That would be a prize, indeed.

CHAPTER TWO

Jesus, the Essenes and the Scandal

Although this is a book about the origins of Christianity, it is more of a detective story than a religious book. If I quote a text from the Bible, it will not be to expound some involved theological belief but to explain what real-life situation I deduce from the quotation. It will be for you to decide whether this is logical and reasonable.

The original research started because I wanted to know exactly what evidence there was for believing in Jesus Christ. I was not a regular attender at my local church nor did I believe in miracles and the power of prayer. However, I did believe in God and that a man called Jesus had lived at some time. It seemed to me unlikely that the stories about him had been made up, as this would have involved a conspiracy beyond the ability of men of those times to organise and bring to such a successful conclusion. Despite this, there were some very odd stories in the Gospels which did not ring true, and which seemed to have been fabricated by man rather than inspired by God.

So, I went to my local library.

I took out an assortment of books by leading theologians and was amazed to find how scanty was the evidence and how little they knew about those early years of the 1st century AD.

Many of their explanations were quite unconvincing. I spent over two years reading and re-reading the whole of the New Testament and became more and more convinced, as my reading continued, that there was something basically wrong with the Jesus story. Never for a moment did I suspect that, like water under a microscope, the seemingly clear writings of the Old and New Testaments contained within them so many hidden secrets.

The breakthrough came quite unexpectedly. I had read that when a number of the Dead Sea Scrolls had been published there were some who thought that the Teacher of Righteousness, a figure worshipped by the Essene sect, bore a remarkable resemblance to the Jesus Christ of our New Testament. There were indeed similarities; but the differences, including the beliefs and the chronology of the two men, seemed to satisfy almost everyone that although one might have influenced the other, they were two different men. For example, the Teacher of Righteousness lived in the 1st century BC whereas Jesus was active in the 1st century AD.

I decided to read up on the Essenes and was most fortunate in the book I chose. I have to thank Stockport Municipal Library for having the good judgement to purchase *The Essene Writings from Qumran* by a French theologian, Professor Dupont-Sommer. Like another theologian who I grew to respect enormously, R. Travers Herford, if he could not explain a difficulty, he admitted it. If a damaged text proved difficult to decipher, he explained why he chose a particular translation. He was never authoritarian, expecting his ideas and opinions to be accepted without question, and he never talked down to his audience.

My experience of life is that when faced with a problem outside one's special subject it is not a bad idea to consult the experts. The trouble is that expert opinion is not quite as expert as it is supposed to be. So, I read a number of books about the Dead Sea Scrolls and then I chose my expert of experts – the man whose views seemed to make more sense than the rest. Professor Dupont-Sommer was my expert. His book proved, for me, to be a fascinating study of a quite amazingly influential sect.

I was, however, disappointed to find that whilst recognising the remarkable similarities between the events in the life of the Essene Teacher and Jesus, he rejected the idea that they were the same man. Nevertheless, I then returned to the New Testament and decided to study the letters of Paul because, despite the uncertainty which surrounded the life of Jesus, no one seemed to doubt that Paul had been active during the 1st century AD or that the letters attributed to him were, for the most part, genuine. I thought that perhaps somewhere among the voluminous correspondence there would be a clue that would take me a little further on the road to the truth. I found it in the Letter to the Galatians.

This was the key which opened the door to the truth about the origins of Christianity and which then opened door after door, leading to a virtual maze of corridors. The conclusion I drew was that the chronology of Christianity was wrong and that our present understanding of the New Testament was just a mirror image of the truth.

The test of a theory is whether the parts fit together, and whether it answers all the questions without raising others to which there are no easy answers. This theory raised no such questions.

The clue in the Letter to the Galatians suggested that Paul could have trained as an Essene; another verse in Philippians supported this. Suddenly, Paul's association with the Essenes and his worship of Jesus Christ made possible a link between Jesus and the Essene Teacher of Righteousness. Now, according to the Acts of the Apostles Paul was involved in some way with the persecution of Christians, and whilst there were no secular accounts of Christians being harassed in Greece, Turkey or Judea, I knew that the Essenes had suffered at the hands of the Romans. Even after the Essene headquarters at Qumran had been destroyed in AD 68, there had been conflict between the Essenes and the Romans. What had happened to the Essenes who had escaped from Qumran and those who had lived in other parts of the Middle East? From being one of the most fanatical, righteous and proselytising sects of any age, the Essenes simply disappeared from the theological scene. Nothing was heard from those persecuted Essenes, but much was heard about the trouble and violence faced by the early Christians. Here, then, was another link. Paul's possible association with the Essenes led to the thought that perhaps the early Christians were simply Essenes on the run from Roman persecution.

If this was correct, then the devastating conclusion to be

drawn was that our understanding of those early years is completely mistaken. If Jesus was the Teacher of Righteousness then the chronology of Christianity, including the activities of Paul, as presented to us by the Church and unquestioned by past and present theologians, would have to be wrong. In fact, as I read more, I became increasingly concerned at the misconceptions of the Church. For example, they thought:

— that Luke and Matthew copied from Mark's Gospel, against clear evidence to the contrary;

— that Jesus lived in the 1st century AD, when not one writer of this time referred to him;

— that the Virgin Mary was the mother of Jesus, without even considering, let alone disclosing to the laity, that evidence from the Talmud identifies Mary Magdalene as the mother of Jesus;

— that Judas was the sole betrayer of Jesus, when the Gospels make clear the friction between Jesus and Peter and that Peter was the principal betrayer;

— that Paul was the sole writer of the Pauline letters, when an analysis of their style and content points clearly to at least three identifiable writers being involved;

— that Psalms and Isaiah were written before 500 BC, on the basis of very little, if any, conclusive evidence.

Theologians are highly intelligent and superbly qualified people, but in important areas of theology – those which could have led them to the truth – they have refused to challenge the traditional beliefs which have come down to them through the centuries.

Even worse, as my reading and research continued it became obvious that there appeared to be a puzzling reluctance by those responsible for the translation of certain Dead Sea Scrolls to publish the results. The Scrolls were found in 1947, and yet in 1992 there still remain some translations which are being withheld from the public. The suspicion has been expressed that the reason for the delay is that the translations would reveal Jesus to be the Teacher of Righteousness. It is a scandal which the Church has tried to play down by the most effective weapon ever used against criticism – silence. If there is no response to the critics, then the public concludes that, perhaps after all, it was much ado about nothing. If there had been anything serious to worry about, someone, somewhere, would have raised his voice and been heard.

What is certain is that it is not really necessary to have these unpublished translations, as I hope the evidence given in this book will prove.

As my reading continued, the whole of the New Testament began to take on a new meaning. Many parts which were previously unintelligible now made sense when read against the Essene background. The Gospel stories cross-checked with the Dead Sea Scrolls which, in turn, cross-checked with certain Old Testament books which no one had previously attributed to the Essene sect.

Such is the brief outline of the beginnings of this book. I hope that you will look on this as a story of detection rather than a theological book, and that you will find it as interesting to read as I found it to research and write.

One final point: in the course of the book I will repeat some of the evidence given earlier. It would be unfair, I think, to suppose that the reader will necessarily recall all the relevant information, particularly as Jewish history will be quite unfamiliar to the average person. I hope that such repetitions as there are will be looked upon as an attempt to be helpful and in no way disrespectful.

CHAPTER THREE

Theologians

The easy answers to difficult questions, as given by William Barclay, a Scottish theologian, persuaded me that theologians were not to be trusted. Barclay was the archetypal apologist for Christianity. No matter what the problem, he had a ready answer. In his book dealing with the Gospels, he explained why Mark's Gospel was not written until approximately AD 65, a date generally agreed for its appearance. After all, one would expect the Gospel to have been written very soon after the death of Jesus. Two of the reasons given by Barclay for the delay were:

1. The sheer cost of producing handwritten gospels. He estimated the cost per line which a scribe might have charged, and, relating it to the number of lines in the Gospel, he reached his verdict: the disciples would find the cost prohibitive.
2. Jesus was expected to return in 40 years time. In these circumstances, why bother writing a gospel account of his ministry?

At first, I was deeply impressed with the trouble Barclay had taken to calculate the cost involved, and also with his perception that this would be a problem. The brain, weighing the explanation, finds it reasonable; we all know that everything has to be paid for. A moment's reflection, however, showed it to be nonsense. Would cost be a problem? What scribe would overcharge, if he charged at all, for producing copies of an account describing the ministry of Jesus? Here was a man who was a miracle worker. He was the Son of God, the creator of the universe. Money was but an earthly consideration. Working for God in this way could provide heavenly benefits which would far outweigh the earthly. Quite contrary to Barclay's proposition, here was a positive reason for wanting to commence writing at the earliest opportunity.

Furthermore, if the writing was delayed because of the expected return of Jesus in 40 years time, why should they decide to produce a Gospel with only five years to go? The reader, trusting the theologian, tends to accept his explanations without too much thought because he is the expert; he is the one who has devoted his life to researching the origins of Christianity and his opinions on his specialist subject are not lightly challenged.

Our theologians have failed us. It is important that the general public recognises that, intellectuals though our theologians may be, on the very subject on which they should be consulted, they are unreliable. Their thinking is so channelled that any challenge to traditional beliefs is rejected. They reason that the Bible is the word of God, and that the beliefs which have been passed down from the 1st century AD come from those close to the events they have recorded. God's word and this evidence cannot be wrong. *Ipso facto*, any new approach to Christian thinking is, by their definition, unworthy of consideration. This attitude is now being seen in the new easy-to-read Bibles where words such as 'elect' and 'perfect', both words used by the Essenes, are rejected in favour of equivalents which conceal the Essene link. By unnecessarily not using the original words, the writers might be thought to be deliberately pointing people away from the Essene connection.

The suppression of some of the Dead Sea Scrolls has been criticised because of the suspicion that they would reveal links between Jesus and the Essene Teacher of Righteousness which the Church is anxious to hide. In one recent instance, certain theologians who had access to the translations assured television viewers that there was nothing in the Scrolls which would upset Christians. Within three months of the interview, reports had leaked that one Scroll contained a reference to a 'leader of a community' being 'put to death' together with

16

mention of 'piercings' and 'wounds'.

From another source it became known that one of the unpublished Scroll translations included verses which were almost identical to those in the Gospel of Luke. They referred to the Essene Teacher of Righteousness and Jesus as 'the Son of the Most High' and the 'Son of God'. Most reasonable people, on reading these links, would begin to question whether Jesus could have been the Essene Teacher.

It is not that the Church or the theologians do not recognise the possibility. Although there are a number of times in this book when I am critical of theologians, I am not denying their undoubted scholarship. They are very clever men and of proven outstanding academic ability. Even at grass roots level, ministers and priests have been educated to university standards. My own investigation into the New Testament writings would have been quite impossible without the skilled translations provided by these men and the research they have done in the service of Christianity. Why have they failed us?

The theologian was probably attracted to Christianity at an early age, and this interest doubtless continued into adulthood where his beliefs were reinforced at high school and university. People hold on to their religious and political beliefs tenaciously. They do not like to hear or read anything which might undermine their confidence. If the facts point in the direction of an unpleasant truth which they cannot answer, they run away. They close their minds; if they do not want to see, they do not see. It is not an uncommon response. So, whilst admiring their talent, I feel justified in criticising their judgement.

They must know that the unpublished, suppressed Scrolls reveal secrets relating to Christianity – but they say nothing.

They have not put any pressure on those who are suppressing publication of these unpublished Scrolls – they have done nothing.

Why have none of these problems been discussed from the pulpit so that the laity are aware of the problems – because they prefer silence.

With the information now being leaked by sources close to

the unpublished Scrolls pointing even more clearly to the Essene/Christianity link, the original misjudgement of the Church is now moving into an area which can only be described as highly sensitive. It will not be long before the Church will have to defend itself against charges of deliberate concealment, and there can be little doubt that their arguments and explanations will be heard by a very sceptical public.

This is unfortunate, because, as I hope to persuade the reader in the final chapter, there is a God and Jesus was very much part of His plan.

The sad verdict on most – but not all – theologians is that they have allowed their strong beliefs to override their undoubted scholarship.

CHAPTER FOUR

The Historical Evidence for Jesus Christ

From the detail given in this chapter the reader will see what minimal evidence there is for a man called Jesus Christ who lived in the 1st century AD.

What the early writers have to say about Jesus is very important. If they give accounts which substantiate those given in the Gospels, then the Jesus story becomes increasingly believable. On the other hand, if they provide little information then, depending upon what is said, the Gospels become much less credible. If the historians say nothing then this is also important, because silence is often valid evidence – it is sometimes possible to recognise the truth of a situation as much by what people do not say, as by what they do say.

The position is that the only evidence we have about Christ which identifies him with the 1st century AD is that provided by the New Testament. When we find, as we shall, that the historians of the day, with the exception of Josephus, seem unaware of the presence and activities of Jesus in the 1st century AD, we are entitled to question the chronology of the New Testament writings. Let us see what they have to say.

Pliny the Elder (*c.* AD 23–79)

Pliny the Elder was a noted historian. He makes no reference to Christianity, and, although some of his histories have been lost, had he done so it is unlikely that some of his contemporaries would have failed to quote him on a subject as important as a new Jewish sect.

19

Pliny the Younger (c. AD 61–113)

Nephew of Pliny the Elder, Pliny the Younger was a political figure and historian whose correspondence is important. The reference made by Pliny the Younger to Christians is of interest for two reasons. First, it is the shortest, and secondly, despite its brevity, it is possibly the most illuminating. Pliny wrote a report to Trajan in AD 112 in which he said that Christians appeared to be harmless people who met at daybreak and who sang hymns to their Messiah.

In the first place, this refers to the activities of Christians in the early part of the 2nd century, so that whilst it is evidence for Christianity it tells us nothing about the period when Jesus lived.

In fact, these few words, seemingly so innocent, give us evidence of a different kind – that the so-called Christians were practicing the Essene ritual of holding a morning prayer meeting at daybreak. This was an important beginning to the Essene day, and of course fits in with our proposition that the first Christians were simply ex-Essenes who were displaced from their communes.

This is the only reference which Pliny the Younger makes to Christianity. Here was a man whose uncle was a historian and who would have known of any leader of Jews who had performed miracles and made his mark upon the Jewish scene as Jesus is said to have done in the Gospel stories. Does not the evidence of silence point to both Pliny the Elder and Pliny the Younger having heard nothing about Jesus?

Suetonius

In the 2nd century, Suetonius made a reference to a revolt of Jews in Rome during the reign of Claudius, who was in office from AD 41–54. Suetonius wrote that this was at the 'instigation of Chrestus'. This has been taken to mean a Christian revolt, although this is not what Suetonius said. Taken at its face value, the reference means that a man called Chrestus started a revolt.

Now, Chrestus was not an unusual name and so this could have been a non-Christian revolt.

However, it can also be taken as meaning 'the cause of the disturbance was Chrestus' or 'Christus', in which case it could mean 'the cause was the Jewish Messiah'. There were certainly no Christians in Rome at that time, but I believe that there were Essenes. They may well have been involved. The evidence, however, is not proof that Jesus Christ was crucified in AD 30, which is what we are concerned about in this chapter. Further, this evidence is not inconsistent with Jesus having been crucified, as I believe he was, in 63 BC.

Tacitus (AD 55 – *c.* AD 120)

According to Tacitus, Nero accused 'the Christians' of setting fire to Rome in AD 64. He said that they derived their name and origin from Christ who, 'in the reign of Tiberius had suffered death by the sentence of the Procurator Pontius Pilate'.

This is not reliable evidence.

Writing around AD 100, Tacitus was reliant on information which had come down to him. He was certainly not an eye-witness to the life of Jesus. Secondly, the detail he gives looks as though it came from the Gospel of Luke. The tradition that Jesus had been killed at the time of Pontius Pilate had ample time to reach Rome, but as a witness Tacitus is so remote that no reliance can be placed upon his evidence.

Suetonius also refers to the persecution of Christians in Nero's reign and writes, 'the Christians were executed – a sect of men who had embraced a new and criminal superstition'. Criminal superstition is hardly the way to describe the true Christian. Nevertheless, it probably describes pretty accurately the feelings which the Romans had towards a sect, the Essenes, which believed that within a relatively short space of time, there would be death and everlasting fire for everyone except themselves.

Tacitus was a noted Roman historian and in his *Historiae*, a history of the Roman Empire, he included anything of outstanding interest in the lands which were under Roman rule. He makes no reference to the rise of a Christian sect in Judea and the sole reference to Christians in his writings is the one we have quoted. It is vague and inconclusive, and points to the sect being Essene rather than Christian.

Flavius Josephus (AD 37–100)

Josephus was a noted historian who wrote *Antiquities of the Jews* and *The Jewish Wars*. In his first book, *The Jewish Wars*, he covers the period of Jesus's ministry but makes no mention of him. Here is a dedicated historian who has access to influential people among the Roman and Jewish hierarchy, and yet in the very book which covers those early years of the 1st century, he finds no place for a detailed reference to Jesus.

In the *Antiquities of the Jews*, however, there are two short passages about Jesus. The first is from Book 18 : 3 : 3. 'And there appeared at this time Jesus, a wise man, if indeed he may be called a man. He was a doer of marvellous acts, a teacher of such men as received the truth with delight. And many Jews and many, too, of the Hellenic race he brought over to himself. He was the Christ. And when, on the evidence of the most influential among us, Pilate had condemned him to the Cross, his first adherents did not forsake him; for he appeared to them on the third day alive again, divinely inspired prophets having foretold this and a myriad other wondrous things about him. And even now the tribe of Christians, named from him, is not extinct.'

A noted scholar, Solomon Zeitlin completely rejects the authenticity of this passage on a number of grounds. For example, it is far too favourable to the Christian view; no Jew would be likely to call Jesus 'the Christ'. Also, when Josephus repeats anything, he invariably introduces it with the phrase, 'this is the same . . .'. He does not do this with a reference to Jesus found later on in Book 20 : 9 : 1, which reads, ' . . . and having brought thither the brother of Jesus, him called Christ (James was his name) and some certain others . . .'. Finally, Zeitlin points out that nobody referred to this passage until Eusebius mentions it, and because Eusebius is the only writer to use the description 'tribe of Christians', he concludes that it was Eusebius who interpolated this passage into the *Antiquities of the Jews*.

There are a number of reasons for thinking that the first

passage in particular, and possibly the second, have been added by a Christian scribe when copying out the book by hand.

1. A 3rd century writer named Origen was anxious to persuade readers that the life of Jesus had been a reality and not fiction. He makes reference to the second passage, involving James, but not to the first.

   Now, Origen had read the book by Josephus.

   He was looking for evidence from an early historian that Jesus had lived.

   It was a longish passage.

   How could he have missed it?

   The conclusion must be, I think, that the original book did not contain that particular text.

   It is widely acknowledged by theologians that Christian scribes, when re-copying religious or historical writings, used the opportunity to add their own contribution so that readers would be influenced by the copyist's beliefs. In Chapter 8, 'The Gospels', I quote the 21st chapter of John's Gospel as an example.

2. Josephus is said to have been trained as an Essene. It is almost certain that he would have known that Jesus was the Essene Teacher of Righteousness. In these circumstances he would not – could not – have written the first passage. He was, as evidenced by his books, a scribe. He was probably involved in that capacity with the Essenes, and as a result of copying scrolls was likely to be very well informed about the Essene Teacher. He also wrote about Onias the Just, who I believe to have been the 'Teacher of Righteousness'. Although he did not describe him as such, it must be remembered that the Essenes were sworn to secrecy to reveal nothing about their sect. By the time that Josephus wrote his *Antiquities of the Jews* and *The Jewish Wars*, the sect had been expelled from Qumran and dispersed. He may, therefore, have felt able to refer to Onias by name, but not to reveal anything further about the man. What he does tell us about Onias, and did not tell us about Jesus in the first passage, squares up with the Gospel accounts of the death of Jesus.

3. Josephus was a writer who was keen to record the history of the Jews. Had there been a man such as Jesus, living in the 1st century AD, who had performed miracles and who was supposedly the Son of God, it is difficult to believe that Josephus would have not written about Jesus in much more detail. With Onias, his vows of secrecy restricted his comment. He was under no oath of secrecy relative to the life of Jesus. In my opinion, it is unbelievable that Josephus would write such a short passage about Jesus when there was so much in his life which would be of interest to students of Jewish history. There were sensational events – how could he virtually ignore them?

4. The particular passage referring to Jesus has all the looks of being interpolated. The preceding paragraph (the second) deals with the massacre of some Jews. The paragraph following the passage starts: 'About the same time another terrible misfortune confounded the Jews . . .'. The two chapters have all the appearance of the second being followed naturally by the fourth. Instead, we find the third paragraph, relating to Jesus, between them.

5. Writers such as Iranaeus, Tertullian and Clement of Alexandria did not refer to the passage from Josephus. This is further evidence of ignorance of the text by those who should have known it, and, reasonably, would have quoted it.

For all these reasons, I, too, regard the Josephus passage as an interpolation.

Philo Judaeus

Philo was a noted Jewish philosopher and writer who lived in the 1st century AD. He would almost certainly have referred to someone who had made a mark on recent Jewish history. There is no mention of Jesus in any of the writings of Philo.

Justus of Tiberias

Another noted historian of the time was Justus of Tiberias. Justus wrote in the second half of the 1st century AD and made no references to Jesus or Christianity in his writings.

We do not have any copies of his works, but a Christian writer commenting on them in the 9th century said that Justus made no reference to the appearance of Christ, his deeds or his miracles. We have to ask ourselves, yet again, why should this be? Can it really be that these able historians missed not only the man himself and his deeds, but the build up of the early Christian Church which took place during the years that followed Jesus's death, supposedly in AD 30?

We will now look at the evidence provided by the Apostolic Fathers. They are as follows:

1. Ignatius (1st–2nd century AD).
2. Polycarp (AD 69–155).
3. Clement of Rome (b. AD 96).

These writers were described as the Apostolic Fathers because they were thought of as the successors to Jesus's apostles. Their writings are of interest because they tell us what they knew about the Gospel stories. These three men were quite influential people in the early Church, so what they knew about Christianity and the early Christian writings is important. What is more important, however, is what they did not know.

Ignatius

As an example let us take Ignatius, who is said to have been thrown to the lions in Rome in about 117 AD. He wrote seven epistles. He should have known of all the Synoptic Gospels, which the majority of theologians date between AD 70 and AD 120. However, there is no reference anywhere in his epistles to any of these. He refers to Paul's Letter to the Ephesians and makes reference to 'a gospel' in some of his epistles, but there is no mention of the particular gospel he had in mind.

It could be that the Gospel he referred to was Matthew's, because there are verses in this which express ideas very similar to some to be found in the works of Ignatius. Ignatius wrote that: 'A star shone in heaven, brighter than any other star, its light was unspeakable and its strangeness caused amazement and all the other stars, with the sun and moon, became a chorus for that star, which outshone them all; all were troubled to know whence came this strange appearance, so unlike them'.

The nativity story in Matthew's Gospel links Jesus and the Star of Bethlehem in a very similar way. Matthew writes in 2 : 3 that, 'When Herod the king heard this, he was troubled . . .' and, referring to the three wise men, he writes in 2 : 10 that, 'When they saw the star they rejoiced exceedingly with great joy'. Being 'amazed' does not quite equate with 'rejoiced exceedingly' but these similarities (and the fact that Ignatius was the first to mention the virgin birth of Jesus and the first to name the mother of Jesus) lead some to suspect that Ignatius was the writer of Matthew's Gospel.

Polycarp

Polycarp, who wrote in the first half of the 2nd century AD is noted for a single epistle which shows some knowledge of the teaching of Jesus. Quotations which he uses suggest that this might have been gained from the Gospels of Matthew and Luke, although he could well have had access to the original Essene gospels. There is nothing in Polycarp's epistle which suggests that he acquired knowledge from special sources other than the Gospels.

Clement of Rome

Clement makes no mention of any particular Gospel, and it is apparent that, where it would have suited his purpose to quote from the Gospels, he chooses to use the Old Testament stories as his authority. Nevertheless, there is evidence that he has used sources which may have been used by those who compiled the Gospels. However, we would have expected a leading Christian like Clement to have had access to some of the Gospel stories and to have included in his writings some evidence that the Jesus Christ he knew was a man who lived some years previously – perhaps by reference to some saying or act which had not been covered by the Gospels. This, he does not provide.

Looking at the writings of the Apostolic Fathers, therefore, we find nothing that adds to our knowledge about Jesus. They only repeated stories which had been written elsewhere, and their evidence is no more informative and no more helpful than that provided by the early historians.

Conclusion

Looked at quite dispassionately, there is no credible evidence that Jesus lived in the 1st century AD. In *The Myth of God Incarnate*, John Hick, a noted theologian, commented on the 'confusion and uncertainty' which are faced when speaking of an historical Jesus. Further, he described the evidence for Jesus as 'fragmentary and ambiguous'. Considering the detail given in this chapter, I think that his comments could be described as a fair description of the position.

CHAPTER FIVE

Why the Chronology of Christianity is Wrong

In this chapter, I will explain why the people in the Gospel stories have been identified with the early years of the 1st century AD instead of the 1st century BC.

After the Essene camp at Qumran was overrun by the Romans in AD 68, some of the escaping Essenes took the Essene teachings of Jesus to the gentiles. It was a very simplified form of Esseneism which dealt with the life of Jesus and the injunctions to live a good life. They needed an account of the life of Jesus for their gentile converts. The similarities between the Gospels suggest that they were drawn from a common source – perhaps an Essene 'Gospel of Jesus'.

I discuss in a later chapter how the Gospels came to be written. As the reader will see, the secrecy adopted by the Essenes with regard to the names of people who played important parts in the life of Jesus and the Essene sect, presented problems to the compilers of the Gospels. They were looking into the distant past without recourse to the help we would get today from newspapers and libraries. Suppose, for example, we were to find an undated letter which made reference to a great War. We would rate World War I and World War II as meriting the description 'great', particularly if we knew they had been fought across the whole of Europe. The writer, however, may have been referring to the Napoleonic Wars. Without some identifying name such as Churchill, Lloyd George or Napoleon we could be completely mistaken.

Jesus was crucified in 63 BC, and the compilers were writing the Gospels perhaps around 100 AD, a distance of 163 years. Without the benefit of historical records we would have exactly the same difficulties linking events and people living in 1829. How many of us could name an event which happened in that year?

Let us examine the people and events which led to the ministry of Jesus being placed mistakenly in the 1st century AD.

John the Baptist

First, we will look at what is known about John the Baptist. I will then present the case for linking him with the reign of Alexander Jannaeus, who was in control of Judea during the period 104–78 BC. Our information comes from Josephus, the Gospels and the Jewish Talmud.

Josephus (writing around AD 80)

The reference to John the Baptist by Josephus is approximately 255 words in length and commences: 'Now some of the Jews thought that the destruction of Herod's army came from God and that very justly, as a punishment for what he did against John that was called the Baptist'.

Along with the accompanying passages, this places John the Baptist in a time-slot around the closing years of the 1st century BC. There is, therefore, a time gap of roughly 70 years between the traditional dating of John and the time-slot proposed by me – some time prior to the death of Queen Alexandra Salome in 67 BC.

Many believe that this passage from Josephus is an interpolation – an addition by a Christian scribe when copying out Josephus's book. The reasons for thinking so are as follows:

1. There is already suspicion that two references to Jesus by Josephus are interpolations. The presence of two suspected interpolations gives rise to the suspicion that the reference to John the Baptist is also a late addition.
2. We will call the passage referring to John 'Passage 2'.

The previous verses ('Passage 1') describe the army of Herod being destroyed, and it would be natural for Josephus to follow it by 'Passage 3' which explains why the army was beaten. Instead, the John the Baptist verses, Passage 2, interrupt the flow from Passage 1 to Passage 3.

3. Josephus was believed to have trained as an Essene under Banus. If he had received any information which suggested that John the Baptist was a contemporary of Herod he would have known it to be untrue.

4. The reason for the death of John given by Josephus differs from that given in the Gospels. According to Josephus, Herod feared the influence of John with the people and thought that John might inspire civil disorder. The Gospels attribute his death to his criticism of Herod for marrying the wife of his brother. This was regarded as unlawful. On this particular point, neither Josephus nor the Gospels are correct for the reasons I shall give.

The Gospels

It was John who introduced the ritual of baptismal washing to cleanse body and spirit. He may also have been the founder of the sect and the one who led pious Jewish dissidents into the wilderness – the Qumran area. There is Biblical support. The Gospels associate Isaiah 40 : 3 with John the Baptist. It reads: 'A voice cries "In the wilderness prepare the way of the Lord and make straight in the desert a highway for our God"'. Incidentally, it might be thought that in this passage 'the way' referred to was a path or clearance. In fact, 'the way' was how the Essenes described themselves and their lifestyle, and this is how the passage should be read. This is one of the many 'Esseneisms' in the New Testament.

The Talmud

References to John the Baptist which, like Josephus, seem to place him in the closing years of the 1st century BC can be found, for example, in Matthew 14 : 1–12. These verses describe the arrest of John because of his criticism of Herod. It was at the request of his step-daughter, Salome, that she be given the head of John. It is my contention that, although the name was correct, the identification was wrong. The Salome

30

who featured in this incident was Salome, the wife of King Alexander Jannaeus (104 – 78 BC). Although she was known as Queen Alexandra, having taken the feminised version of her husband's name, her original name was Salome.

There is a passage in the Jewish Talmud (b. Sanh. 107b) which specifically identifies Jesus with this period because it refers to an incident involving Jesus '. . . when Jannai the king killed our Rabbis . . .'. The passage is difficult to understand because, over a period of years, it has become confused either in the re-writing or the re-telling. Interestingly, in it an incident is described in which there is a reference to Alexandria (in Egypt). The suspicion arises that over the years the name of the lady became misunderstood so that Alexandria, the place, was written instead of Alexandra the woman.

Jesus and a companion – Jehoshua Ben Perahjah – are involved in a discussion and a lady is insulted. Although not named as such, I believe the companion to be John. I believe it is possible to distill a core truth from the confused Talmudic passage and it is this: that John the Baptist was executed because of an insult made to a leader of the Jews; this was not Herod, but King Alexander Jannaeus or Queen Alexandra Salome. The reasons for so thinking are as follows:

1. The overwhelming evidence throughout this book places Jesus – and, by association, John the Baptist – as being active during the reign of King Alexander Jannaeus.
2. The Talmudic passage places Jesus – and possibly John the Baptist – in the same period. Theologians have never been able to explain the Talmud reference to Jesus. In my opinion, and this applies here, the Talmud tradition is to be preferred to other writings. Even when distorted, there is usually some valuable truth to be wrested from the text.
3. John the Baptist and Jesus were known to each other. John speaks of Jesus as the one who 'is coming after me'. As the leader and prospective leader, it would be natural for them to accompany each other on at least some journeys. If so, then the companion – Jehoshua Ben Perahjah – in the Talmudic passage could have been John the Baptist.
4. Although the lady in the Talmud passage is described as

31

'innkeeper' or 'hostess' I think there must be a mistranslation here, probably as the result of a damaged Scroll. In Hebrew, the written word for 'hostess' is very similar to the word for 'wife'. There is, therefore, a conjunction of references to Alexander Jannaeus, Alexandria or Alexandra, and then the possibility of a mistranslation which might have originally referred to 'wife'. It could therefore be that the passage actually referred to Alexandra, the wife of Alexander Jannaeus.

It is unlikely in the extreme that an insult to a lady innkeeper would have qualified for inclusion in the Talmudic teaching. The lady in question simply must be someone of high status, and the Alexandria/Alexandra connection referred to earlier points to a possible link with the royal family ruling in the early years of the 1st century BC. I believe that this incident was the one responsible for John the Baptist being executed.

Interestingly, there is also a reference in the Talmud to Mary, the mother of Jesus, being connected to 'princes and rulers'. The Gospels also connect Mary with Elizabeth, who was of 'the daughters of Aaron' and therefore of the priestly tribe of Levi.

The evidence points clearly to Mary being born into a very influential family. By association with his mother, therefore, we would expect Jesus to move in royal circles. Hence, my suggestion that the insult mentioned above was not to a lady innkeeper but to Queen Alexandra Salome would not be inconsistent with the information we have about Jesus and his family roots.

For these reasons, I think that the Gospels mistakenly place John the Baptist in the period around the end of the 1st century BC. In my opinion, he is to be placed firmly in the first half of the 1st century BC, when he was killed as a result of an insult to Queen Alexandra Salome.

The two High Priests

In the opening verses of chapter 3 of his Gospel, Luke refers to leading Roman and Jewish leaders whose presence seems to date the ministry of Jesus firmly in the 1st century AD.

His reference to 'the High Priesthood of Annas and Caiaphas' as occurring in the year AD 29 is incorrect. The only year when both men held that office was AD 14 when the retiring Annas handed over responsibility to Caiaphas. The High Priesthood was never shared.

Information had obviously come to Luke that the death of Jesus occurred in the year when there were two High Priests. Looking back from AD 100 or later, Luke probably thought he had identified the period correctly when he found that Annas and Caiaphas, although not holding office together in the same year, at least were both alive at that time.

Had he had access to an earlier history of Judea, he would have found the year when there were two High Priests. They were in dispute and were very much involved in the death of Onias the Just (Jesus). On the death of their mother, Queen Alexandra Salome in 67 BC, Hyrcanus II was appointed High Priest but was deposed by his brother, Aristobulus II; the dispute continued until the arrival of Pompeius Magnus, the Roman general, who finally appointed Hyrcanus II to the office.

In the Essene Dead Sea Scrolls, there are bitter references to 'the Wicked Priest' who persecuted the Teacher of Righteousness, and it is my opinion that Hyrcanus II was the 'Wicked Priest'.

Luke therefore identified the wrong High Priests. They were Hyrcanus II and Aristobulus II, the quarrelsome brothers.

Tiberius Caesar (AD 14–37)

Again, in the opening verses to chapter 3, Luke says that in the 15th year of the reign of Tiberius Caesar, 'the word of God came to John [the Baptist]'. This suggests that John commenced his activities in AD 29 and conflicts with Matthew 3 : 1 which appears to describe John preaching shortly after the birth of Jesus. The only Caesar to be associated with the early development of the Essene movement was Julius Caesar, who formed the ruling triumvirate with Pompeius Magnus and Crassus in 60 BC. Luke, therefore, identified the wrong Caesar.

Quirinius, governor of Syria

In the same chapter, Luke refers to Quirinius as the governor of Syria. This has been disputed by historians.

Herod

A very powerful and influential family dominated Judea during the 1st century BC and the early years of the 1st century AD. According to legend preserved by Julius Africanus, the great-grandfather of the family was a temple attendant named Herod. Grandfather Antipater was an extremely forceful and enterprising leader. He was the man involved with the people and events leading to the crucifixion of Jesus in 63 BC. The father, Herod the Great, ruled Judea from 40 BC until his death in 4 BC, when he was succeeded by Herod Antipas in Galilee and Peraea.

It is my contention that Luke has associated the grandson, Herod Antipas, with Jesus instead of Herod Antipater, the grandfather. Why should he have made this mistake? The similarity between the names of the two Herods is because 'Antipas' is an abridged form of 'Antipater' – in the same way that 'Bob' is an abbreviated form of 'Bobby'. If, with the passage of time, Luke had to choose between an 'Antipas' living in the 1st century BC and an 'Antipas' active in the 1st century AD, it is understandable that he would choose the latter because the date would seem to coincide with the lives of his other identifications. Luke, therefore, identified the wrong 'Herod Antipater'.

Pontius Pilate

Pontius Pilate features so strongly in the trial of Jesus that there seems little doubt that he ruled in Judea around the time of the crucifixion.

In fact, as sometimes happens with historical dates, the Jesus/Pontius Pilate link is a proof that goes round in circles. The death of Jesus in AD 30 would seem to be proof that Pilate held office in that year. For anyone questioning the time when Jesus was put to death, the fact that Pontius Pilate was governor of Judea in AD 30 would support the belief that he was killed around that time.

It may come as a surprise to learn that there are no official records which identify a Pontius Pilate as being the holder of any office in Judea or anywhere else. Of the origin of Pilate we know nothing. His very name is a puzzle; his praenomen, or Christian name, is unique to him and his cognomen, or surname, is unusual. There are references to Pilate in the books of Josephus and later writers, but they may well have been misled by a tradition which came down to them that a Pontius Pilate was involved in the death of Jesus.

The only writer who was a contemporary of Pilate and who refers to him in a letter is Philo of Alexandria, and this could be produced as evidence that a Pontius Pilate did live around the opening years of the 1st century AD. Philo lived during the period 20 BC–AD 40.

Because a Pontius Pilate was thought to have played a part in the life of Jesus, attempts have been made to fake evidence. A series of letters allegedly written by Pilate include references to Jesus Christ, but there is widespread agreement that they are forgeries. Some years ago, Italian archaeologists found a damaged stone believed to have part of a dedication to a building in Caesaria. The preserved right hand side of the stone bears an inscription which, some might think, rather conveniently seems to support Luke's reference to Tiberius Caesar and Pontius Pilate. What appears to be the top line ends with '. . . TIBERIEVM' and underneath, the word '. . . VSPILATVS'. There is another word at the end of the next line which cannot be deciphered. By producing only part of the stone – what happened to the rest of the stone? – the inscriber, if forger he was, avoided providing a more comprehensive wording which, if in error, would have brought his fraudulent work into question. The inscription is so badly done, with ill-formed letters which are cramped almost to the point of distortion, that it is difficult to believe that, even in those days, officials would have found the workmanship acceptable. It has all the hallmarks of being a fake.

The case for identifying Jesus as the Teacher of

Righteousness does not rest on whether or not Pontius Pilate ever lived. However, it is my opinion that he did not, and for the reasons I shall now give.

We have seen that 'Pilate' was not a recognised surname of the time. It has been suggested that it was derived from 'Pileatus' – one who wore the pileus of the slaves, the inference being that he was a freedman or descended from one. This is, however, regarded as unlikely. Others have derived 'Pilatus' from 'pilum', which means javelin or spear. Hence 'Pilatus' could be a way of referring to the leader of the spear carriers, the Roman soldiers. The only serious evidence for a 'Pilate' who lived in those eventful years of the 1st century AD comes, as we have seen, from Philo; it may be that in using the word 'Pilate' he was using the word to indicate a military governor who lived at that time, and who would in his capacity as governor, be responsible for the actions of his spear-carrying soldiers.

However, the overwhelming evidence linking Jesus with the Teacher of Righteousness leads to an examination of the people who were involved with the death of the Teacher in 63 BC. It is here that we find the Roman soldier who was the official responsible, along with the Pharisees, for the trial of Jesus. That long chain of oral and written evidence contributed to a smudging of the name of Pompey, the Roman general, and, as a consequence, confused the writers of the 1st century AD. There seems little connection between Pontius Pilatus and Pompey, but 'Pompey' was the nickname of Pompeius Magnus. As the general leading an army of spear-carriers, it is not too difficult to see how Pompeius Pilatus became corrupted to Pontius Pilate.

The Gospels are, therefore, incorrect in identifying Pontius Pilate as the Roman leader involved in the death of Jesus. They should have identified Pompeius Magnus, whose name became distorted to 'Pontius Pilate'.

Despite the 167 years or so separating Jesus from the Gospel writers, some events and some names have come down the long chain of story tellers and re-tellers unchanged, thus enabling us to provide further links with the early 1st century BC.

A ruler of the Jews

In the Gospel of John (3 : 1) there is reference to a 'man of the Pharisees, named Nicodemus, a ruler of the Jews . . .'. It is a description which must indicate close association with those who were running the affairs of Judea at that time. This quotation obviously places Nicodemus with Jesus mistakenly in the 1st century AD. However, if we go back to the period around 63 BC, Aristobulus II (one of the two brothers disputing the office of High Priest) had an assistant named Nicodemus, and this would qualify him, I think, to be described as 'a ruler of the Jews'. Aristobulus II was a Sadducee, not a Pharisee, and looked on the Essenes as friends, whereas the Pharisees were very much the critics of Jesus and his followers. The Gospel of John is, therefore, incorrect when describing Nicodemus as a Pharisee. However, Josephus correctly places Nicodemus, and hence Jesus, around 63 BC.

Malchus

There is a curious story in the Gospel of John, repeated in less detail in the other Gospels, which is actually based on truth but had somehow become distorted when it finally reached the Gospel writers.

In John 18 : 10 it reads: 'Simon Peter having a sword, drew it and struck the High Priest's slave and cut off his right ear. The slave's name was Malchus'. Luke agrees with John that it was the right ear, whereas neither Mark nor Matthew indicate whether it was the left or the right ear. An understanding of the history of those times enables the origins of the story to be explained:

1. At the time of the arrest of Jesus, Hyrcanus II and Aristobulus II, who were brothers, were disputing the office of High Priest.
2. In Hebrew, the written words 'slave' and 'brother' are similar and could be confused, particularly if a scroll was damaged.
3. The original wording of the Essene writing would refer to the loss of an ear by the brother of the High Priest; the

Essenes would regard Aristobulus as the High Priest and Hyrcanus II as his brother.

4. Why should the loss of an ear be featured in the story? The original account would refer to the loss of an ear by Hyrcanus II and it is, in fact, a true story, although in circumstances quite different from those described in the Gospels. In 40 BC, Antigonus, who replaced Hyrcanus II as High Priest, was determined that Hyrcanus II would never hold that office again. There was a rule that no one who had a bodily blemish could be appointed High Priest. Antigonus, therefore, tore off the ears of Hyrcanus II with his teeth.

5. The 'core truth' is that the brother of the High Priest lost his ears, but that the scribe transcribed his information into 'the slave of the High Priest'. Further, in view of the unlikelihood of the ears having been bitten off, he attributed the loss to a blow from a sword.

6. According to Josephus, Hyrcanus II had an assistant called Malichus who met an untimely end. The spelling of the name is so close to that of 'Malchus' that it does not seem unreasonable to conclude that we are referring to the same man. There is unlikely to have been anyone other than the original Malichus who was so closely associated with any of the High Priests during those turbulent centuries.

Even taken in isolation, it would be difficult to ignore these coincidences and to dismiss them as sheer chance. There is no written work, apart from the Gospels, which links a Nicodemus and a Malichus with any of the leaders in the 1st century AD. There is, however, evidence from Josephus, an independent source, that Nicodemus and Malichus were people who were connected with leaders who featured in the events leading up to the stoning of Onias the Just (Jesus) in 63 BC.

History also enables us to connect, with a reasonable degree of confidence, events reported in the Gospels as having occurred in the 1st century AD, when they actually involved people active in the 1st century BC who were of interest to the Essenes. Here are two such events.

The War

In Luke 14 : 31–32 it reads: 'Or what king, going to encounter another king in war, will not sit down first and take counsel whether he is able with ten thousand to meet him who comes against him with twenty thousand'. This is almost certainly a reference to the Parthian attack on Jerusalem in 40 BC, and is a sneering reference to the incompetence of the High Priest, Hyrcanus II.

The bank

In Luke 19 : 43, Jesus is described as telling of a time of tribulation which was coming. He says: 'For the days shall come upon you, when your enemies will cast up a bank about you and surround you, and hem you in on every side, and dash you to the ground, you and your children within you . . .'.

Josephus, in *Antiquities of the Jews* (14 : 4 : 3) describes the Roman preparations for the attack on Jerusalem: 'The Romans . . . threw nothing at the Jews . . . but raised up their earthen banks, and brought their engines into much forwardness that they might do execution the next day'. When the assault did take place, it led to mass slaughter of the Jews and Josephus tells us that, 'some there were who threw themselves down the precipices'.

There is correspondence between the two accounts – the enemy with his surrounding forces, banks being raised and the unfortunate Jews being dashed to the ground. This description links a Gospel story with events dating back to 63 BC and the seige of Jerusalem by Pompey, the Roman general.

These are just some of the people whom the Gospel writers placed in the wrong century.

There is much more evidence that Jesus was active in the 1st century BC. The writings and diligence of Josephus in recording the history of the Jews has been critical in identifying the people involved with the events unfolding in those early years of the century. If the Gospel compilers had been able to draw upon the books of Josephus they may have been able to link the real names with the code names given in the original Essene writings. Instead, the High Priests, Tiberius Caesar, Herod Antipas and Pontius Pilate were wrongly identified.

I think it fair to conclude that the Gospel writers were wrong in their dating of the life and mission of Jesus.

CHAPTER SIX

The Essenes

In this chapter I outline some of the rules, customs and beliefs which were followed by this quite remarkable Jewish sect.

That very well-known saying 'Truth is stranger than fiction' was coined for one very good reason – it is true. When fiction writers tell a story, they have to keep the content within what the reader will regard as the bounds of possibility. This need not be too restrictive providing the writer makes some effort to justify the unbelievable. Science fiction writers have gained wide acceptance for their stories because they mix a considerable amount of scientific fact with a vivid imagination, and the end product is something which the reader is ready to accept. Truth can be as outrageous as it likes but science fiction writers must keep within reasonable limits.

But how many readers would accept a storyline about Jesus Christ, the surprise ending to which is that for nearly 2,000 years, the educated world of religion was wrong; that what they thought to be true was a mirror image? Like all mirror images, there is little difference between reality and the image. It is only when one looks closely that one sees that the positions are reversed and that what is right hand in truth is left hand in image. Jesus Christ certainly lived, but he lived in the 1st century BC not the 1st century AD. He was the Teacher of Righteousness of the Essene sect, and, for reasons to be explained later, a man referred to by Josephus, the historian, as Onias the Just.

Josephus and Philo had both written briefly about the

Essenes. In 1947, however, a Bedouin boy stumbled into a cave in the Judean hills and discovered earthenware jars which contained scrolls. Further caves were searched and more jars were found.

The Dead Sea Scrolls were revealed and a new branch of theology was born. The translations of the Scrolls gave an opportunity to learn some of the secrets of the sect. The Scrolls covered different aspects of the life and procedures of the Essenes.

The following sets out some of the most important Scrolls and gives a summary of their contents.

The Community Rule Scroll — sets out the rules relating to joining the community and statutes regarding the council.

The Damascus Rule Scroll — this Scroll contains more exhortations to the members and rules to follow, including some duplication of those in the Community Rule Scroll.

The War Rule Scroll — this sets out various military plans for the final conflict between the spirits of Light (the Essenes) and Darkness.

The Temple Scroll — sets out the design requirements of the Temple, the feasts to be observed and the sacrifices and worshipping practices to be observed.

The Messianic Rule Scroll — these were rules to be observed by the sect in the final days of the Messianic war.

The Thanksgiving Hymns — most begin 'I give thee thanks, O Lord . . .' but include references to the tribulations of a man who must be the Teacher of Righteousness (Jesus).

The Biblical Commentaries — in this Scroll, the Essenes quote Old Testament verses and interpret them to show how they foretell events in the life of the sect and of their Teacher of Righteousness.

Of all the books written about the Essenes, the most outstanding, in my opinion, is *The Essene Writings from Qumran*, written by Professor Dupont-Sommer. If the reader cares to carry on a deeper study of the Essene sect he can do no better than read this book, which was described by one theologian as a 'magisterial work'. Originally written in French, it has been translated into English by Geza Vermes, another outstanding theologian, who has written his own book on the Scrolls entitled *The Dead Sea Scrolls in English*.

The following resumé gives an idea of the rules, practices and beliefs of the Essene sect.

1. The Essenes rejected pleasure and regarded continence and the conquest of their passions as a virtue. This attitude included the rejection of sexual pleasures and gives the lie to suggestions made from time to time that Jesus and his disciples were homosexuals. Moreover, their attitude to women, seen in the next paragraph, was one of suspicion. It was clear that it was from women, not their fellow males, that temptation would come.

2. They were on their guard against the lascivious behaviour of women and were convinced that none preserved their fidelity to one man. Those at Qumran were not married, but there were Essene supporters among the Jews of the Dispersion who were married and had families.

3. They adopted children and instructed them in Essene beliefs. I believe that Jesus was adopted by the sect, and the reasons for my thinking this are given in Chapter 13.

4. They despised riches and, on joining the sect, newcomers were required to give all their goods to the commune. This explains the answer given by Jesus to the young man who asked what he should do to inherit eternal life. In Luke 18 : 22 Jesus says, '. . . sell all you have and give to the poor . . .'. The word 'poor' was how the Essenes described themselves because, as individuals, they had no wealth. Jesus was, in effect, saying that the man should give his wealth to the Essenes. Even property had to be sold and there were penalties for those who disobeyed the rule. This explains the grim story in the Acts of the Apostles where Ananias and Sapphira lost their lives as a result of laying only part of the proceeds of a property sale at the feet of the apostles.

5. When Essenes travelled from their homes to distant parts, their fellow Essenes treated them as one of the family. Hebrews 13 : 2 reflects this attitude where it reads, 'Do not neglect to show hospitality to strangers'.

6. At sunrise, they offered up prayers to the sun, which they regarded as a manifestation of God's power. Pliny the Younger reports having seen 'Christians' meeting at daybreak and singing hymns.
7. Whatever they said was the truth and was as good as having been given on oath. However, swearing was avoided for they believed that he who could not be believed without swearing was already condemned. Very much in sympathy with this is the verse in Matthew 5 : 34 where Jesus says, 'But I say to you do not swear at all by Heaven or by earth'.
8. Members were forbidden to lie.
9. Members guilty of 'silly laughter' would be punished.
10. Whosoever uttered a foolish word would be punished.
11. None should speak to his brother in anger, disrespect, impatience or a spirit of wickedness.
12. Members were not to insult a colleague or to speak to him arrogantly.
13. Each member was to sit at meetings according to his numbered rank.
14. In matters of property and work, the lower ranked would obey the higher.

It is my suspicion, but as yet not substantiated by any of the Scrolls, that the Essenes looked upon themselves as Elijah's remnant of 7,000 which appears in 1 Kings 19 : 18. This reads, 'I will leave seven thousand in Israel, all the knees that have not bowed to Ba'al and every mouth that has not kissed him'. These are the words of the Lord, speaking to Elijah. If I understand them correctly, they mean that those who have resisted the sinful influence of Ba'al will be the Lord's remnant.

The Essenes would look on this as the raison d'être for the sect. The sect must, they would think, become perfect, a sinless brotherhood ready to serve the Lord at the end of time. The need to achieve a specific target membership of 7,000 would explain their numbering system (described later in Chapter 13). The need to avoid sin would explain their efforts to achieve perfection. The rules were designed to ensure these standards.

The Essenes also believed that in the last days there would be a Holy War between the spiritual and human forces of Light against the forces of Darkness and they, the Essenes, would be those land forces, worthy of representing the Lord because of the state of perfection they had reached. They would be victorious and had prepared a prayer to God to extend the day so that they could persue the forces of Darkness and end the final day in triumph. However, a sect which was intent on expansion simply had to prepare an account of the life of their leader, the Teacher of Righteousness. How else could they explain to new members aspects of the life of their outstanding leader?

Moreover, they lived in violent times. If there were only one copy of the story of their Teacher, what would happen if the commune holding the writing was attacked and the record lost? What if disease struck at the main camp and this was subsequently carried to other camps, killing the Elders? The story of Jesus could be lost for ever, and it was a risk that they could not take. We have evidence of a highly organised scriptorium at Qumran which was designed to turn out a considerable amount of those scriptural works which the Essenes favoured, and which would be distributed to their various communes and colonies. Although a copy has not been found, it is almost certain that a 'Gospel of Jesus' would have been written.

Professor Dupont-Sommer believes that the Biblical Commentary on the Book of Habakkuk was written sometime after 40 BC. The Scroll of the War Rule was another piece of writing which was prepared at the same time. It is clearly based upon Roman military practice and is evidence of the Essene belief and intention to be involved in a Holy War.

They lived their lives, building up moral strength and increasing their membership so that they might represent the forces of Light in the confrontation with the forces of Darkness.

The War Scroll set out in some detail the plan of battle which would enable the Essenes to defeat their opponents – and there is a strong suspicion that the hated Romans would be those representing the Prince of Darkness. The coming

45

confrontation explained their aim for the very highest standards of conduct. It probably also tells us why they were so secretive in their writings, and why all members undertook never to reveal the secrets of the sect. Had the Romans discovered that they were to be the target of Essene action, they may well have taken action unexpectedly against the sect.

The War Scroll plans were based on Roman military practice, and expert opinion regards them as quite useless. Further, whether 7,000 men would have been adequate to take on the Roman forces is not known, but when Philo wrote about the Essenes he estimated that the Essenes numbered approximately 4,000. If he was privy to the numbering system, it could be that his estimate was reasonably accurate. This would indicate that the Essenes had still some way to go in building up their membership.

The chronology of the Essene sect

A number of coins have been found at the Qumran site. Those which can be dated give a reasonably clear picture of the periods when the camp was occupied.

Coins dated 104 – 76 BC	:	144 coins
Coins dated 75 – 40 BC	:	6 coins
Coins dated 39 BC – AD 6	:	30 coins
Coins dated AD 7 – AD 68	:	272 coins

The sect move into Qumran – c. 104 BC
I do not know if it would be correct to describe the group which occupied Qumran as a sect. They were a group of dissidents, certainly, possibly including some of those pious Jews who were concerned that the Judaism of the Pharisees did not fully reflect the Laws of Moses.

Josephus, the historian, makes reference to Essenes active around 146 BC and to a certain Judas, who was an Essene, as active around 104 BC. Nevertheless, the evidence of the coins suggests that most of the Essene activity was some time after 104 BC.

There were, I believe, two factors responsible for the sect leaving Qumran around 76 BC and eventually fleeing to

Egypt following the crucifixion of Jesus, their Teacher of Righteousness, in 63 BC.

In Chapter 5, 'Why the Chronology of Christianity is Wrong' I set out my reasons for thinking that Jesus and John the Baptist were involved in an incident, recorded in the Talmud, wherein Queen Alexandra Salome was insulted, and that this led to the death of John the Baptist. This may have been one of the factors responsible for Jesus being harassed by the authorities, and the pressure would almost certainly be felt by anyone associated with him. In Mark 9 : 30 we read that Jesus went into hiding. It tells us that Jesus and his disciples, 'went on from there and passed through Galilee. And he would not have anyone know it'. A similar story is told about the Teacher of Righteousness in Hymn 'I' of the Hymn Scroll, where the Teacher writes: 'I give thee thanks, O Adonai that Thou didst not abandon me when I was in exile among a strange people . . . and Thou hast set me in a place of exile among many fishers that stretch a net on the face of the water'. There is a strong suspicion that the place he is alluding to is Galilee.

When a group is distressed, members usually begin to question the leadership. We find the same story told in both the Scrolls and the Gospels. In Hymn 'J', the Teacher of Righteousness records: 'And I, I was the butt of the insults of my enemies, an object of quarrelling and dispute to my companions'.

Jesus had the same experience, described in John 6 : 66 thus: 'After this, many of his disciples drew back and no longer went about with him'. Later, in John 7 : 5, we are told that '. . . even his brothers did not believe in him'. It is impossible to date these happenings to a particular year, but those turbulent years ending in 63 BC influenced world history.

During the reign of Queen Alexandra Salome, from 76–67 BC, there had been a constant jockeying for position between Hyrcanus II and his younger brother Aristobulus II. This broke out into open conflict upon the death of their mother. Hyrcanus II, with the help of Aretas, the King of the Arabs, beat Aristobulus in battle and beseiged him in Jerusalem.

Hyrcanus II then made what proved to be a momentous decision. Josephus tells us that a Jewish priest named Onias the Just had successfully prayed for rain following a period of severe drought. He was brought to the camp and was asked to pray for the success of the seige. He refused. Onias was then killed by stoning, or, if we are to accept the Dead Sea Scrolls and Acts 10 : 39 as being accurate, Onias was stoned and then hung on a tree to die. Note the man well, for there is a volume of evidence that brings Onias the Just alongside the Teacher of Righteousness and Jesus, until there can be little doubt that the three are one and the same. The year was 63 BC.

The sect leave Qumran – 63 BC
Frightened, the Essenes fled. They went to a place they describe as the 'Land of Damascus'. Many theologians have taken this description to indicate an area near to Damascus. On the face of it this is a reasonable enough assumption. But at a time of trouble, the Essenes could be expected to move, not north to Damascus, but south to the region of Mount Sinai where Moses, their revered prophet, received the tablets from God. The whole of Essene theological thinking originated with Moses, and knowing this it is unlikely that they would go, at a time of danger, anywhere else.

There are two other reasons for thinking that Egypt was their goal. Josephus tells us that when Onias the Just – Jesus – was killed in 63 BC, other 'principal Jews' had previously moved away from Jerusalem to Egypt – in other words, they had gone to the new home of the Essenes. The second reason for thinking that Egypt was their 'Land of Damascus' is that Essene writings were designed to conceal rather than reveal. For them to identify an area so clearly gives rise to the suspicion that this was merely a code name designed to mislead.

The return to Judea – c. AD 6
When the Essenes deserted Jesus and fled to Egypt, they would know that they had made a mistake. They would be aware that God had expressed his anger at the treatment meted out to Jesus by the Jews and of how God had punished them.

48

This probably persuaded the leaders to return to Judea when it was safe to do so. Hyrcanus II was the High Priest who had persecuted Jesus and only on his death, in 30 BC, would the Essenes be likely to return. The coins found at Qumran lead to the conclusion that the return was probably effected in the final years of the 1st century BC.

It was almost certainly at this time that the sect began to organise not only its beliefs but also the rules and regulations we find in the Scrolls.

The sect, its aims and its organisation show a remarkable degree of ambition, drive and sophistication for a society whose lifestyle 2,000 years ago was really quite primitive. But not its thinking. The Dead Sea Scrolls provide ample proof of the organisational abilities of those who framed the ordinances of the Essene sect.

Anyone wishing to join the community was given 'postulant' status, which he held for one year. He then spent two years as a 'noviate' and, if finally accepted, would be required to give his wealth to the community. It was the period of three years which Paul records in Galatians 1 : 18 which led me to suspect that he had trained as an Essene.

There were three different categories within the Qumran community. The executive head of the sect appears to have been a council of 12 men, perhaps representing the 12 tribes of Israel or the 12 apostles, and three priests, perhaps representing the three priestly families descended through the three sons of Levi. This is the view put forward by John Allegro in his book *The Dead Sea Scrolls – A Reappraisal*. However, I think it likely that the three priests would represent the original trio of Peter, John and James whose names, as I suggest later, would be passed on to their successors.

The third group, the laity, were the general membership. They were examined each year to determine their intelligence, strength, valour and, most important of all, their zeal for the cause of virtue. This examination established their numbered position in the community.

The leadership would all be 'Men of Knowledge'; those who had the Essene 'gnosis' which enabled them to

49

understand the secretive, covert writings of the sect.

Many communities formed among the Jews of the Dispersion, and these were under the control of an 'Overseer' or 'Bishop'. The Essenes may have found it difficult to attract members to the ascetic life led by those in the all-male commune at Qumran, because there were reported Essenes who were married and living in Egypt and Rome. It is certain that those Churches mentioned in the New Testament were also Essene communities. Not surprisingly, there are many similarities between the Essene and Christian customs:

— both were Jewish sects originally;
— both practiced the ritual of baptism;
— both featured a communal meal as part of their practices;
— both included the breaking of bread and the drinking of wine as part of their communal meal;
— both required the disposal of worldly goods prior to a member joining the sect;
— both sects had three special priests – the Levite priests and Peter, John and James;
— both used a veiled form of writing – the Biblical Commentaries and the evidence of 2 Corinthians 4 : 3 – 4;
— both buried their writings in earthenware jars – the Dead Sea Scrolls and the evidence of 2 Corinthians 4 : 7;
— both had as the focus of their writing leaders who were linked together (as detailed in Chapter 11: 'Jesus Identified').

One would have thought that surely, with so many links between the two sects, the Church might have at least suspected there might be something wrong with the chronology of Christianity.

AD 66–70 – The Jewish War

When the Romans began their war against the Jews in AD 66, perhaps the Essenes thought that this was the beginning of their Holy War. It could be that when Nero accused the followers of 'Chrestos' of setting fire to Rome in AD 64, there were Essenes behind the disturbances and that this led to the

Roman authorities persecuting the Essenes in Judea.

The end for the Essenes at Qumran came in AD 68 when the 10th Roman Legion marched in and routed the Essenes. Theologically speaking, they were never heard of again. From being the most energetic, the most devout, the most honest and upright sect ever known in Judea, they disappeared almost literally overnight.

In reality, the Essenes were still active in all those areas where the Romans had not been able to identify Essene communes and colonies. They were to hang on to their beliefs for another 50 years or so before some, like Paul, began passing them on to the gentiles.

Others were active and began to develop into new groups. These reveal their Essene origins by the names which became attached to them. Theologians, however, still look on them as Christian sects. But the Gnostics, for example, got their name from their claim to have the Essene 'gnosis' – knowledge. Perhaps they were led by one or more men who had been Essene 'Men of Knowledge'. The Ebionites, whose name means 'the poor ones' were poor because, as Essenes, they gave all their wealth to the sect, leaving themselves with nothing bar small personal items.

The dispersal of the sect – and its reformation into the Christian Church

The fall of Jerusalem in AD 70 was almost a disaster for the Jews, but with the Temple in ruins and Judaism in disarray, they reacted in typically enterprising style. Under Rabbi Zakkai, who established a school at Jamnia, the Jewish religion developed into the Church that it is today. For the Essenes, things were different.

Whilst the ordinary Jews had a loose relationship with their Church, the Essene commitment was rigid and severe with strict codes of behaviour and a discipline that originated, and was controlled, from Qumran. During the early period following the War, the distant communities would miss the social and theological direction which they had previously received from Qumran.

The so-called Pauline letters give some idea of the areas

that were active after the War, and there seem to be none in Judea or Egypt. The Churches referred to in the Pauline correspondence are almost all situated in Asia, Greece or Syria, suggesting that of all the Essene communes or colonies those in Judea and Egypt received very severe treatment from the Roman soldiers. If any of the Churches outside these areas remained effective Essene units, one would have thought that they, too, would have received visits and letters from the Jerusalem trio of Peter, John and James. The fact that they did not suggests that it was because of Roman action. There were none left to receive letters.

And then, sometime between the end of the Jewish War in AD 70 and perhaps the early years of the 2nd century AD, Paul stepped onto the theological scene.

It may be that Paul found the Essene teaching too selective and felt that a God of love would look on all his children, Jew and gentile, with equal affection. In opening the door to Esseneism for the gentiles, Paul changed the course of world history. It was a simple enough change which, on the face of it, had only minor implications. In fact, it became a completely new religion. God was now everybody's God and all were now God's children.

If the worship of the Jewish God were now open to the gentiles, then some far-reaching changes would have to be made. Circumcision would not be compulsory and certain foods would not be unclean.

These were changes which the Essenes found impossible to accept, and although there seemed at first to be limited acceptance of the gentiles, gradually the problems and frictions created led to the Essene Jews slowly returning to the Jewish fold. Little is heard of the Essenes – except perhaps a suspicion that they were involved in the Jewish rebellions in AD 116 and AD 132 – and, ironically, the belief in Christ was taken up by the gentiles, the last people with whom the die-hard Essenes would want to be involved.

The Gospel stories of Jesus suddenly appeared in that twilight period between AD 100 and 200. They were based on a basic Essene 'Gospel of Jesus' which had been written, perhaps, late in the 1st century BC – a hundred or more years before. The Gospels surfaced without anyone recording when or where. No one knows who compiled them, but the source material was undoubtedly the Essene 'Gospel of Jesus'.

The Essene Teacher of Righteousness, who probably never claimed to have performed a miracle, who had little love for gentiles and perhaps regarded women as a source of temptation for his 'perfect' companions, became, in the writings of the gentiles, Jesus the miracle worker and lover of humanity, who gave his life that we might all be saved.

CHAPTER SEVEN

The Biblical Commentaries

I seek to show, in this chapter, that the Essene Biblical Commentaries describe events in the life of their Teacher of Righteousness which find their counterparts in the New Testament Gospels. Further, that these correspondences show that Jesus was the Essene Teacher.

Before we look at the Essene Biblical Commentaries, which give us a clear link with the New Testament writings, we must examine the evidence for thinking that these refer to one particular Teacher of Righteousness and not to a number of Teachers. There are theologians who believe that the name was the title of a position within the Essene sect, and that the veiled references to incidents involving the Teacher of Righteousness actually happened to a number of holders of that position at different times during the history of the sect.

This concept, however, does not really make sense. If the Essenes took all the trouble to record important events in the life of the sect, they would surely not do so in a way which could be misinterpreted. During the period 63 BC to AD 68 – 131 years – there could have been perhaps ten or more holders of the office of 'Teacher of Righteousness' – assuming that this was a continuing office within the sect. The Essenes would, in these circumstances, have had to devise a way of identifying which Teacher was being referred to in their Biblical Commentaries. If they took the trouble to record the event, it would have been equally important to them to know which particular Teacher had featured in that event.

Although we know, thanks to our historians, that the Essenes were dispersed by the Romans in about AD 68, the Essenes were not to know this when they devised their system of writing during the 1st century BC. If the Teacher of Righteousness had been a continuing office, they would have had to have made sure that each one, when referred to in their writings, was clearly identified, otherwise there would have been considerable opportunity for the history of the sect to become confused and inaccurate.

When we look at the writings in the Dead Sea Scrolls, we find no clues to suggest that the Essenes were trying to identify one particular 'Teacher' in one piece of writing and a different 'Teacher' in another. The following references to the Teacher, which I have taken from the Essene Commentary on the Book of Habakkuk (translated by Professor Dupont-Sommer) are quite straightforward and uncomplicated:

VIII (2 and 3). God will deliver them from the House of Judgement because of their affliction and their faith in the Teacher of Righteousness.

VIII (16 and 17). The explanation of this word concerns the Priest who rebelled and violated the precepts of God and persecuted the Teacher of Righteousness.

XI (4). The explanation of this concerns the Wicked Priest who persecuted the Teacher of Righteousness.

In these three examples, and in others which could be quoted, no attempt is made to differentiate one 'Teacher' from another. The conclusion must be that there was one, and only one, Teacher of Righteousness. There will be adequate support proof for this later on.

But why should the Essenes write in this secretive, veiled way? Why did they not refer to the 'Teacher of Righteousness' as Jesus, and the 'Wicked Priest' as Hyrcanus? Why did they not name the towns where the incidents happened? An appreciation of the importance to the Jews of 'pesher' provides part of the answer.

Pesher

To understand the Essene writings, it is necessary for the reader to appreciate the meaning and significance of 'pesher'.

The Jews, from the time of Moses, looked on the Pentateuch (the first five books of the Old Testament) and the oral law which was being built up, as setting out their duty to God. It was the basis of Judaism, with its pre-eminent belief that it was the duty of the Jew to 'love God, with all his heart, with all his mind and with all his soul', and it gave guidance to the Jews on how this might be achieved.

However, to the ever scholarly minds of the Jews, the explicit teaching of the written and oral laws was not enough. They were eager to discover not only the obvious meaning of the texts, but also the hidden, implicit meaning of their teaching, the Torah. The hidden meanings, the new interpretations of texts or of the pronouncements by Rabbis were known as the 'Pesher'.

The Essene Biblical Commentaries

Many years later, the Essene Jews were to turn the system round in a unique way. Instead of writing the account of the important events in the life of the sect and of their Teacher of Righteousness in plain everyday language which could be readily understood, they adopted a secret, cryptic style which required interpretation – pesher. They took Old Testament verses and interpreted them as though they were predicting some incident in the life of the sect, even though sometimes there was not, by any sensible judgement, the slightest connection between the verses and the incident. We find 'pesher' being used in this way in the Biblical Commentaries which were among the Dead Sea Scrolls. But to make understanding the 'pesher' even more difficult, they used their coded style of writing to conceal from the reader the identities of the people being featured.

Where an important personality is referred to, they adopted a pseudonym to conceal his identity. For example, 'Teacher of Righteousness' (Jesus), 'Wicked Priest' (Hyrcanus II) and 'Man of Lies' (Peter) appear in the Commentaries.

Sometimes, because great use is made of pronouns such as 'he' or 'they', it is difficult to know precisely which 'he' or 'they' is indicated. This is why the link between Jesus and the Teacher, and Christianity and Esseneism, has eluded the theologians. In this way, the explanation itself required a further explanation. This final 'pesher', or explanation, would be known to the 'Men of Knowledge' of the sect but not to the junior members of the community. It may be that they were recorded and that somewhere, perhaps among the unpublished translations, there will be a complete record of the history of the sect and of Jesus.

Why there was a need for secrecy

One of the beliefs of the sect was that at some stage in the future, there would be a confrontation between the forces of Light (Essenes) and the forces of Darkness. It is reasonable to assume that the Romans and Pharisees, who had jointly deposed Aristobulus II and persecuted the Teacher of Righteousness, would be regarded as the enemy forces.

If, in their writings, the Essenes were to have made quite clear their battle plans for the final conflict, that they regarded the Romans and the disloyal Pharasaic Jews as the enemy, then they would all be in danger should their scrolls fall into the wrong hands. The Holy War was to be at the instigation of God and the signs that he sent to the Essenes, not due to some chance discovery of their writings by their future enemy.

The Jewish War of AD 66 – 70 broke out in circumstances which are not clear. The Essene camp at Qumran was overrun by the Romans in AD 68 and it is likely, though speculation only, that the Essenes were involved in some way with the beginning of that War. Perhaps they thought that some local disturbances were a sign from God that the conflict should begin.

From the time of the destruction of the Qumran camp the Essenes were never heard of again. The disappearance of these devout men would be amazing if it were true. As this book seeks to show, the Christian Church being built up for gentiles and Jews alike, which we read about in the New

Testament letters, was the work of these energetic but displaced Essenes from Judea.

The Essenes had decided that the Biblical Commentaries should be written in veiled terms so that no one but the Elders would understand them. There was, however, a snag. It could happen that death by persecution or an epidemic could quickly deprive the community of those who knew what these veiled interpretations meant. They lived in troublesome times, and if too much were committed to the memories of the Elders the most important part of Essene history, the life story of their Teacher of Righteousness, could be lost forever. The true meaning of the veiled interpretation could not be committed solely to memory.

It is my belief, therefore, that the Essenes wrote a 'Gospel of Jesus' in which all the people who featured in the life of Jesus were named. It is obvious from what Papias had to say about the writings of Mark and Matthew that they drew upon both memory and written work for material on which to base their Gospels. Mark 'remembered' as best he could and Matthew 'interpreted the oracles' to the best of his ability. The inaccuracies of the Gospels and the variations between these two Gospel accounts point clearly to neither using a complete text of the 'Gospel of Jesus'.

Many Essene scrolls were found in the caves, but there was not a Gospel of Jesus among them. From this I deduce that whilst there simply had to be some record of the life of Jesus in which the people involved were named, a very limited edition was made and held in safe-keeping. Thus, no matter what happened to the Elders, those who followed would have access to the facts about Jesus.

One really has to sit back in amazement at these people. At a time in history when our forefathers were in animal skins and woad, the Essenes were writing literature which would compare with any written at the present time. Not only that, they were examining moral issues and promoting theologies which were many hundreds of years in advance of their time. And finally, in order to keep their secrets, they devised a code which almost achieved its objective.

The reader will shortly get the flavour of the Essene

method of writing and will see how their secrets were protected. They revealed only part of their history by vague allusions to events with no identification of who was involved.

The Biblical Commentary links between the Scrolls and the New Testament

We now come to two important questions. What evidence do we have that Jesus was the Teacher of Righteousness, and exactly how do the Gospel stories tie up with the Biblical Commentaries in the Qumran Scrolls?

Even when the two are studied side by side, the links between the Gospels and the Biblical Commentaries are not readily appreciated. It was an ingenious system. Let us see how it worked. Take the following example from the Biblical Commentary on the Book of Habakkuk.

Old Testament quotation from Book of Habakkuk 1 : 10	*Essene Biblical Commentary*
At kings they scoff and of rulers they make sport.	The explanation of this is that they are insolent to the great and contemptuous of the respected. At Kings and leaders they jeer, and despise a multitude of people.

This Commentary ties up with Mark 15 : 16 which reads as follows:

'And the soldiers led him away inside the palace (that is the Praetorium) and they called together the whole battalion. And they clothed him in a purple cloak and plaiting a crown of thorns, they put it on him. And they began to salute him "Hail, King of the Jews"'. In Luke 23 : 27 it reads: 'And there followed him a great multitude of the people and women who bewailed and lamented him'.

Let us see just how closely the Gospel and the Biblical Commentary are in agreement.

Biblical Commentary	Gospel story
Most scholars agree that the word 'they' refers to Roman soldiers.	The word 'they' refers to Roman soldiers allegedly belonging to Pontius Pilate.
'They are insolent to the great and contemptuous of the respected.'	The soldiers are insolent to Jesus. They clad him in a purple cloak and place on his head a crown of thorns.
'At kings and leaders they sneer.'	They salute the Essene leader and describe him as 'King of the Jews'.
'They despise a multitude of people.'	Luke refers to the multitude of people who followed Jesus.

There can be little doubt that the two accounts tie together neatly, and that both Commentary and Gospel refer to the same man – Jesus, the Teacher of Righteousness of the Essene sect.

Briefly, then, the system works this way:

1. The Old Testament verses are quoted.
2. The Essene 'pesher' would then blandly explain the actual circumstances without too much detail and with code names rather than real names.
3. The 'Men of Knowledge' would be able to interpret the code names and fill in the detail of the actual circumstances surrounding the story.

We will now look at a number of Biblical Commentaries and identify them with their respective Gospel quotation, or with the history of the time where an event or events had influenced the life of the sect in some way. But before I do so, one point should be made clear. Whilst the Essenes preferred the quotation from the Old Testament to be a fairly precise forecast of the event, it did not need to be.

Where they had a true life situation for which they could not find an Old Testament quotation, they did what I illustrate in the next example – they selected the Old Testament prophecy, and then wrote a Biblical Commentary which described the Gospel event and completely ignored the words of the prophecy.

Old Testament quotation from the Book of Habakkuk 1 : 5	*Essene Biblical Commentary*
Look among the nations and see; wonder and be astounded. For I am doing a work in your days that you would not believe if told.	The explanation of this concerns those who have betrayed with the Man of Lies: for they have not believed the words of the Teacher of Righteousness, which he received from the mouth of God, and it concerns those who betrayed the New Covenant: for they did not believe the Covenant of God and profaned His Holy name.

Notice how the Commentary has no apparent connection with the quotation from Habakkuk. What has 'looking among the nations' and 'doing work in your days' got to do with the betrayal of those with the Man of Lies?

However, the really important part is the actual Commentary; this connects with the original Gospel story or with the history of the sect. I shall therefore only quote the Essene Biblical Commentary in future and omit the Old Testament quotation.

What connection, then, does this Commentary have with the Gospel?

1. The 'Man of Lies' is Peter. I present the arguments supporting this identification in Chapter 12, 'The Crucifixion, the Resurrection and Peter'.
2. The reference to the Teacher who received words from the mouth of God links up with Matthew 17 : 1 where Jesus, together with Peter, John and James, meets God and the two prophets, Moses and Elijah.
3. Those who betrayed the covenant are those followers of Jesus, the Essenes, who did not believe the words of Jesus.

In John 6 : 64 Jesus says, 'But there are some of you that do not believe', and later, in John 6 : 66, it tells of many of his disciples drawing back and that they 'no longer went about with him'.

Here, we find two apparently different men – Jesus and the Teacher – each in the same unique situation: Jesus met God, and later his disciples did not believe; the Commentary tells us that the Teacher met God and that his words were not believed.

When their supporters commit these events to writing using identical words, then one simply has to consider seriously the possibility that the two are, in fact, the same man.

Essene Commentary on the Book of Habakkuk 1: 13

> The explanation of this concerns the House of Absalom and
> their members of the council who were silent at the time of
> the Chastisement of the Teacher of Righteousness and
> gave him no help against the Man of Lies who despised the
> Law in the midst of their council.

The Commentary describes the situation set out at length in the 7th and 8th chapters of John's Gospel. The basic story behind the Commentary tells of a meeting, perhaps in the Temple, of the Essene 'Men of the Holy Council' in front of which the Teacher is challenged by the Man of Lies, who rejects the Teacher's insistence on the need to adhere to the Law of Moses. There are a number of points of contact between the Gospel account and the Essene Commentary, and these are best dealt with separately.

Chastisement of the Teacher

The two chapters of John's Gospel clearly deal with a situation wherein Jesus is defending himself against criticism, this is summed up in John 8 : 49 where he says, '... you dishonour me'. Jesus was, therefore, chastised, as was the Teacher.

Criticism of Moses's Law

Again, the Gospel parallels the Commentary and in John 7 : 19 Jesus says, 'Did not Moses give you the Law? Yet none of you keeps the Law'. Again, there is correspondence between the two.

Threat to the Teacher's life

In the Gospel, verse 7 : 19 describes Jesus asking the congregation, 'Why do you seek to kill me?', and whilst there is no specific mention of a threat to the Teacher's life in the Commentary, the actual verse 4 from Habakkuk, which the Commentary is seeking to explain, reads: 'O traitors, why do you look on and keep silent when the wicked swallows up the man more righteous than he?'. Now, the Jewish term 'swallow up' invariably means 'to kill' and it could be that there was a threat to the Teacher's life. The actual verse from Habakkuk, therefore, does tie up with John 7 : 19.

Reference to the House of Absalom

At the time of the challenge to the Teacher, Aristobulus II would have been the Chief Priest, and he was a Sadducee. He was the nephew and son-in-law of Absalom, and, as such, would be linked with the Absalom family.

As enemies of the Pharisees, therefore, the Essenes and the Sadducees were allies. This is why the Commentary speaks bitterly of having been let down by the friendly Absalom faction.

There is correspondence, therefore, with the history of those times as recorded by Josephus. Although there is no specific reference in the Gospels to the Absalom family, there is a specific link with Jesus recorded in John's Gospel. There was a man who was a faithful lieutenant of Aristobulus II and the Absalom family, and his name was Nicodemus. He is referred to twice in the Gospel – once when he visited Jesus and once when he helped Joseph of Arimathea with the body of Jesus at the crucifixion.

The writer of John's Gospel was mistaken in thinking

Nicodemus to be a friendly Pharisee. Rather, he was an influential member of the House of Absalom, and one who is seen in the Gospel to have spoken in support of Jesus.

This mistake on the part of the writer of John's Gospel is typical of many to be found in the Gospel, which has stories and sayings which seem to be out of place or which present a distorted picture of the events which were taking place. These differences are due, I believe, to some of the verbal accounts having come down over a long period – from 63 BC to well into the 2nd century AD – and having become twisted in the re-telling. In addition to this, the secrecy adopted by the Essenes in their writings presented many problems to those who made up the Gospels from the Essene Commentaries and incomplete written accounts of the life of Jesus – what would be, in effect, the original Gospel of Jesus.

Teacher betrayed by the Man of Lies

There can be little doubt that the Man of Lies is Peter. Although Professor Dupont-Sommer identifies the Man of Lies as Hyrcanus II, I differ from him on this point because, having referred to Hyrcanus as the Wicked Priest, I think it unlikely that the Essenes would adopt a singularly different description for the same man. This is discussed in detail in Chapter 12, 'The Crucifixion, the Resurrection and Peter'.

When it is possible to link the words of the Commentary to specific situations in the Gospel in this way, there is a build-up of evidence which makes it as clear as it can be that the Teacher and Jesus were involved in them, not by coincidence, but because they were the same man.

Essene Commentary on the Book of Habakkuk 2 : 1–2

> The explanation of this concerns the Teacher of
> Righteousness to whom God made known all the mysteries
> of the words of his servants the Prophets.

This particular Commentary ties up with the account of the Transfiguration of Jesus which is described in the Synoptic Gospels. In Matthew, the story is set out in verses 17 : 1–13.

This describes Jesus going up a high mountain accompanied by Peter, James and John. Here, Jesus meets and talks with Elijah and Moses, the Old Testament prophets. It is at this time that a bright cloud overshadows them and a voice from the cloud says, 'This is my beloved Son with whom I am well pleased: listen to him'.

The link is obvious; the Commentary says that God made known all the 'mysteries of the words of his servants the Prophets' to the Teacher, and here is the Gospel account showing that God had arranged a meeting between Jesus and the two great Jewish prophets, Elijah and Moses. Not only do the accounts complement each other, but the Gospel story records the event as witnessed by the three leading disciples of the sect.

This Commentary, one of the shortest, is perhaps one of the most powerful proofs that Jesus was the Essene Teacher. The situation described is exceptional. In two quite different writings, the leader of the sect is described as having met God and the prophets. In the history of the world, how many people have been so favoured? We have to make a judgement, and in my opinion there can be no doubt that the two different writings from two apparently different sects refer to the same man.

Essene Commentary on the Book of Habakkuk 2 : 7–8

> The explanation of this word concerns the Priest who rebelled and violated the precepts of God and persecuted the Teacher of Righteousness. And they set upon him to smite him in virtue of the Wicked Judgements and evil profaners committed horrors upon him and vengeance upon his body of flesh.

This Commentary deals with the general persecution of Jesus and would not be linked with any particular verse. It refers to Hyrcanus II who rebelled against his brother Aristobulus II and who, with the aid of the King of Arabia and the Romans, successfully overthrew Aristobulus. The Commentary is fully supported by the recorded history of the time, that Hyrcanus 'rebelled' and that he did persecute and crucify Onias the

Just, whom I identify as Jesus, the Teacher of Righteousness.

Finally, Hyrcanus got his just reward when he was captured by the Parthians – the evil profaners – in 40 BC. He was later assassinated at the instigation of Herod in 30 BC. As discussed previously, Hyrcanus, when captured in 40 BC, had his ears torn off by Antigonus who had been installed in his place. By this act, and by the assassination, the known life of the man ties up neatly with the Commentary. In all details, therefore, the Commentary and history are in agreement.

Essene Commentary on the Book of Habakkuk 2 : 14

> Interpreted, this means that when they return . . . the lies.
> And afterwards knowledge shall be revealed to them
> abundantly, like the waters of the sea.

The dots indicate words which are indistinct. What the Commentary seems to be saying, however, is that despite having been told lies, the disciples who had been influenced by them were given knowledge which revealed the truth. I take this to refer to those who had deserted Jesus, the Teacher of Righteousness as a result of lies told by the Man of Lies (Peter), and who were given knowledge from God. How this was transmitted to them is not explained. The whole point of this Commentary is to account for their return to the Qumran area sometime after the death of Hyrcanus II in 30 BC, and for the rebirth of belief in the Teacher which led to the organisation of this amazing sect.

Essene Commentary on the Book of Habakkuk 2 : 15

> The explanation of this concerns the Wicked Priest who
> persecuted the Teacher of Righteousness swallowing him
> up in the anger of his fury in his place of exile. But at the
> time of the Feast of the Rest of the Day of Atonement, he
> appeared before them to swallow them up and to cause
> them to stumble on the Day of Fasting, their Sabbath of
> Rest.

The situation described in the opening sentence is the crucifixion of Jesus – Matthew 27 : 50. The Jewish term 'swallowing up' usually means putting to death. This is described as happening at 'his place of exile' but it is not clear who is meant by 'his', because both the Wicked Priest and the Teacher of Righteousness could be described as being in exile. The Wicked Priest, Hyrcanus II, had been ousted by his brother Aristobulus and, to that extent, could be described as being in exile. The Teacher of Righteousness had also been ousted from his position as leader of the sect, so that he too was in exile. Further, was 'the place of exile' intended to describe the place from which he had been exiled, or the place to which he had been exiled?

The city of Jerusalem fits both the Teacher and Hyrcanus II in the sense that they had both been exiled from the theological centre of the Jews. The situation set out in the Commentary above is described by Josephus in his *Antiquities of the Jews*, Book 14, chapter 2, verse 1. Hyrcanus II had defeated his brother Aristobulus II in battle and had besieged him in Jerusalem. It was to the headquarters of the Hyrcanus camp that Onias the Just – Jesus – was brought. Onias had earlier successfully prayed for rain to end a drought. Hyrcanus II asked Onias to pray for a curse to be placed upon Aristobulus who was besieged in the city, and on his refusal, Onias was stoned to death. In other words, Onias was swallowed up – crucified – at his place of exile – Jerusalem.

The second part of the Commentary has presented all students of the Essene writings with a considerable problem, but Professor Dupont-Sommer gives what seems to be by far the best explanation. He believes that the catastrophe which was to cause 'them' i.e. the Jews of Jerusalem to stumble, was the violent capture of Jerusalem by the Roman general, Pompey, in 63 BC. Josephus tells us that 12,000 Jews lost their lives. This happened on the Day of Fasting i.e. on the Day of Atonement and is attested by Josephus.

Again, the text in the Commentary is consistent with the events which were experienced by Onias the Just and Jesus, bringing the Teacher alongside not just one man, Jesus, but a second, Onias the Just.

Essene Commentary on fragment 2 of Psalm 37 : 32–33

The explanation of this concerns the Wicked Priest who laid

hands on the Priest, the Teacher of Righteousness to put him to death . . . (But God . . .) and he awakened (?) him (because of the Spirit) which he sent to him. And God will not let (the Wicked Priest go) un(punished for the blood which) he has shed but (God will) pay him his reward by delivering him into the hands of the violent of the nations to execute (vengeance) upon him.

In Chapter 12, 'The Crucifixion, the Resurrection and Peter' I set out evidence which leads to the conclusion that Jesus, the Teacher of Righteousness, did not die upon the cross – that he was, in fact, rescued by Joseph of Arimathea. There is much to support this contention. The Commentary certainly supports my argument. There is no mention of the Teacher being killed. Although the Wicked Priest 'laid hands' on the Teacher and blood was shed, death is not mentioned. Further, the reference to being 'awakened' seemingly recorded in Matthew 28 : 9 is consistent with an unconscious Jesus being taken from the cross and later revived. Had the Essenes wished to indicate that the Teacher was killed they could have made a reference to his spirit being in Heaven and then returned. Professor Dupont-Sommer specifically writes that the 'appearance' of the Teacher after his supposed death was not described with words which suggested a spiritual return.

The actual Commentary above covers Psalms 37 : 33 which also makes clear that there was no betrayal by God. It reads: 'The Lord will not abandon him to his power or let him be condemned when he is brought to trial'. This supports the contention that the Teacher did not die. This, again, is further strong evidence linking Jesus and the Teacher of Righteousness, for, as Chapter 12 demonstrates, Jesus did not die on the cross. Although the Wicked Priest is not identified, there can be little doubt that he is Hyrcanus II. He had his ear bitten off by Antigonus so that he could never again hold the office of High Priest, and was later killed in 30 BC. In this sense, therefore, history supports the Commentary in that the 'nations did execute vengeance upon him'.

> The explanation of this concerns the furious Young Lion
> (who took ven) geance on those who seek smooth things –
> he who hanged living men (or wood . . . which was not)
> formerly (done) in Israel; but he who was hanged alive
> upon the wood . . .

The dots and the brackets indicate parts of the Scroll which are indistinct. The 'furious Young Lion' was Alexander Jannaeus who, according to Josephus, hanged 800 Pharisee Rabbis 'on the wood', which was the Jewish way of describing crucifixion.

But what of the reference to 'he who was hanged alive upon the wood'? This is the way Professor Dupont-Sommer translates the Scroll. In writings whose sole purpose was to focus on the life of the Teacher of Righteousness, the single 'he' must refer to him. Like Jesus, the Teacher was hung on a tree; this is just one more important piece of evidence which connects the two men.

Other theologians do not translate the text in this way. Theodor H. Gaster in his book, *The Scriptures of the Dead Sea Sect* believes that the 'he' has been used in the general sense of 'anyone'. Another respected theologian, G. Vermes, translates that particular passage as: 'Because of a man hanged alive on the tree, He proclaims "Behold, I am against (you says the Lord of Hosts)"'. The Vermes translation seems to indicate opposition from the Lord because of treatment given to a particular man and, in that sense, is in accord with the Dupont-Sommer translation.

The 'raison d'être' of the Commentaries was to show how the Old Testament prophets had foretold the events and personalities involved in the history of the sect. The actual killing of the 800 Rabbis was not of particular importance to the Essenes, but the manner of their deaths served as an introduction to the death of their revered Teacher. The precise word 'crucifixion' is not used, but references to Jesus having been 'hung on a tree' to die appear in the Acts of the Apostles, Galatians and 1 Peter, and this is consonant with being 'hanged alive upon the wood'. The fact that both the

Teacher of Righteousness and Jesus were 'hanged alive upon the wood' is more extremely strong evidence that the two men were actually the same man, but referred to in two different writings.

Essene Commentary on Psalm 37 : 7, 19 and 20

> The explanation of this concerns the wicked who will perish
> by the sword and by famine and by plague. The
> explanation of this is that He will cause them to live during
> the famine at the time of affliction; but the wicked who
> have not gone out of the land of Judah will perish from
> famine and plague.

The Essene writer is making some important points here.

He tells us that the wicked will perish by the sword, and Josephus confirms that when Pompey stormed the walls of Jerusalem, Roman swords accounted for the deaths of 12,000 Jews.

Further, that some will perish from famine and plague. In Matthew 27 : 51 there is reference to an earthquake happening after the crucifixion; clouds of dust are associated with earthquakes and these affect crops. There is, therefore, this correspondence between the Commentary and the Gospel in that both are linked with famine. In Josephus explicitly, and in the Gospel by inference, these natural disasters are a result of God's actions and are His response to the treatment of Onias/Jesus.

Finally, those who 'He will cause to live' and who, by implication again, have gone out of the land, are those described by Matthew in 26 : 56, which reads: 'Then all the disciples forsook him and fled'. Josephus confirms the exodus from Israel at the time of the death of Onias the Just – he tells us that immediately prior to his capture, 'the principal men among the Jews' had left the country.

Summary

The following summarises the links between the Commentaries and the Gospels.

Habakkuk	1 : 10	– links with Mark 15 : 16 and Luke 23 : 27
	1 : 5	– links with John 6 : 64 and 66 and Matthew 17 : 1
	1 : 13	– links with John 7 : 19, 8 : 49
	2 : 1–2	– links with Matthew 17 : 1–13
	2 : 7–8	– links with history of the time described by Josephus
	2 : 14	– links with history of the sect
	2 : 15	– links with Matthew 27 : 50
Nahum	2 : 13	– links with 1 Peter 2 : 24
Psalms	37 : 32–33	– links with Matthew 28 : 9
Psalms	37 : 7 and 19–20	– links with Matthew 26 : 56 and 27 : 51

These correspondences are not an accident of chance. They not only confirm, through the writing of Josephus, the period when these events happened, but also link with the Gospels. Recognising as we must that the Gospels were compiled from the secretive Essene writings, with the inherent problems which they posed, the Commentary/Gospel links match with satisfying accuracy.

The Church is not unhappy at the failure of theologians to agree about the identification of the Teacher of Righteousness and the period when he lived. Where there is confusion and disagreement there is unlikely to be much risk of a proof being presented which shows that Jesus was the Essene Teacher.

For these reasons, it has been an upsetting experience for them to find one theologian – Professor Dupont-Sommer – who has not only demolished some of the wilder arguments put forward by fellow theologians, but set out closely argued reasons for placing the crucifixion of the Teacher at the time of the Hyrcanus II/Aristobulus II confrontation in 63 BC. He has further upset them by making translations in the Biblical Commentaries which suggest that the Teacher was, like Jesus, 'hung on a tree to die' and was awakened after his apparent death. The detailed knowledge, understanding and judgement Professor Dupont-Sommer shows in his *Essene*

Writings from Qumran make his book required reading for those who want an authoritative work on the Essenes and the Scrolls.

Conclusion

It cannot be just coincidence that the Biblical Commentaries tie up so clearly with events which happened around 63 BC and with Gospel incidents. Again, it is the 'coincidence factor' operating; when it is possible without bending or distorting the meaning of words, to link the Commentaries, one after another, to verses in the Gospels or the history of the time, then I think the admission must be made that chance has played no part and that Jesus is clearly identified with the period and with the Teacher of Righteousness.

CHAPTER EIGHT

The Gospels

In this chapter I hope to persuade the reader that the four Gospels were based on an Essene 'Gospel of Jesus' which was written sometime during the period 63 BC – AD 68.

It is my contention that the Essenes wrote a 'Gospel of Jesus' possibly towards the end of the 1st century BC, and that it was from this original Gospel that the writers of Matthew, Mark, Luke and John compiled their Gospels.

It will come as no surprise, therefore, to find the Church, with the belief that Jesus was crucified in AD 30, somewhat worried at the lack of detail about when, where and by whom the New Testament Gospels were written. What information we do have from the early Christian fathers comes from people who were commenting 50 to 90 years after the Gospel writers were supposed to have published their work.

Briefly, this is what theologians think about the origins of the Gospels. It must be stressed that these are pure guesses; there is no accurate information.

The Gospel of Matthew

Author   Some suggest the apostle Matthew, but there is no evidence to support this supposition apart from the name which has become attached to the Gospel.

Date   Sometime after AD 70; no evidence produced to support any particular date.

Place   Perhaps Caesarea or Antioch (Syria) but there is no clear evidence for either place.

The Gospel of Mark

Author	Some suggest the Mark named in Acts of the Apostles 12 : 12 based on his association with Peter and the information from Papias, Bishop of Hierapolis.
Date	Between AD 65 and AD 70; there is little evidence to support this date.
Place	Antioch or Rome; Rome is favoured because Mark was an associate of Peter, and Peter was supposedly martyred in Rome.

The Gospel of Luke

Author	Luke, who was a physician and friend of Paul (Col 4 : 14). No evidence apart from the name which has become attached to the Gospel.
Date	No evidence – most theologians guess around AD 70 – 85.
Place	Rome and Achaia suggested; no clear evidence to support either place.

The Gospel of John

Author	According to Irenaeus (AD 180) John, the disciple of the Lord, published this Gospel.
Date	Usually dated early 2nd century AD–AD 125 perhaps, but no clear evidence.
Place	Ephesus (Turkey) and Alexandria mentioned as possible places.

When attempting to date a Gospel or, perhaps, the Pauline letters, the technique used by theologians is, to say the least, arbitrary. If, for example, writer 'A' lived around AD 80 but makes no reference to John's Gospel, and writer 'B', who lived around AD 140 does refer to the Gospel, then a date of AD 115 for John's Gospel does not seem out of place. Use is made of assumption – that writers 'A' and 'B' actually did live around the dates quoted. This is not a criticism of theologians who, in the absence of hard fact, have to try and make some estimate. The trouble is that after a suggested date is repeated a number of times, it becomes a fact. The names of the writers and the place of publishing are equally unreliable.

Looking back over the evidence available about the authors of the Gospels, the main point to note is that it is, by any standards, highly unreliable.

If the chronology of the ministry of Jesus was as the Church presents it to us, we would expect to find manuscripts dating back to the 1st century AD. The following list sets out the dates of the oldest ones held today:

1st century AD	Nothing.
2nd century AD	There is a papyrus fragment at the John Rylands Theological Library in Manchester. It is roughly two inches square and it records verses from the 18th chapter of John's Gospel. It was found in Egypt.
3rd century AD	The Chester Beatty Papyri include nearly the whole of the New Testament.

It would be reasonable to expect earlier manuscripts to be available. This is all part of the Synoptic problem which not only deals with the combination of similarity and differences between the Gospels, but also seeks to explain the delay in writing and other associated problems. Let us look at these in detail.

Why were the Gospels not written immediately following Christ's death?

Most theologians would accept that the dates of authorship for all the Gospels are later than AD 60. The reasons they give for the delay seem quite plausible. The early Christians, they explain, were not well-educated men, and those with the ability to write were few. If, however, we are to accept the Epistles as evidence, then Peter, John and James could write – why were they not inspired to record the life of their leader, a man with whom they had journeyed to the top of a mountain and met the prophets, Elijah and Moses? It is my opinion that the Gospels were not compiled until the escaping Essenes organised themselves and prepared the Gospels for the communities in which they were working. This was at a time much later than AD 60.

Finally, the theologians tell us that the early Christians thought the Parousia, the second coming of Christ, would be upon them within 40 years, and if this was so then it was unnecessary to write a Gospel. If the world is to end in 40 years, who will there be to read a Gospel in 41 years' time? And yet, persuasive though this might seem, it is a nonsense. The earliest Gospel was supposedly written about AD 65. If the writers were deterred from writing because the end of the world was coming 40 years after AD 30, how much more would they be deterred in AD 65 when there were only five years left? Furthermore, the imminence of the end of the world should have acted as a stimulus to the recruitment of Christians. The disciples would need a life story of their revered Jesus to leave with their new converts before they passed on to new areas.

What at first seem to be reasonable explanations for the delay in writing the Gospels suddenly dissolve into nothing. They are the easy answers, ones which seem logical at first sight but which, on close examination, can be seen to have little substance.

Why do some of the sayings of Jesus show him to be anti-Jewish and anti-gentile?

Most of the problems raised by the Gospel stories can be solved once their Essene origin is understood. The Church tells us that Jesus came to save all men, and just as He loves us, so should we love our fellow humans. In Luke 6 : 27 Jesus says, 'Love your enemies: do good to those who hate you'. How is it possible to equate this injunction with the hatred and contempt he shows for the Pharisees in Matthew 23 : 33 which reads: 'You snakes, you vipers brood; how can you escape being condemned to Hell?'. It is clear from this quotation, and other passages in the Gospels, that Jesus hates the Pharisees and sees no salvation for them – they are condemned to Hell.

76

It is not a question of Jesus being misquoted or the Gospel having been mistranslated, because this is just what could be expected from an Essene. Anyone outside the faith would perish. See what Jesus says of the Jewish villages who do not receive his disciples: in Luke 10 : 12 he says: 'I tell you, it will be more bearable for Sodom on the Great Day than for that town'. According to Matthew 18 : 15–17, the gentiles fare no better: 'If thy brother sin against thee ... and hear thee not ... then let him be unto thee as the Gentile and the publican'.

The selective nature of Jesus's mission is obvious from John 17 : 9 where he says: 'I am praying for them; I am not praying for the world, but for those whom thou hast given me, for they are thine'. Jesus is speaking of the remnant, the select few, not gentiles, not all Jews but just those few, the Essenes who accepted the Law of Moses and aimed at the very highest of standards – perfection. These passages, and others, present theologians with problems which they find impossible to explain. They remain in the Bible, surprisingly not deleted by the early Christians, as a reminder that the Church has completely misunderstood the writings of the New Testament.

Why are the early years of Jesus hardly mentioned?

Apart from a very brief reference to his disappearance when he was later found teaching in the synagogue, there is no mention in the Gospels of the childhood years of Jesus. In fact, when the Gospel stories are examined closely, the reader will be struck by the absence of the sort of detail expected in a biography.

There are no descriptions of the years before reaching manhood and there is little of his reaction to events which would give us a picture of the man. The Essenes, however, were not interested in giving that sort of description. They were concerned only with the life of their Teacher and the history of the sect, and how the events in the lives of both were foretold by the Old Testament prophets. The early life of Jesus was, with this objective, of no importance.

Why did Jesus wrongly forecast the end of the world as coming within the lifetime of his hearers?

The Parousia – the end of the world which would be signalled by the second coming of Jesus – is prophecied in Matthew 16 : 28 and reads: 'Truly, I say to you, there are some standing here who will not taste death before they see the Son of Man coming in his Kingdom'. There are other similar predictions elsewhere in the Gospel stories.

The theologians accept that he made these statements but cannot explain why he was wrong and failed to show a precise knowledge of the future or the infallibility which we would expect from the Son of God. The prophecies of Jesus were wrong because he had no special powers.

Why do the Synoptic Gospels agree in some parts and differ in others?

The Synoptic Gospels are so called because the first three – Matthew, Mark and Luke – give roughly the same synopsis or account of the life of Jesus. However, the combination of similarity and difference in the wording is unusual; this is well illustrated by a comparison of the passages naming the disciples:

Matthew 10 : 2–4. 'These are the names of the twelve apostles: first Simon, also called Peter, and his brother Andrew; James, son of Zebedee, and his brother John; Philip and Bartholomew, Thomas and Matthew the tax gatherer, James, son of Alphaeus, Thaddaeus, Simon, a member of the Zealot party and Judas Iscariot, the man who betrayed him.'

Mark 3 : 16–19. 'So he appointed the Twelve: to Simon he gave the name Peter: then came the sons of Zebedee, James and his brother John, to whom he gave the name Bo-anerges, that is, sons of thunder; then Andrew and Philip and Bartholomew and Matthew and Thomas and James the son of Alphaeus and Thaddaeus and Simon a member of the Zealot party and Judas Iscariot, the man who betrayed him.'

Luke 6 : 13–16. 'When the day broke he called his disciples to him and from among them he chose twelve and named them Apostles; Simon, to whom he gave the name Peter, and Andrew his brother, James and John, Philip and Bartholomew, Matthew and Thomas, James, son of Alphaeus and Simon who was called the Zealot, Judas the son of James and Judas who turned traitor.'

The list of the disciples illustrates the problem neatly – so very much alike but not identical. The explanation is, I think, that all the Gospels are made up of basic Essene Gospel material in which errors have occurred in copying and remembering over a period of years. Some errors would be made by both Essene and later Christian writers when making copies of the Gospel of Jesus. There were also deliberate additions to the Gospels by writers who sought to portray Jesus as a miracle worker and one whose mission was the salvation of all the peoples of the world.

The 'Priority of Mark' theory

It is understandable that theologians should try to discover who wrote the first Gospel, and there developed what is known as the 'Priority of Mark' theory. The assumption was that the first Gospel inspired others to write their own version and that they used Mark's Gospel as a source of information about Jesus. This would explain the similar and sometimes identical wording to be found in the Gospels of Mark, Matthew and Luke. What they had not considered was that an Essene 'Gospel of Jesus' had provided the information about the life of Jesus. Instead of using Mark's Gospel, therefore, Matthew, Luke and John had worked from either a remembrance or an actual copy of the Essene 'Gospel of Jesus'.

Even so, the 'Priority of Mark' theory does not stand up to examination. It puts forward, for example, that the shorter Gospel is likely to have been written first because had Mark copied Matthew or Luke, he would not have omitted so many verses. In Mark's Gospel there are 661 verses, in Matthew's 1,068 and in Luke's 1,149. Comparing the three Gospels, Matthew uses 606 of Mark's verses and Luke uses 630 verses so that, on the face of it, there seems some reason for accepting the theory. But is it really logical to argue this way? It could be that Mark's Gospel was originally much longer but that some pages were lost. Suppose Mark was not as expansive in his writing as Matthew and Luke – this would account for the Gospel being shorter but not necessarily having been written earlier. It could be that Mark, having read Matthew or Luke, decided to be more selective in his choice of material and abbreviated the Gospel.

Some theologians, when trying to show that Matthew the tax collector was the writer of the Gospel, come across the problem of answering the question, 'If Matthew was an eye-witness, why would he need to copy Mark?', to which the easy answer comes back: 'Any words about the Lord would be so treasured, so valuable that writers like Matthew and Luke would make the maximum use of every piece of written work available'. This begets another question: 'If they found written material about the Lord so treasured, why did Matthew omit 55 verses and Luke 31 verses from Mark?'.

Another argument in support of the 'Priority of Mark' theory is that, generally, Matthew and Luke follow the order of events in Mark. Notice, however, the word 'generally', because this enables us to re-state the argument as follows:

1. Generally, Matthew follows Mark's order of events, but not always.
2. Generally, Luke follows Mark's order of events, but not always.

Conclusion: Matthew and Luke copied Mark.

This statement could be turned round in order to argue the opposite: that neither Matthew nor Luke copied Mark:

1. Matthew does not always follow the order of events in Mark.
2. Luke does not always follow the order of events in Mark.

Conclusion: neither Matthew nor Luke copied Mark.

If the arguments can be turned round in this way, it shows that both are unreliable.

It is, however, possible to demolish the theory beyond any doubt.

When the Gospels of Matthew and Luke are examined closely we find that there are a number of verses which are duplicated and even triplicated. This points to the Gospels of Matthew and Luke having been compiled from two or more gospels. Now if two or more gospels have been used, we cannot be sure that Mark was one of them. When we find that none of the wording in the following quotations from Matthew and Luke ties up exactly with the comparative wording in Mark, then the 'disproof' of the 'Priority of Mark' theory is as complete as it could be.

Let us look at the verses in question:

Matthew 13 : 12. 'For to him who has will more be given and he will have abundance; but from him who has not even what he has will be taken away.'

Matthew 25 : 29. 'For to everyone who has will more be given and he will have abundance; but from him who has not even what he has will be taken away.'

Luke 8 : 18. 'Take heed then how you hear; for to him who has will more be given and from him who has not, even what he thinks he has will be taken away.'

Luke 19 : 26. '. . . that to everyone who has will more be given; but from him who has not, even what he has will be taken away.'

Mark 4 : 24–25. '. . . the measure you give will be the measure you get, and still more will be given you. For to him who has will more be given; and from him who has not, even what he has will be taken away.'

I will not quote all the examples of duplications in the Gospels, but here are some which the reader can check if he so wishes:

Matthew 12 : 38/ Matthew 16 : 1 and 4/ Luke 11 : 16 and 29/ Mark 11 : 13.
Matthew 11 : 15/ Matthew 13 : 9/ Mark 4 : 23.
Luke 7 : 36/ Luke 8 : 16/ Luke 11 : 37/ Mark 4 : 21.
Luke 11 : 43/ Luke 20 : 45–46/ Mark 12 : 38–39.
Luke 9 : 1–6/ Luke 10 : 1–16/ Mark 6 : 7–12.
Luke 6 : 6–11/ Luke 13 : 10–17/ Luke 14 : 1–6/ Mark 3 : 1–6.

If both Matthew and Luke have used two or three sources for their particular wording, none of which match with that of Mark's Gospel, then the evidence clearly points to there having been other sources; other copies or fragments of the Essene 'Gospel of Jesus' which have been used and not Mark's Gospel.

The 'Priority of Mark' theory is untenable. The only part of the theory which must now be refuted is the dating of the writing of Mark's Gospel. This needs to be earlier than the other Synoptic Gospels if it is to fit the theory. Once again, the examination of the facts by the theologians is superficial, thus ensuring that the conclusions drawn do not conflict with the theory. Paul, who is supposed to have died in Rome in about AD 64, did not appear to know of any gospel, so that Mark's Gospel must, the argument goes, have been written after AD 64. Bearing in mind that Paul's death in Rome is pure speculation and that there is nothing in the Pauline letters which even places Paul on the theological scene before AD 64, the dating of the Gospel is off to a very uncertain start.

The theologians then point to the references in Mark 13 : 1–2 where these two verses are interpreted as being a prophecy by Jesus that the Temple in Jerusalem would be destroyed. Because Mark does not include any comment to show that the prophecy was fulfilled, it was assumed that he wrote it whilst it was an event still to come. The Temple was destroyed in AD 66–70 during the Jewish War. The conclusion drawn is that Mark's Gospel was written some-time between AD 65 and the end of the Jewish War.

An examination of the relevant verses in Mark's Gospel

reveal, however, that Jesus was talking about the desolation and destruction which will precede the end of the world. He was certainly not referring to the Jewish War.

The dating of Mark's Gospel can only be set with certainty as sometime before AD 140, when it was first referred to by Papias. Much as they would like to place Mark's Gospel earlier, if only to keep the delay in the writing of the Gospels after the supposed death of Jesus in AD 30 within reasonable bounds, the theologians will have to accept that they have misled us by presenting us with a flimsy, unsubstantiated, misinterpreted and ill-argued theory.

The Essene connections in the Gospels

There are many stories and incidents in the Gospels which are impossible to explain unless the Esseneism of Christianity is understood.

Matthew, in 26 : 36–46, tells a story of Jesus finding the disciples asleep not once, nor twice but three times. The inclusion of this in the Gospel seems to have little point; there is nothing in Christianity to prevent followers falling asleep. But there was an Essene rule which required that 'the many watch in common for a third of all the nights of the year, to read the book and study the law and bless in common'. The night was divided into three watches so that if each member took one of the watches, he was effectively keeping the rule. In this story, Matthew is telling of a happening which his readers – the Essenes – would understand without explanation. He was making the point that the disciples had not only broken the rule by falling asleep during each of the three watches, but had done so at just the time when Jesus was to be arrested and when the events foretold by the Old Testament prophets were beginning to unfold.

There is an unusual reference in Luke 23 : 27–28 to a multitude of people following Jesus as he goes to be crucified. The women bewailed and lamented him, 'But Jesus turning to them said "Daughters of Jerusalem, do not weep for me, but weep for yourselves and for your children"'.

The Essene Biblical Commentary on Habakkuk 1 : 10

supports this verse. Now, if the Gospels had been written by man but inspired by God, one could have expected them to record that the crucifixion of Jesus was a time for rejoicing rather than weeping. The crucifixion was, after all, a sign that God so loved the world that he gave his son. There is another explanation for the verse.

I think that it was written by a scribe, looking back on the crucifixion and the punishment which, according to Josephus, was inflicted on the Jews by God for their treatment of Onias the Just. The famine which followed must have caused distress in the area which would have affected parents and children.

Essene beliefs explain a passage in Luke 8 : 18 which reads, 'For him who has will more be given, and from him who has not, even what he thinks he has will be taken away'. This is certainly not the teaching of the Church today. It seems cruel and harsh, but this was Esseneism. To those who aspired to perfection, the Essenes, life after death would be given, but for those who rejected their beliefs and way of life, even what they had would be taken.

It did not matter how early or late a man accepted 'the faith'. This is brought out in an otherwise puzzling parable found in Matthew 20 : 1–15. In this some labourers work only one hour in the vineyard while others work longer, but at the end of the day they all receive the same payment. Again, this seems unfair, but what Jesus was saying was that no matter how late they forsook the evil life for the Essene good life, their payment in Heaven would be just the same as for those who had changed earlier. It would be a persuasive point, particularly as they also preached that the end of the world was coming within a generation. John the Baptist said that the Lord would 'gather the wheat into the granary and the chaff he would burn with unquenchable fire'. The Essenes were determined to secure their place in the granary.

John the Baptist also gives more evidence of his origins when he says in Luke 3 : 11, 'He who has two coats, let him share with him who has none and he who has food, let him do likewise'. Jesus expressed the same thinking to a would-be follower in Matthew 19 : 21: 'If you would be perfect . . . sell what you possess and give to the poor'. In this context, 'perfect' and 'poor' were words used by the Essenes to describe themselves. They aspired to perfection, and by giving all their wealth to the community when joining the sect, they merited the description 'poor'.

Another instance of a statement made by Jesus for which there seems to be no rational explanation can be found in Mark 13 : 20, which reads, '... and if the Lord had not shortened the days, no human being would be saved, but for the sake of the elect, whom he chose, he shortened the days'. Readers will recognise the word 'elect' as an Essene word describing themselves. Jesus was, therefore, referring to the Essenes. Again, a knowledge of Essene writings enables us to recognise this as being an Essene belief, but one which has been misunderstood by whoever wrote Mark's Gospel. The Essenes believed that they would be required to pray for a lengthening of the day so that in those final days of the Holy War they could emerge victorious.

Now, there is no Christian belief that the final days of the Holy War should be either lengthened or shortened and no other religious group holds such a belief. What has happened is that by the time the compiler of Mark's Gospel received this Essene belief, it had become distorted in the telling so that the prayer for a lengthening was written down as a shortening of the day.

There can be little doubt that the New Testament Gospels and letters are from Essenes, to Essenes and about the Essene life. I think the sheer weight of evidence leads to no other conclusion.

Why have no copies of the Essene 'Gospel of Jesus' been found?

There may, of course, be a copy of the Essene Gospel among the so far unpublished Scroll translations. However, because it would be essential for the Essenes to have some permanent record of the life of their Teacher, I am inclined to the view that a few copies were made but with a very restricted circulation.

If there was only one copy, then it would be hidden in a

place known only to the Elders, and I think it would be memorised not only by the Elders but by the Overseers of the main Churches in the Middle East before they took up their appointment. It was not unusual in those times – and even for today – for Jewish religious leaders to memorise large tracts of Judaic texts. The secrets of the sect would be double-protected if the Overseers of the Essene Churches knew the location of the hidden Gospel – or Gospels – and if they had also memorised the content.

I am inclined to think that a copy of the 'Gospel of Jesus' would be given to each main Essene Church throughout the Middle East and, perhaps, the Elder was required to commit it to memory. We do not know where the main Churches were, but my guess is that Qumran, Rome, Corinth, Alexandria, Damascus, Antioch and perhaps Ephesus were the ones likely to control other smaller Churches in these main areas.

How were the New Testament Gospels compiled?

The original Essene Gospel would have been written perhaps at the end of the 1st century BC.

When the Essenes at Qumran were routed in AD 68 those Essenes who sought to bring the life of Jesus to the gentiles would need some record of his life for their converts.

Authorship	It is not really important who compiled the individual Gospels. The Church obviously finds it attractive to suggest that Matthew and John were responsible for the Gospels named after them, but the chronology of Christianity makes this quite impossible – the apostles Matthew and John lived in the 1st century BC. Mark and Luke, mentioned in the New Testament epistles could have written the two other Gospels.
Place	It seems likely that the Gospels were compiled in different areas. The traditional places named are somewhat unreliable, but it is unlikely that two nearby places would produce

their own copies of the Gospel. Because the Jews of the Dispersion, which included the Essenes, were present throughout the Middle East, the individual Gospels could have been written anywhere in that part of the world.

Date   The only date one could put forward for all the Gospels is sometime after AD 68 and, perhaps, sometime before AD 150.

Why were the other Essene writings not used by the new Essene Christians?

The evidence we have from Papias tells us that Mark 'remembered' the teaching of Peter and that Matthew interpreted the oracles as best he could. This probably explains some of the problems associated with the Gospels – the compilers were reliant on memory and, even where they had the actual oracles, there could be problems of interpretation. This would explain the identical wording of some Gospel passages and the slight differences between other texts in the Gospels.

It is noticeable, however, that although one or more copies of the Essene 'Gospel of Jesus' must have been available, none of the other Essene writings such as the War Scroll, the Thanksgiving Hymns and the Damascus Document seemed to circulate in the new Christian Churches.

This may be due to the sharpness of the Roman attack on the Qumran camp and the difficulties in taking the Scrolls from their secret hiding place. In the event, the teaching which was taken to the gentiles was a very simple form of Esseneism, one which stressed the need for high standards of conduct and a belief in Jesus. There was no need to plan for a war that had been fought and lost, and there would be no strict rules of conduct for those who were not living in controllable communes but in the everyday circumstances of village life.

The Gospel of John

There is one Gospel which deserves rather special comment,

and that is the Gospel of John. It provides another reason for the differences between the Gospel accounts of the life of Jesus. Interpolaters – those scribes who re-copied the Gospels for new communities – were able to insert verses of their own creation in order to project ideas which they thought would persuade people to believe in the Gospel. John's Gospel is an example. The 20th chapter seems to end the Gospel and the 21st chapter therefore appears to be an addition. There seems to be confirmation of this when one examines the contents. In it, there is a story of Peter and the disciples catching fish and Jesus helping to increase the catch. The story in John occurs after the death of Jesus, whereas a similar story in Luke's Gospel appears before his death. What has probably happened is that a scribe, who had read the story in Luke's Gospel, or had received it from another source, noticed it was missing from the Gospel he was copying. He therefore included it in a new chapter he was to write – the 21st – and in addition to this wrote into this chapter and into previous chapters references to 'the disciple who Jesus loved', a storyline which was false but ingenious.

Who was the beloved disciple? The debate has engaged theologians for countless years and the general opinion seems to be that John was the favoured disciple. It wasn't John; the disciple was Lazarus. The interpolater would be amazed to find how his clues to the identity of the beloved disciple have been ignored. Really, he could not have made the identification clearer.

In John 11 : 1–3 the verses tell of Lazarus falling sick and the sisters sending for Jesus with the words, 'Lord, he whom you love is ill'.

Further, when Lazarus died and Jesus wept, it was said, 'See how he loved him'. The conclusive passage is in John 21 : 20–23 which tells of Peter seeing the beloved disciple and of Jesus saying to Peter, ' "If it is my will that he remain until I come what is that to you? Follow me." The saying spread among the brethren that this disciple was not to die . . .'.

Now the only disciple who could have inspired such a thought was Lazarus. He had been dead once and brought back to life. There is no reason given anywhere which might suggest that any other disciple was being referred to. What Peter was really saying to Jesus was, 'You have died Lord. What about Lazarus who has already died but whom you brought back to life? Is he not to die? Will he remain alive until you return for a second time?'.

The interpolator had a reason for writing the Lazarus incident into the 21st chapter; the 24th verse makes it clear that Lazarus was the writer of the Gospel. Here was someone even more impressive than Peter. Here is a Gospel written by a disciple who had actually been brought back to life by Jesus and who was, together with the Gospel, proof of the power of Jesus. It was, of course, a complete fabrication, as were the other verses he wrote earlier into John's Gospel.

It is a reminder to us that although there is a considerable amount of truth in the Gospels, there are also verses which have been included which are false and there solely to deceive the reader.

On this occasion, the interpolater developed his deception by including references to the 'disciple who Jesus loved' in other chapters of his Gospel. As we shall see in Chapter 13, 'Mary, the Mother of Jesus', this enables us to identify the real mother of Jesus.

The original 'Gospel of Jesus'

When the founding fathers of the sect set about the task of recording the life of their Teacher of Righteousness – Jesus – they designed a system which was to deceive the world of theology for over 2,000 years. They needed material which could be used for their evening services where, after the traditional Essene supper, the members of the sect received further instruction. At the same time, it would be necessary for the written material used at these evening services to contain only material which did not breach the secrecy rules of the sect.

It is my belief that Psalms and Isaiah and other Old Testament books were used at these evening services; they clearly project Essene thinking, with a number of chapters specifically describing the torment and unhappiness of Jesus.

89

Anyone reading these chapters would not know what was behind the bland wording. Obviously, we cannot know what the members were told about Jesus, but it seems reasonably clear that only the 'Men of Knowledge' would know the secrets and that the ordinary members would be told only the broad history of the sect. It was an ingenious way of recording the history of the sect and it would have continued to succeed in keeping the Essene secrets had not that Arab boy, in 1947, made what was a momentous discovery.

It revealed the truth about the origins of Christianity in general and the identity of Jesus in particular.

Conclusion

I hope that I have demonstrated the Essene links with the information we get in the Gospels about Jesus and the sect, and that the evidence points to an Essene 'Gospel of Jesus' being the basis for most of the contents of the four Gospels.

CHAPTER NINE

Peter, John and James

The reader may have wondered how it is possible for Peter, John and James to be associated with the time of Paul, during a period roughly AD 68 to AD 150, and also with Jesus in 63 BC. They obviously cannot be in two chronological periods at the same time.

Although there is no reference to any special arrangement in the Scrolls that have been translated to date, it is my opinion that the Essenes wanted to continue the links with the Teacher of Righteousness until the final Parousia. In order to do this, I think they made it a requirement that whenever an Elder of the Church died, his replacement took his name. When the original Peter died, therefore, his replacement would take on the name 'Cephas' and when John and James died, their replacements too would take on their names. In this way there would always be a Peter, John and James at the head of the Church.

In actual fact, the name Cephas is more a description than a name – Cephas means 'Rock' and means 'Peter', so that heading the Church there would always be the 'Rock'. In the Gospel of Mark, verse 3 : 17 it reads: '. . . James the son of Zebedee and John, the brother of James he surnamed "Bo-anerges", that is, sons of thunder'. It is a name which does not make sense and theologians have been at a loss to explain it. I think it is a mistranslation. The Gospels were written in Greek and the word 'thunder' is written in a style similar to the word 'column' or 'pillar'. The Elders of the sect were known as 'Pillars', and I think a damaged scroll could explain how 'pillar' came to be translated as 'thunder'. The

Peter, John and James of the Pauline letters and Acts of the Apostles were not the same trio who accompanied Jesus, and the 'John the Elder' referred to by Papias was, again, a man who was the Pillar of the Church in the 2nd century AD who had been given the name 'John' in accordance with Essene custom.

The appearance of various Johns, James' and Peters has caused some confusion due to their appearance in different time-slots; this has proved difficult to explain. The Essene custom – as I believe it to be – solves the puzzle.

CHAPTER TEN

Miracles, Prophecies and the Old Testament

In this chapter, I explain why I do not accept the reality of miracles and prophecies, and why I am certain that the Essenes made many contributions to the Old Testament.

The various Christian Churches do not seem to have a consistently expressed belief about miracles. Everyone seems to have their own opinion, and this is helpful to the Church – it is able to speak with many voices. Generally speaking, however, the Roman Catholic Church accepts miracles, both scriptural and those from specially attested sources – for example, those reported from Lourdes. The Protestant Churches tend to accept only miracles found within the scriptures. The reader may not agree with me, but I do not believe that God interferes with life on earth. I would agree that there are many happenings which are so unexpected that it is difficult to account for them. However, this applies to both good and bad events. The tragedy at Aberfan, where almost a generation of children from the village were killed when a landslide buried their school, and the droughts in Africa which have killed millions of poverty-stricken natives are just two examples of opportunities for God to perform a miracle. But the protective hand to hold the landslide was not there. An instant supply of food for the starving millions never appeared.

If God had wanted us to recognise His power by working miracles into our lives, then these disasters would have been the time to demonstrate His might and His concern. Instead, when we read of miracles, they tend to be associated with the sudden cure of an illness of the psychosomatic kind which has the basic problem hidden within the body or mind. I have never read or heard of a change in the health of a patient which has been identified beyond any doubt as being due to some miraculous force. For example, there has never been a case of an amputated limb suddenly being replaced by a new one growing from the socket. That would have been impressive; providing that there were credible witnesses, it would be believable to the point where I might reconsider my views.

Spiritualism could be classed as a form of miracle. I have noticed, however, that there are charlatans who, for profit and prestige, are prepared to play upon the foibles of human nature. There is considerable money to be made by unscrupulous mediums who profess to have contact with those who have died. In front of a paying audience, they will cleverly sound out their audience in this way: 'I am hearing a voice – the name given is John or Jack – he died of an illness – something to do with the chest – the lungs or heart I think – does this have any meaning for anyone in the theatre tonight?'.

The names and illnesses are common and, as a consequence, there is always someone in the audience to whom they have meaning. The mathematics of probability have worked again.

Probably because the audience wants to believe that the medium has made a contact, this deception succeeds.

Does the medium really have to go through this charade? If there is genuine contact with the deceased, why is the full name and address of the deceased not passed on so that the audience knows precisely who is calling from 'the other side' and so any relatives or friends in the audience will instantly recognise the person involved? And, it has to be asked, does God perform at music-hall level?

There are, however, people who find it satisfying to think that God intervenes in our lives. When they hear of reported miracles affecting others, they want to believe the story. They reason, perhaps subconsciously, that if God intervenes on behalf of others, then He might at some time of need give them the same sort of help.

Onias the Just (whom I identify as Jesus) is described by Josephus as a miracle worker. But it was one miracle – the successful prayer for rain. In John 7 : 21 Jesus says, 'I did one deed and you all marvel at it . . .'. Given that one miracle was attributed to Jesus, the Gospel compilers probably thought that there was little harm in adding others; it would help them to persuade potential converts of the awesome power of Jesus.

For these descriptions of miracles to be persuasive, we would expect witnesses to be impressed and for the display to influence their subsequent behaviour. In fact, those who witnessed the miracles behave as though there had been no supernatural event. It is noticeable that:

1. The disciples do not react as though Jesus was a worker of miracles. If they really had witnessed them, they would have been completely convinced of the claim by Jesus that he was the Son of God. No disciple would have dared to betray him. To do so would be to risk the wrath of God. Furthermore, they should have responded by showing absolute loyalty to Jesus, even in the face of pressure from the Pharisees – such support would doubtless be rewarded by God either in this life or the next. In fact, knowing the power of God and Jesus they should have had every confidence that in the confrontation with the authorities, Jesus would have the power to win. Instead, when the soldiers arrested Jesus, the disciples fled.

   It is obvious that they had no confidence in Jesus nor believed that he had the protection of God.

   The lack of confidence in Jesus is made quite clear in John 7 : 3 where his brethren say to him, '. . . go to Judea that your disciples may see the works that you are doing'. If this appears to suggest that they believed in Jesus, the position is made quite clear two verses later. These read: '. . . his brothers did not believe in him'. The invitation to go to Judea was simply a sneer.

2. The Pharisees do not react to Jesus as one who has performed miracles. The argument is similar to that used above – that, like the disciples, had they witnessed the

miraculous powers of Jesus, they would not have dared to persecute him as they did.

The response of the disciples and Pharisees to the works of Jesus is not consistent with them having witnessed any miracles. Even the one deed which is attributed to Onias the Just (Jesus), the successful prayer for rain, seems to be explained by Jesus in verses from Matthew 16 : 1-4. Abbreviated, these read: '... the Pharisees and Sadducees ... asked him to show them a sign from heaven. He answered them "When it is evening, you say 'It will be fair weather; for the sky is red'. And in the morning, 'It will be stormy today for the sky is red and threatening.' You know how to interpret the appearance of the sky ... an evil ... generation asks for a sign, but no sign will be given"'. Here, Jesus seems to be saying that even the prayer for rain was more of an intelligent assessment of the weather by him, and that as far as miracles are concerned, no such sign will be given.

There are many unusual happenings reported in the press which are difficult to explain. When the outcome is good, there are always some who attribute the happy result to Divine intervention. It is a miracle, they say. To balance these incidents there are many more tragic events, but no one criticises God for having failed to intervene nor suggests that there may have been Satanic intervention. The Church plays a very one-sided game. Miracles involving the lives and health of people are occasionally reported, and this is why Lourdes attracts so many visitors. No one can deny that psychological influences can bring about impressive improvements in health. The problem with these is that it is impossible to identify what has happened to cause the improvement because it has occurred internally. If the internal improvements were due to miracles, it would be reasonable to expect that external damage would also be restored miraculously. There is, after all, no reason why God should work only internally when, for a display of his powers, an external and visible miracle would be more convincing. As I wrote earlier, there has never been an authenticated case of an amputated limb being miraculously made whole, thus being seen to have contravened the laws of nature. It simply does not happen.

I conclude, therefore, that miracles do not happen and that the other form of miracle – the prophecy – is also fiction. A consideration of the theory of 'free will' gives support to this conclusion.

Free will versus predestination

It can be argued that, without recourse to complex semantics, the Church should reject all miracle stories from whatever source.

The Church believes that man was given freedom to choose good or evil. Because man was choosing sinful ways, God sent Jesus to save mankind. Now, there is a contradiction here. The mission of Jesus was a deliberate interference in the activities of man. Man was not being given the freedom to make a choice, free of Godly influence, between good and evil. Despite this, the Church manages to straddle both concepts – free will and the mission of Jesus – without a blush.

Predestination seems a much more sensible approach, and one which would encompass the mission of Jesus without any problem. He would be – as I shall argue later – part of the Great Design.

Miracles and prophecies

If there is free will, then there cannot be miracles – which would be an interference from God – nor can there be prophecies. If we have free will, then even God cannot know how we are to behave in the future, and if He does not know, it is hardly likely that He would grant a human the ability to predict the future. If He did, then this act itself would be an interference from God.

Now, in a world which was predestined, it is possible that miracles and prophecies have been built into the Great Design. Have we any evidence that they are a part, even an exceptional part, of our lives?

If anyone should have been given the power to perform

miracles it should have been Jesus. The evidence points clearly to Jesus not performing any miracle or magic which impressed those around him. As we have seen earlier, even 'his brothers did not believe in him'.

Similarly, prophecies about the future are never made in such detail that they qualify, without question, for that description. An accurate prophecy about the future would, in fact, qualify for description as a miracle. Judging from experience of life today and applying it to life at the time of Jesus and before, I conclude that neither miracles nor prophecies are a natural part of life. The ability to perform supernatural acts is not given to us.

The origins of certain Old Testament books

The Jews were never deliberately secretive in their Biblical writings. They were recording their history. Names of people and places were given and the events and happenings were described in detail. There are many books in the Old Testament which are evidence of this.

There are, however, certain books which are distinctive in their content. With one exception, there are no other writings in the world of Jewish religious literature which compare with them. The exception is the Dead Sea Scroll containing the Hymns of Thanksgiving. There is a remarkable correspondence between these Hymns and the books of Psalms and Isaiah.

These two books are written in typical Essene fashion. Few names or places are mentioned. Like the Essene Hymns of Thanksgiving, there is a profusion of pronouns – 'I', 'he', 'them' and others – to the point where it is sometimes difficult to understand which 'he' or 'them' is being referred to.

The Hymns of the Essenes and the books of Psalms and Isaiah have one other extremely important feature in common. Many of the chapters describe the trials and tribulations of an unknown man and his responses to the hardships he is facing. They are repetitive, even boring, frustrating because they are so vague and secretive and yet at the same time fascinating because they give an insight into the mind of a man obsessive in his love of God. He is a man of suffering; he is scorned and betrayed by friends, threatened by his enemies; death is close at hand but despite the bitterness he feels, never does his love and confidence in God falter.

There are only two men in the religious history of Judea to whom these writings can refer. One is Jesus Christ and the other is the Teacher of Righteousness of the Essene sect. We have an abundance of evidence to show that, beyond any reasonable doubt, Jesus was the Teacher of Righteousness.

The conclusion must be that, like the Hymns of Thanksgiving, the books of Psalms and Isaiah were, for the most part, written by the Essenes. No wonder that the Essenes frequently quote from the Old Testament books of Psalms and Isaiah.

This conclusion conflicts with the current thinking of the Church. Many of the psalms have a heading which seems to attribute them to the time of David – roughly 1,000 BC. It is, however, generally agreed that the headings were added by an unknown writer and were not part of the original works. Apart from the headings there is nothing in the content which might link Psalms with David because whatever problems were experienced by David, they were nothing like those of Jesus.

Theologians date the book of Isaiah at between 500 and 800 BC; it is possible that a minority of chapters are of non-Essene origin. But those which are written in that bland, enigmatic and secretive style of the Essenes show, beyond doubt, that they were originated by that Dead Sea Scroll sect.

This was a very important breakthrough. Once I realised that the Essene writers were actually recording history in their bland Psalms and Isaiah verses I was able to examine them in detail for information on other aspects of the life of Jesus. They provided it in abundance, not only referring to the birth, but also to the betrayal, crucifixion and resurrection of Jesus. The Essenes thought that they could reveal the circumstances relating to Jesus in detail but maintain their secrets by not naming the participants.

However, once it was possible to relate actual people to the 'I' and 'he' pronouns used by the writers, the Essene 'mysteries' were secrets no longer.

The criticism which could be levelled at theologians is that they are too ready to accept traditional beliefs without question. The early Christian fathers, they think, were guided by the Holy Spirit and were therefore honest and completely reliable in their reporting of events. To doubt and question them would be tantamount to blasphemy.

Theologians have not identified, nor would they be looking for, any connection between the Essenes and the books of Isaiah and Psalms. Prior to the discovery and publication of the Dead Sea Scrolls, there was no particular reason for doing so. But even when the translations of some Scrolls were published and the Essene Hymns of Thanksgiving were there for all to read, there were few who saw a link between them and the Old Testament books. There were none, certainly, to take the thinking a stage further to consider the questions:

1. If the Essene Hymns were in style and content similar to Isaiah and Psalms, were these Old Testament books also written by the Essenes?
2. If so, then must not the prophecies previously associated with Jesus actually refer to the Essene Teacher of Righteousness?
3. If this is so, then was Jesus the Teacher of Righteousness?

Had any theologian actually suspected a link with the Essenes he would immediately have rejected it. For theologians the interests of Christianity require them to place as great a distance as they can between Jesus and the Teacher of Righteousness. Anything which brings them closer together, they fear, might lead to further questions and such confusions within the Christian Churches which could lead to their collapse. This is why the theological advisers to the media – TV contractors, radio stations and the press – take care to obstruct any discussions about the Dead Sea Scrolls and the Jesus connection. It also explains why there are a number of Dead Sea Scrolls which, after a period of over 35 years, have been translated but remain unpublished.

The reality of the prophecies relating to Jesus

There have been two theories about the Old Testament prophecies:

1. That they are genuine prophecies. A prediction is another kind of miracle. It goes against our experience of life, but for those who accept miracles as a possibility, this is explanation enough.
2. That the Gospels were written with specially fabricated incidents designed to be in accord with the Old Testament verses. This is possible, but improbable if a third possibility is considered.

I believe that many chapters in Psalms and Isaiah were written by the Essenes. This would date them between 63 BC, the year of the death of Jesus, and the routing of the Essenes from Qumran in AD 68. In other words, the chapters were written after the event, and instead of being predictions they are a supporting account of incidents and experiences in the life of Jesus and the Essene sect. The writers were not looking forward, but looking back and recording history.

This is of extreme importance when examining the Gospels in general and the crucifixion/resurrection accounts in particular, because the Old Testament writings now make for a clearer understanding of the Gospels. It is not known how the Essenes used these particular writings, but it would seem likely that they were intended to be instructive for the Essene congregation. The clear messages of these hymns is that despite the turbulence of the life of their Teacher of Righteousness and the life-threatening problems he faced, God protected him – and as God did for Jesus, so He would do for all others who loved the Lord and lived the righteous life.

With Proverbs and Lamentations, which exhibit the same Essene stamp, and together with the Essene Hymns of Thanksgiving, the number of chapters exceeds 250; perhaps with other material, one chapter was used each evening at the time of their traditional supper.

For example, as an incident in the life of Jesus, Psalms 69 :

21 would be quoted. This reads: 'They gave me poison for food and for my thirst they gave me vinegar to drink'.

This would be related to a verse in the Essene 'Gospel of Jesus' – probably the one which appeared in Matthew 27 : 34 which reads: '. . . they offered him wine to drink mingled with gall . . .', or perhaps the later verse in 27 : 48, which may be one of Matthew's duplications, which reads, '. . . and one of them at once ran and took a sponge, filled it with vinegar . . . and gave it to him to drink'.

Referring back to Psalms 69 : 21 there is that typical Essene combination of precision and vagueness. There can be no doubt about what happened – someone was offered vinegar to drink and poison (gall), and this is described precisely. The vagueness, to be found in all the prophecies in Psalms and Isaiah, relates to the identity of the people featured in the verses.

Pronouns such as 'he', 'she' and 'they' abound. In this way, the secrecy of the sect is protected. If someone outside the sect happened to see some of the writings, they would find accounts of incidents but never any clues as to who featured in the writing. Thus, it was difficult to identify the Essenes as being involved in any of the events chronicled in their scrolls.

The writer of 2 Corinthians 4 : 3 makes clear his Essene connections with his comment: 'And even if our Gospel is veiled, it is veiled only to those who are perishing', i.e. those outside the sect.

Quotations which link the Dead Sea Scrolls with the Old Testament

The secrecy adopted by the Essenes has led to important books in the Old Testament being attributed to writers dating back to 1,000 years BC when, in fact, they were written by the Essenes sometime after the crucifixion of their Teacher of Righteousness in 63 BC.

Fortunately, it is possible to prove, beyond any reasonable doubt, that the so-called prophecies were written by the Essenes looking back on the event and not forward, prophetically, to the future. Consider these:

1. The birth of the Teacher of Righteousness

Dead Sea Scrolls Hymn P	From the time of my father Thou hast known me and from the womb of my mother Thou hast established me, and from the belly of my mother Thou hast attended to me and from the breasts of her that conceived me . . .
Psalm 22 : 9	Yet Thou art he who took me from the womb, Thou didst keep me safe upon my mother's breasts . . .
Isaiah 49 : 1	The Lord called me from the womb, from the body of my mother he named my name . . .

2. Rejected by his father

Dead Sea Scrolls Hymn P	For my father knew me not and my mother abandoned me to Thee . . .
Psalm 10 : 14	. . . the hapless commits himself to Thee, thou hast been the helper of the fatherless.

3. Metaphorical description of birth

Dead Sea Scrolls Hymn J	And Thou hast sent out a sprouting as a flower that shall bloom forever, that the Shoot may grow into the branches of the eternal planting.
Psalms 80 : 14–17	. . . Look down from Heaven and see; have regard for this vine, the stock which thy right hand planted . . . let thy hand be upon the man of thy right hand, the son of man whom thou hast made strong for thyself . . .
Isaiah 11 : 1	There shall come forth a shoot from the stump of Jesse and a branch shall grow out of his roots.

4. The Holy Spirit is with the Teacher

Dead Sea Scrolls Hymn D	I give Thee thanks, O Lord, because of the Spirits thou hast put in me . . .
Psalms 51 : 11	Cast me not away from thy presence

| | and take not thy Holy Spirit from me . . . |
| Isaiah 11 : 2 (also see Isaiah 53 : 2) | . . . and the Spirit of the Lord shall rest upon him. |

5. He writes as one who is afflicted

Dead Sea Scrolls Hymn O	. . . for my strength had vanished from my body, And my heart ran out like water and my flesh melted like wax and the strength of my loins was prey to terror.
Psalms 22 : 14	I am poured out like water and all my bones are out of joint my heart is like wax it is melted within my breast my strength is dried up like a potsherd.
Isaiah 53 : 3–5	. . . he was despised and we esteemed him not . . . smitten by God and afflicted. But he was wounded for our transgressions he was bruised for our iniquities.

6. Teacher's voice is silent

Dead Sea Scrolls Hymns J and O	I clothed myself in black and my tongue cleaved to my palate. But Thou hast made the tongue in my mouth to grow without going back.
Psalms 38 : 13	Like a dumb man who does not open his mouth . . . and in whose mouth there are no rebukes.
Isaiah 53 : 7	He was oppressed and he was afflicted yet he opened not his mouth.

7. Life of the Teacher redeemed

| Dead Sea Scrolls Hymn D | Thou hast redeemed the soul of the poor one whom they planned to remove by shedding his blood because of Thy service. |
| Psalms 31 : 5 | Into Thy hand I commit my spirit; thou hast redeemed me, O Lord, faithful God. |

| Isaiah 51 : 13–14 | And where is the fury of the oppressor? He who is bowed down shall speedily be released; he shall not die and go down the Pit . . . |

8. A trap is set for the Teacher

Dead Sea Scrolls Hymn C	And the net which they stretched out for me catches their foot; they have fallen into the traps which they hid for my soul.
Psalms 57 : 6	They set a net for my steps; my soul was bowed down. They dug a pit in my way but they have fallen into it themselves.
Isaiah 29 : 20–21	For the ruthless shall come to naught and the scoffer cease and all who watch to do evil shall be cut off, who by a word make a man out to be an offender and lay a snare for him who reproves in the gate . . .

9. Rejection of the Teacher

Dead Sea Scrolls Hymn J	And I, I was the butt of the insults of my enemies, an object of quarrelling and dispute to my companions, an object of jealousy and wrath to those who had entered my Covenant . . . and all who ate my bread lifted the heel against me.
Psalms 41 : 5–9	My enemies say of me in malice 'When will he die and his name perish?' . . . All who hate me whisper together about me . . . Even my bosom friend in whom I trusted, who ate of my bread has lifted his heel against me.
Isaiah 53 : 3	He was despised and rejected by men; a man of sorrows and acquainted with grief; . . . he was despised and we esteemed him not.

10. The Teacher and the covenant

Dead Sea Scrolls Hymn L	And Thou in Thy righteousness hast appointed me unto Thy covenant
Psalms 50 : 5–6	Gather to me my faithful ones, who made a covenant with me by sacrifice. The heavens declare his righteousness for God himself is the judge.
Isaiah 49 : 8	I have kept you and given you as a covenant to the people ...

11. The drinking of vinegar

Dead Sea Scrolls Hymn H	And they stopped the thirsty from drinking liquor, the liquor of Knowledge, and when they were thirsty they made them drink vinegar, that their straying might be gazed on, that they might be foolish concerning their feasts.
Psalms 69 : 21–22	They gave me poison for food, and for my thirst they gave me vinegar to drink. Let their own table before them become a snare; let their sacrificial feasts be a trap.

12. The Teacher of Righteousness' special relationship with God

Dead Sea Scrolls Hymn C	They knew not that my being proceeds from Thee and that Thou wilt save my soul by Thy favours.
Psalms 119 : 73	Thy hands have made and fashioned me: give me understanding that I may learn thy commandments.
Isaiah 42 : 1	Behold, my servant, whom I uphold, my chosen, in whom my soul delights; I have put my Spirit upon him.

Is not the correlation between these writings remarkable?

The Dead Sea Scrolls, Psalms and Isaiah are supposedly from different periods spanning a thousand years. We find, however, that in most verses identical words are used to describe exactly the same situation.

If it had been possible to find verses from the Scrolls and the Old Testament which corresponded to just one particular connection with the Teacher of Righteousness this could be regarded as minimal evidence.

When the group of verses from the Scrolls and Old Testament involve first one important linkage – for example: 1. The birth of the Teacher of Righteousness, coupled with another, 2. Rejected by his father, connected with another, 3. Metaphorical description of birth . . . and so on, down to 12, The Teacher of Righteousness' special relationship with God, we are back to the 'coincidence factor' and the mathematics of probability. Coincidences like this reveal the truth – that they are not coincidences. The mathematics of probability tell us that the likelihood of these three different books referring to three different men in such detail is as near as anything could be to being a mathematical impossibility. Further, when we find that they are all written in that distinctive, cryptic, Essene style where situations are alluded to but with no real names or identities being revealed, then the proof is complete. It can be stated, without equivocation or qualifying caveats, that these particular verses from Psalms and Isaiah, and many others in these books and others in the Old Testament, were written by the Essenes and refer to their revered leader, the Teacher of Righteousness.

It might be argued – someone surely will do so – that the writers of the Dead Sea Scrolls, reading the verses in the Old Testament, decided to write about the life of their Teacher in a way which was in accord with these texts. However, thanks to Josephus and the cross-reference linkages between Onias the Just and the Teacher, we know that two of these connections apply to Onias: number 6, Onias, too, was silent and number 12, Onias had a special relationship with God for he was 'beloved'. Thus, these verses tell the truth of a man who lived in the 1st century BC. These, therefore, were not fabricated, nor were the rest. I do not think that theologians would use this argument, for to do so would invite the accusation that the Gospels too could have been written, not based on the truth, but simply to match the Old Testament verses.

107

Few theologians would question the miracles associated with Jesus, because to them they are an important part of the proof that Jesus had been invested by God with special powers. Without the New Testament miracles being credited to him, Jesus would lose that supernatural aura. The prophecies in the Old Testament seem to add further credibility to his unique origins, for here was a Saviour whose coming was predicted many hundreds of years before his actual birth.

Theologians, therefore, use their undoubted scholarship to reinforce these concepts and to protect the image of both Jesus and the Old Testament prophecies.

A Scottish theologian, W. Graham Scroggie DD, wrote a book entitled *Psalms*, and in it he made the following statement: 'It can be confidently asserted that we have no irrefragable [sic] proof that there is in the Psalter, a single Psalm of the Maccabaean period ... but a heavyweight of evidence that the major part of Books I – III originated in the period 1,000 BC–700 BC'.

I think, however, that the evidence given earlier shows clearly that this is wrong. They were written – must have been written – in the 1st century BC at the earliest.

The importance of recognising the Essene origins of parts of the Old Testament

One final comment on the comparisons of the Dead Sea Scroll verses and those of the Old Testament seems worthwhile.

The reader will have noted that the extracts from Isaiah are generally written in the third person whilst the other two are written as though by the sufferer himself. From a distance of 2,000 years, it is impossible to be certain, but there are a number of chapters in Psalms, including those which I quote from above, which seem to have been written by Jesus – the pain, the suffering, the disappointment and heartache are expressed clearly, and yet despite the reproaches of the writer his faith and loyalty to God remain undiminished.

The style of writing and the actual situations described,

together with the same or similar wording, are such that there can be little doubt that all three writings come from the same source – the Essenes. This is extremely important when examining the Gospels and the Scroll writings because the verses in the books of Psalms and Isaiah provide a further cross-check on actions and incidents in the New Testament, particularly the betrayal of Jesus and his subsequent crucifixion. I am not suggesting that all the chapters in Psalms and Isaiah were written by the Essenes, and some may have been written hundreds of years before the ministry of Jesus. Why the Essene and non-Essene chapters should have been merged is a puzzle. We can only speculate. Perhaps, when the Essenes were preparing their writings, they included their own with other ancient scrolls to give the impression that their work had originated many years previously.

Conclusion

I hope that this chapter has persuaded the reader that:

1. There are no miracles.
2. There can be no prophecies.
3. Certain chapters in the Old Testament books of Psalms and Isaiah were actually written by the Essenes – some, perhaps, by Jesus.

109

CHAPTER ELEVEN

Jesus Identified

In this chapter, I will present evidence to show that the Jesus Christ of the Gospels was the Teacher of Righteousness of the Essene Dead Sea Scroll sect. Further, that he was also the priest, Onias the Just referred to by Josephus in his book *Antiquities of the Jews*.

Jesus Christ

Was there a Jesus Christ? If so, can he be identified? Just as important, does it really matter? To many people it does; when people face a bereavement or some personal crisis in their lives, they may feel alone and need to believe in God. They do not want vague reassurances; they want a certainty supported by convincing proof.

Despite the many thousands of books which have been published about Christianity, there remains one major difficulty – no theologian has proved that Jesus Christ ever existed. In a book called *The Myth of God Incarnate* one theologian wrote that the evidence for Jesus is 'fragmentary and ambiguous', whilst Professor G.A. Wells in his *The Jesus of the Early Christians* drew on a host of theologians and writers to prove that the Jesus story is a myth.

The discovery of the Dead Sea Scrolls brought to light details of the life of the Teacher of Righteousness of the Essene sect which seemed to mirror events in the life of Jesus. The world of theology patiently waited for the remainder of the Scroll translations to be published but, for some undisclosed reason, they have not been released. Many people suspect the reason to be that the suppressed translations would reveal further connections between Jesus and the Essene Teacher which would make it clear, beyond any doubt, that Jesus was, in fact, the Teacher of Righteousness.

In 1991, an unexpected development brought hope to the waiting theologians. It was revealed that photographs had been taken of all the Dead Sea Scrolls and that these would be made available for translation by the museum which owned them. This was good news for some, bad news for the Church. When the new translations will be available is not known. What is certain, however, and I hope this book will persuade the reader to agree, is that it is not necessary to have any further translations for the truth to be known. Those translations of the Scrolls which have been available now for some years, together with the Gospels and the writings of Josephus, provide all the information needed to identify Jesus with absolute certainty.

Exactly who was Jesus?

It has to be understood that different names may be ascribed to people depending on the writer and the timescale. Mrs Margaret Thatcher MP has been variously referred to by different names – the positions she held in Parliament, for example. She was Parliamentary Secretary to the Ministry of Pensions and National Insurance; Secretary of State for Education and Science; Leader of the Opposition and Prime Minister; and in addition she has collected descriptions such as 'The Iron Lady', 'Maggie' and 'TINA' (There Is No Alternative). A male, for example, could be referred to as a 'son' by his parents, 'husband' by his wife, or 'father', 'brother' or 'nephew', depending on the relationship. It all depends upon the perspective from which one person views another. In the same way, various writers have used different names when referring to Jesus.

In different writings, Jesus has been named as 'the Teacher of Righteousness', 'Onias the Just', 'Honi the Circle Drawer', 'Jeshu Ben Pandira', 'Ben Strada', 'Balaam' and 'a certain person'.

In Chapter 13 I will deal with each of these names in some detail to show how the reported lives of these people correspond to the life of Jesus. I think it fair to claim, however, that the following series of coincidences provides quite overwhelming evidence for the identification of Jesus as the Essene Teacher and Onias the Just.

Evidence that Jesus was the Teacher of Righteousness

The coincidence that Jesus and the Teacher were described as 'Son of God'

Although the translations of certain Scrolls have not yet been published, news has been leaked of a text which compares very closely with verses in Luke's Gospel.

Taken from the unpublished Scroll and referring to the Essene Teacher of Righteousness	*Taken from the Gospel according to Luke and referring to Jesus*
He shall be great upon the earth. He shall be called the Son of God and they shall call Him the Son of the Most High	He will be great and will be called the Son of the Most High (chapter 1 : 32) . . . and will be called holy, the Son of God (chapter 1 : 35)

Now, it could be argued that Luke, the Christian, quoted Essene verses which referred to the Teacher of Righteousness and applied them to another man, Jesus Christ. However, this would be to dent the originality of the Gospel and would bring into question the rest of Luke's Gospel. A more reasonable explanation would be that the same words were used in two different written works because they had the same source and referred to the same man.

The majority of people comparing the two quotations would, I think, concede that the seeming coincidence is, for Christianity, an unsettling link between Jesus and the Essene Teacher of Righteousness, and one which should be investigated further. The Church, however, would prefer it to be quickly forgotten, discarded as an interesting connection but no more than that.

The coincidence of references to being 'pierced' in both Gospel and Scroll

At the time of writing (1992) another link between the two men has emerged from the translations now being made from photographs of the unpublished Scrolls. There is a reference to the 'leader of a sect' being 'pierced'. Obviously, the leader referred to is the Teacher of Righteousness and students of theology will doubtless recall the verse in John's Gospel (19 : 34) which reads: 'But one of the soldiers pierced his side'.

The coincidence that Jesus and the Teacher received God's words from the prophets

In Matthew 17 : 1–13 the Transfiguration of Jesus is described. Jesus is accompanied by Peter, James and John up a high mountain. There appeared before them Moses and Elijah, who talked to Jesus. God spoke to them.

A Dead Sea Scroll passage, written by the Essenes explaining a text taken from Habakkuk, reads, 'They [the Teachers' followers] did not listen to the word received by the Teacher of Righteousness from the mouth of God', and later in the explanation tells of the Teacher, 'in whose heart God set understanding, that he might interpret all the words of His servants the prophets, through whom he foretold all that would happen to His people and His land'.

The essential correspondences are these:

— Jesus met God (Matthew);
— the Teacher of Righteousness received the 'word' from the 'mouth of God' (Scrolls);
— Jesus met the prophets, Elijah and Moses, and talked to them (Matthew);
— the Teacher of Righteousness received predictions about the land and people from God via the prophets (Scrolls).

No other religious figure, apart from Jesus and the Teacher, has experienced a personal meeting with God and two prophets. It is an experience unparalleled in Judaic history. The only reasonable explanation must be that Jesus and the Essene Teacher of Righteousness were the same man.

113

The coincidence that Jesus and the Teacher claim God as their father

In Matthew 16 : 17 Jesus refers to 'my Father who is in Heaven' and later, in 17 : 5, God tells the disciples, 'This is my beloved Son, with whom I am well pleased'. In the Essene Hymn Scroll, recorded as Hymn C by Professor Dupont-Sommer, it reads: 'They knew not that my being proceeds from Thee', and in Hymn J the writer records: 'And Thou hast created me for Thy sake to fulfil the Law'.

Throughout the Hymn Scroll, there are references to the special bond between God and the writer – and there can be no doubt that it was either the Teacher of Righteousness (Jesus) or someone writing in his name. For example, he claims, 'Thou manifest the powers in me', 'unto judgement hast Thou established in me' and 'Thou hast poured thy Holy Spirit within me'. This last text might well be compared with Luke 3 : 22 which reads: '. . . and the Holy Spirit descended upon him in bodily form'.

The coincidence that Jesus and the Teacher preached the Law of Moses

One of the jars rescued from the caves around Qumran protected the Scroll of the Rule which sets out the doctrines, ceremonies and rites practiced by the Essenes. In Chapter V of this Scroll it reads: '. . . and let him [the newcomer to the sect] undertake by oath of obligation to be converted to the Law of Moses . . .'. There are a number of references to the Law of Moses in the Gospels, and the verses which encapsulate the regard Jesus has for it are John 7 : 16 and 19 : 'So Jesus answered them, "My teaching is not mine . . . did not Moses give you the Law?"'.

The coincidence that the death of Jesus and the Teacher involved Roman soldiers

The presence of the Roman leader Pontius Pilate and his soldiers at the crucifixion of Jesus is described in the Gospels. There is not general agreement amongst theologians as to the time-slot in which to fit the Teacher of Righteousness. The Dead Sea Scrolls, written as they are in a cryptic, secretive way, make no reference to Roman soldiers. Theologians have suggested a variety of dates for the activities of the Essenes. One has suggested the time of the Crusades, others the 9th century AD, the 6th century AD, the 1st century AD, the 1st century BC and the 2nd century BC, leaving the eager student somewhat bewildered at their lack of unity. Professor Dupont-Sommer, a theologian of outstanding calibre, whose *The Essene Writings from Qumran* has been described as a 'magisterial work' dates the death of the Teacher at around 63 BC. Further, it was the year that Roman soldiers captured Jerusalem. The death of Onias the Just in 63 BC, his links with Jesus, and the cross-reference links with the Teacher of Righteousness all provide evidence which supports the Professor.

In addition to this, there is a reference in the Nahum Commentary to 'Emilius' who almost certainly was M. Aemilius Scaurus, the first Roman governor of Syria. There is also reference in an unpublished liturgical calendar to Alexander Jannaeus and his wife, Queen Alexandra Salome, together with 'Hyrcanus', a name which probably refers to the son of the King and Queen.

The whole weight of evidence converges on the events which culminated in the death of Jesus and the Teacher, in the presence of the Romans, in 63 BC.

The coincidence that Jesus and the Teacher were hung on a tree to die

Although the Gospels tell us that Jesus died on the cross, evidence from other verses in the New Testament tells us otherwise. In Acts 10 : 39 it reads, 'They put him to death by hanging him on a tree'. This is supported in Galatians 3 : 13 and 1 Peter 2 : 24.

In the Commentary on Nahum, there appears a reference to 'he who was hanged alive on the tree' (in the G. Vermes' translation) and 'on the wood' (in the book by Professor Dupont-Sommer). The Professor comments that following this passage there are words which could suggest that the person who had been hanged 'suffered punishment and became an object of invocation', i.e. an object of prayer. There are only two persons in Judaic writing who could be described thus – and they are the Teacher of Righteousness and Jesus. Not only does this link the two men, but there is also the additional connection that both were 'hung on a tree to die'.

The coincidence that Jesus and the Teacher returned after death
The return of Jesus, his resurrection, is clearly set out in the Gospels, and John, in 20 : 19, describes it in these words: 'Jesus came and stood among them and said to them "Peace be with you"'.

In the Commentary on Habakkuk, there is a verse which reads, '. . . but at the time of the feast of rest of the Day of Atonement he appeared before them . . .'. Professor Dupont-Sommer comments that this does not have supernatural implications and, as I later argue, this is because there is considerable evidence to show that Jesus did not die on the cross – that he was taken alive, and that this was not a supernatural, spiritual appearance.

According to the Dead Sea Scrolls, therefore, the Teacher of Righteousness appeared after his supposed death, and this is precisely what the Gospels tell us about Jesus after being taken from the cross.

The coincidence that Jesus and the Teacher became the revered figureheads of their sect
The New Testament tells us of the reverence for Jesus expressed by many writers. The Dead Sea Scrolls tell us of the reverence expressed for the Teacher of Righteousness by the writers of the Scrolls.

The coincidence that a Roman leader was involved with the lives of both Jesus and the Teacher
The Gospels tell us that Pontius Pilate was involved with the death of Jesus. In this book I explain why I believe that Pontius Pilate, unknown to secular historians of the time, was actually Pompeius Magnus whose name, because he headed the soldiers who carried the 'pilum' or javelin, was corrupted to Pompeius Pilatus. Even so, there can be no doubt that a Roman leader – or someone representing him – was involved in the death of Jesus.

116

In a still unpublished but partly disclosed fragment of the Scrolls, there are references to 'Emilios' and 'Hyrcanus' who are identified by Professor Dupont-Sommer as Hyrcanus II and Emilius Scaurus, the latter having been sent to Jerusalem in 65 BC to help Hyrcanus II. A Roman leader was therefore involved in the lives of the Teacher of Righteousness and Jesus, and provides yet another link between the two men.

The coincidence that Jesus and the Teacher required followers to sell their goods
A ruler asked Jesus what he should do to inherit eternal life and Jesus told him, in Luke 18 : 22, '. . . sell all that you have and give to the poor'.

Understandably, this is generally interpreted as meaning that the man should give his wealth to those who are destitute. This is wrong.

The Essenes referred to themselves as 'the poor'. They had no goods or money because it was a requirement that before joining the sect, members had to sell all that they had and give the proceeds to the brotherhood. In the Scroll of the Rule it lays down that: 'His property and also his wages shall be handed over to the overseer of the revenues of the Many'; readers will recognise 'Many' as being another word used by Essenes to describe themselves.

There can be no doubt that this was recognised as a rule followed by the early Christians because in Acts 5 : 1-11 a situation is described wherein Ananias and Sapphira sold property and laid only part of the proceeds 'at the apostles' feet'. For this dishonesty, both lost their lives. Does not the practice of giving away one's wealth give us another connection between Jesus and the Teacher?

The coincidence that the followers of Jesus and the Teacher rebelled
In Matthew 26 : 56 it reads: 'Then all the disciples forsook him and fled'. In Hymn J of the Dead Sea Scrolls it reads: 'And all who ate my bread lifted the heel against me'. In this context, 'lifting the heel' means rebelling. There is, in fact, an almost identical passage in John 13 : 18 which says: 'He who ate my bread lifted his heel against me'.

The almost identical wording gives us another important link between the two leaders.

The coincidence that Jesus and the Teacher were betrayed by a friend

Later, I argue that both Judas and Peter betrayed Jesus, but I do not think I need to quote verses as evidence that Jesus was, in fact, betrayed by a friend. In the Essene Dead Sea Scrolls, there are bitter references to the Man of Lies, and recorded in the Commentary on Habakkuk are the words: 'The explanation of this concerns those who have betrayed with the Man of Lies'.

I discuss the betrayal of Jesus by Peter in more detail later. It is suffice to comment here that irrespective of whether Judas or Peter is regarded as the betrayer, they were both friends of Jesus.

This is yet another unhappy experience that both men shared. Is not the weight of singular correspondences leading to the certainty that Jesus was the Essene Teacher?

The coincidence that Jesus and the Teacher were harassed by the authorities

In Luke 20 : 19, we are told that: 'The scribes and the chief priests tried to lay hands on him . . .'.

In the Essene Biblical Commentary on verses from the Book of Habakkuk 2 : 15 it reads: 'The explanation of this concerns the Wicked Priest who persecuted the Teacher of Righteousness . . .'. I identify the Wicked Priest as Hyrcanus II, and this verse tells of the harassment of the Teacher which led to his arrest and an act described as 'swallowing him up' (usually interpreted as 'killing' him). Does this evidence not add to a list which permits no other conclusion but that Jesus was the Essene Teacher?

The coincidence that the followers of Jesus and the Teacher 'murmur' at them

In John 6 : 61 it reads: 'But Jesus, knowing in himself that his disciples murmured at it, said to them, "Do you take offence at this?"'. To 'murmur' is to complain, to express dissatisfaction with something, so that the disciples were dissenting and opposing Jesus.

In the Essenes' Hymn J, it reads: 'And I . . . an object of

118

murmuring and contention to those I had gathered together'. The same story is told quite clearly in both quotations, and is another unhappy experience shared by the two men.

The coincidence that Jesus and the Teacher were killed in the year of two High Priests

According to the Gospel of Luke, 3 : 2, there was a time which he describes as the 'High Priesthood of Annas and Caiaphas', and these are present at the trial of Jesus later in his ministry. This is incorrect because the handover of this high office from Annas to Caiaphas took place in AD 14 and they did not actually hold office at the same time.

All the evidence points to the Teacher having been killed in 63 BC, which was a year in which two brothers fought for the office, each claiming to be the High Priest. The information which had come down through the years that Jesus was killed in the year when there were two High Priests was correct – Luke, looking back over many, many years, identified the wrong High Priests. This is another connection between the two leaders.

The coincidence that Jesus and the Teacher were killed in the year when the two High Priests were related

The fact that the two High Priests, mistakenly identified by Luke, were related deserves to be registered as yet another, separate, coincidence. Annas was the father-in-law of Caiaphas, and Hyrcanus II and Aristobulus II were brothers.

The coincidence that the followers of Jesus and the Teacher wrote in a cryptic style

The Biblical Commentaries of the Dead Sea Scrolls are testimony to the veiled style adopted by the Essenes in order to keep their history secret. The code names used, such as 'Wicked Priest' and 'Man of Lies', keep the identity of some secrets known only to the 'Men of Knowledge' of the sect.

In 2 Corinthians 4 : 3 it reads: 'And even if our gospel is veiled, it is veiled only to those who are perishing', indicating secrets of the sect which would remain veiled to those outside the sect – those who were to perish at the end of time.

How fortunate we are that casual comments such as this,

and the next example, reveal so much – that the two groups, Essene and Christian, adopted the same practice. This is just one more coincidence which adds to the proof that the early Christians were Essenes.

The coincidence that the followers of Jesus and the Teacher stored their writings in earthenware jars

According to the writer of 2 Corinthians 4 : 7: '. . . we have this treasure [knowledge of God and Jesus] in earthenware vessels'.

The Dead Sea Scrolls were also stored in earthenware vessels.

The followers of Jesus and the Teacher used the same words to describe themselves

In the New Testament and in the Dead Sea Scrolls the writers refer to themselves in the same way – 'poor', 'perfect', 'elect' and 'saints'. No other group uses this combination of terms. If seemingly different groups share expressions in this way, the suspicion must be that they are the same group.

The coincidence that Jesus and the Teacher are associated with extreme light

The Transfiguration of Jesus is described thus in Matthew 17 : 2: 'And he was transfigured before them, and his face shone like the sun and his garments became white like the light'. This was the occasion when Jesus was accompanied by Peter, James and John and met God and the prophets.

The Hymn Scroll, Hymn L, reads: 'And Thou, O God, hast succoured my soul and lifted my horn on high. And I will shine with a seven-fold light . . .'. It is easy to see how the words in the Hymn have inspired the verse which is found in all three of the Synoptic Gospels. No other figure in Jewish history has been associated with illumination such as described for Jesus and the Teacher. Is this not further persuasive evidence of the common identity of the two men?

The coincidence that the sects of both Jesus and the Teacher held God's secrets or 'mysteries'.

There are references in the Essene Hymn Scroll to the writer – seemingly, the Teacher of Righteousness himself – knowing the 'marvellous mysteries' given to him by God.

Similarly, in the Gospels – Mark 4 : 11, 13 : 11 and Luke 8 : 10 – and in the New Testament letters such as Ephesians 3 : 4 there are references to the 'mysteries' of Jesus.

No other sects held to their secrets and actually referred to them in this way; in so doing they provide further evidence that the Essenes and the early Christians were the same sect.

Evidence that Jesus was Onias the Just

In his book *Antiquities of the Jews*, Book 14, Chapter 2, Flavius Josephus describes the situation in Judea after the death of Queen Alexandra Salome in 67 BC. Her two sons, Hyrcanus II and Aristobulus II, were fighting for position and Aristobulus defeated Hyrcanus in battle. By agreement, Aristobulus became King, and Hyrcanus became, in Josephus's words, 'as a private man'.

However, Hyrcanus was given support by those who did not like Aristobulus gaining power by force, and who preferred to see Hyrcanus (the elder son and therefore legally entitled to the throne) in power in Judea. Aristobulus was defeated in another battle and fled to Jerusalem where he was beseiged by the King of Arabia who was helping Hyrcanus. The people generally were supporters of Hyrcanus and assisted him in the seige, while only the priests continued to support Aristobulus.

We now come to the really interesting quotation from *Antiquities*: 'As this happened at the time when the Feast of the Unleavened Bread was celebrated, which we call the Passover, the principal men among the Jews left the country and fled into Egypt. Now there was one, whose name was Onias, a righteous man he was, and beloved of God, who, in a certain drought, had prayed to God to put an end to the intense heat and whose prayers God had heard, and had sent them rain. This man had hid himself because he saw that this sedition would last a great while. However, they brought him to the Jewish camp, and desired that as by his prayers he had once put an end to the drought, so he would in like manner make imprecations on Aristobulus and those of his faction. And when upon his refusal, and the excuses that he made, he was still by the multitude compelled to speak, he stood up in the midst of them and said "O God, the King of the whole world; since those that stand now with me are thy people, and those that are beseiged are also thy priests, I beseech thee that thou wilt neither harken to the prayers of those against these, nor bring to effect what these pray against those." Whereupon such wicked Jews as stood about him, as soon as he made this prayer, stoned him to death.'

Now, consider these coincidences:

The coincidence that Onias the Just and Jesus were priests

Implied in the passage from Josephus is that Onias was, like those who had fled, a principal man – a priest. Honi the Circle Drawer (referred to later and identified as Onias the Just) was a priest. Jesus also was a priest. He is referred to as 'Rabbi' by other Gospel writers but also in John 1 : 49.

The coincidence that Onias the Just and Jesus were killed at the time of the Passover

Onias the Just was killed at the time of the Passover.

Jesus was killed at the time of the Passover.

There can have been few priests killed at the Passover and this fact, together with two or three other correspondences, identifies the two men as being the same man with certainty.

Although Josephus was reputed to have trained with the Essenes and was possibly a scribe, it is unlikely that he would have been involved with any of the highly secret scrolls of the sect. He is unaware that Jesus did not die on the cross.

The usual death for those guilty of apostasy was punishment by stoning and then being hung on a tree to die. Josephus obviously knew of the stoning but was not *au fait* with what happened afterwards. He reported and was aware of only part of the story. I think this explains the omission of any reference to the crucifixion and the subsequent escape by Jesus.

The coincidence that Onias the Just and Jesus were workers of miracles

Onias the Just was a miracle worker – he had successfully prayed for rain. He was required to perform another miracle to help the supporters of Hyrcanus. He refused. Let us now take a look at a quotation from Matthew 16 : 1–4. Jesus is required to perform a miracle by the Pharisees but refuses. It looks very much as though the Pharisees have referred to a past miracle involving the weather.

See what the Gospel verses say: 'And the Pharisees and Sadducees came and to test him they asked him to show them a sign from heaven. He answered them "When it is evening you say 'It will be fair weather: for the sky is red'. And in the morning 'It will be stormy today for the sky is red and threatening'. You know how to interpret the appearance of the sky but you cannot interpret the signs of the times. An evil and adulterous generation seeks for a sign but no sign shall be given to it except the sign of Jonah." So he left them and departed'.

Now the reference to weather must have some special significance. Such a reference must have some relevance to the special situation in which Jesus found himself. Look at another quotation, this time from John 7 : 14, where Jesus is preaching in the Temple, in the 'middle of the feast'. Although the Jews apparently marvel at his teaching, the atmosphere is not being described honestly because, within three verses, there is an argument and mention of killing Jesus. And then Jesus says, in 7 : 21, 'I did one deed and you all marvel at it'.

The coincidence that Onias the Just and Jesus only performed one miracle

One deed? We have a situation here where, if Jesus is telling the truth, then the Gospel accounts are untrue. According to John's Gospel, Jesus had already performed the feeding of the 5,000 and walked on water. It has always been assumed that the single deed he referred to was the healing of the man on the Sabbath, but that happened much earlier in the story. The one deed Jesus is referring to here must, I think, be his prayer for rain, and even the Gospel account quoted above from Matthew 16 : 1–4 seems to show Jesus saying that it wasn't really a miracle, that anyone can interpret the appearance of the sky. I should add that Onias also prayed for the

123

termination of the rain; this was also answered. As this was the same incident, I think it would be fair to claim that the 'single deed' could be reasonably applied to both instigation and termination. Does not the alleged 'miracle working' abilities of the two men lead to the suspicion that they were the same man?

The coincidence that Jesus and Onias the Just were linked with prayers for rain

We have evidence from Josephus that Onias successfully prayed for rain and that this was regarded as a miracle. He also prayed for the rain to end.

Jesus is also linked with such a prayer. In James 5 : 16–18 it reads: 'The prayer of a righteous man has great power in its effects. Elijah was a man of like nature with ourselves and he prayed fervently that it might not rain and for three years and six months it did not rain on earth. Then he prayed again and the heavens gave rain and the earth brought forth its fruit'.

It is possible – and I may be wrong to do so – to read into this passage by James an implication that, 'You know about the successful prayer for rain from our righteous man – Jesus – well, the prayer of a righteous man has great power and as another example of someone who successfully prayed for rain, take Elijah who was of like nature with us – he too was righteous'.

If this is invalid, then there is the previously mentioned quotation from Matthew 16 : 1–4 where Jesus seems to be explaining his success by an understanding – which everyone had – of how to interpret the sky.

I have already referred separately to the coincidence of both Jesus and Onias being miracle workers, and of there only being one miracle. I think it fair to present as a different 'coincidence' the fact that both appear to have been associated with rain.

The coincidence that Onias the Just and Jesus were judged before the High Priest

At the time of the arrest of Onias the Just, Hyrcanus II was disputing the High Priesthood with his brother. Having besieged his brother, Aristobulus II, in the Temple, Hyrcanus

II was technically the winner and therefore the High Priest. Onias the Just was brought 'to the Jewish camp', and although the presence of Hyrcanus is not recorded in the extract I quoted earlier, Josephus refers to the support of local Jews for Hyrcanus II. It is not unreasonable to assume that Hyrcanus was present at the Jewish camp outside the Temple, where Aristobulus was besieged. If this is accepted, then Onias was brought before the High Priest for judgement. Jesus also was brought to the High Priest for trial. Is this not further support evidence for my contention that Jesus was Onias the Just?

The coincidence that Onias the Just and Jesus lived in the 1st century BC

The account given by Josephus of the death of Onias the Just associates him with Hyrcanus II and Aristobulus II, both of whom were vying for power at the time that Onias was killed – 63 BC.

Alexander Jannaeus was the father of these two brothers, and there is a Talmudic text which clearly links Jesus with Alexander. It appears in b. Sanh. 107b in a passage which is difficult to understand. In it, Jesus is involved in an incident during the reign of Alexander Jannaeus (from 104–78 BC).

Theologians have been unable to explain a reference to Jesus which seems to place him during the wrong period. Does not the Talmud and the account of Josephus clearly link Jesus and Onias in the first half of the 1st century BC?

The coincidence that Onias the Just and Jesus were killed in the year of two High Priests

The struggle described above, between Hyrcanus II and Aristobulus II, was to establish the right to be High Priest. Hyrcanus had been deposed by Aristobulus and so both laid claim to that office: Hyrcanus because he had been illegally deposed and Aristobulus because of the dictum, might is right. In that sense, therefore, both men were, technically at least, High Priests.

The Gospel of Luke, in 3 : 2, refers to two men holding the office of High Priest. It reads, 'In the High Priesthood of Annas and Caiaphas . . .', and is historically incorrect if he is suggesting that it was jointly ministered. In AD 14, Annas handed over his responsibilities to Caiaphas (who was his son-in-law), so the two never held office together. Nevertheless, a reading of John's Gospel seems to indicate a belief that at the time of Jesus's death, the two men held office jointly. In 18 : 19 John writes: 'The High Priest then questioned Jesus . . .', and it is apparent that Annas is the interrogator. Later, in verse 24, it reads: 'Annas then sent him bound to Caiaphas, the High Priest'. Thus, John refers to both men as High Priest.

There is, therefore, correspondence between the accounts written by both Josephus and John, that there were two High Priests in office at the time of the death of both Onias the Just and Jesus. Is this not one more important element in the case supporting my contention that Jesus and Onias were the same man?

The coincidence that Jesus and Onias the Just were described as 'righteous'
Josephus, when recording the death of Onias, describes him as 'a righteous man'.

In 1 John 2 : 1 Jesus is also described in this way; the verse reads: '. . . we have an advocate with the Father, Jesus Christ the righteous'. Is this not another small but important link between Jesus and Onias?

The coincidence that Onias the Just and Jesus were linked with 'stoning' and that they 'hid' themselves
The links between the two men continue.

In John 8 : 59 and John 10 : 31 there are references to the Jews trying to stone Jesus, but they do not succeed because Jesus 'hid himself'. In a passage from Josephus, he describes Onias the Just as having 'hid himself'.

The punishment for those found guilty of apostasy was stoning, followed by being hung on a tree to die. If, as I suggest, Onias and Jesus were the same man, then the accounts of their death, if combined, are in line with this punishment – Onias was stoned and Jesus was 'hung on a tree to die'.

Again, the unusual coincidences of 'hiding' and the method of execution are a further link between the two men.

126

There are other interesting verses in the Gospel which throw more light on the links between Jesus and Onias. First, let us consider the name 'Onias the Just'. Why was he called 'Just'? Presumably because he judged people. In what circumstances would he be likely to judge people? Well, there is no doubt that if he was an Essene leader – the Essene leader – that he would judge one brother's complaints about another. This would explain the name.

The Essenes had their own court. They were not to judge one another but to leave any disputes to settlement by their own commune council judiciary. In Matthew 5 : 22 Jesus says, 'But I say to you that everyone who is angry with his brother shall be liable to the council, and whoever says "You fool" shall be liable to the hell of fire'.

There are a number of quotations from the Gospels which could be cited which do not make sense unless they are seen against the Essene background we have described in this book. In this quotation, Jesus lays down standards of behaviour, and punishments for deviations therefrom, which have no known parallel in the world. No civil authority would sentence anyone to the 'hell of fire' because he called his brother a fool. None, that is, except the Essenes.

Their standards were the very highest, and the quotation above is described in similar words in the Dead Sea Scrolls. When Jesus refers to a 'council' he does not mean a civil council. A case would be laughed out of court if the plaintiff complained that he had been insulted by his brother. Jesus is referring to the Essene council and, in fact, in Matthew 5 : 25 he makes specific reference to civil courts and the dangers which can arise from appearing before them. These verses from Matthew can only be understood when the Essene origin of the Gospels is recognised.

Let us look at two quotations from the New Testament and see how they are relevant to our identification of Onias as Jesus:

John 5 : 30. 'I can do nothing on my own authority; as I hear, I judge: and my judgement is just, because I seek not my own will but the will of him who sent me.'

Acts 22 : 14. 'The God of our fathers appointed you to know his will, to see the Just One, and to hear a voice from his mouth.'

In the John quotation, when Jesus said, 'as I hear', was he meaning when a complaint was being judged? Possibly. In his position as Essene leader, he would judge, and in the John quotation he is claiming that he is a just man. In the quotation from Acts, Ananias is speaking to Paul and is referring to the vision of Jesus which Paul had received on the road to Damascus. Here, it is obvious that the name 'the Just' or 'the Just One' had come down from a generation of Christians.

It is, I think, reasonable to argue that the implication of these two quotations is that Jesus was a judge who was 'just' and to conclude that 'Jesus the Just' was Onias the Just.

Does this evidence not draw the two a little closer so that, when considered with other coincidences, they merge into the same man?

The coincidence that Nicodemus is linked with both Onias the Just and Jesus
The presence of a man named Nicodemus in the lives of Onias the Just (killed 63 BC) and Jesus (supposedly killed AD 30) is an important link between the two men. Here are the facts:

1. John's Gospel tells us in 3 : 2 that '. . . there was a man of the Pharisees named Nicodemus, a ruler of the Jews. This man came to Jesus by night . . .'. There are two points to note. Nicodemus did not visit Jesus to discuss theological points as the verses which follow suggest. He could have discussed these at any time. Further, he was not a Pharisee. He was a senior adviser to Aristobulus II and, as such, was a supporter of both the Essenes and the Sadducees. Evidence for this comes from John 7 : 51 where he defends Jesus and later in 19 : 39 where he helps Joseph of Arimathea to recover the body of Jesus. The real

128

reason for the visit by night is explained by Josephus.

2. In *Antiquities of the Jews* Book 18 : 16 : 5, Josephus tells us that: 'Aristobulus . . . stole away secretly by night with only one of his servants, and went to the fortresses wherein his friends were such from the days of his father were settled . . .'. Aristobulus was mustering support to enable him to take the High Priesthood away from his brother.

   Although the text refers to him being accompanied by a 'servant', in my opinion the companion was Nicodemus. In an earlier passage, Josephus records that Nicodemus represented Aristobulus in negotiations with Pompey, and, on another important mission to gain support, I cannot believe that he would take a servant in preference to a trusted and experienced adviser. Further, the friends 'from the days of his father' would be the Essenes and Sadducees. If I am correct in my analysis of the circumstances, then Jesus/Onias would have been visited at Qumran by Nicodemus, as described in John 3 : 2 where he 'came to Jesus by night . . .'.

3. Another interesting reference to Nicodemus appears in *Antiquities of the Jews* Book 13 : 3 : 2 and reads: 'In a little time afterward came ambassadors again to him, Antipater from Hyrcanus and Nicodemus from Aristobulus; which last also accused such as had taken bribes, first Gabinius and then Scaurus . . .'. This tells us that Nicodemus, as an ambassador, was truly a 'ruler of the Jews' and that he was involved in bribery. I discuss the relevance of this later in Chapter 12 but, in the meanwhile, it is a further link between the lives of Jesus and Onias the Just.

It would be an outrageous coincidence if two different 'rulers of the Jews' both named Nicodemus and both living at different times, just happened to be involved in similar circumstances with controversial Rabbis who were leaders of dissident groups. In my opinion, the evidence points to the Nicodemus of the Gospel being the same Nicodemus referred to by Josephus.

The coincidence of both Onias the Just and Jesus refusing to speak
The small and easily missed events in the lives of these two

men are just as important as the major happenings.

Josephus tells us that Onias the Just refused to speak until 'the multitude' compelled him to do so.

Similarly, in John 19 : 10 we are told: 'Pilate therefore said to him "You will not speak to me?"'.

Josephus, as I have said, was well informed and was not one, fortunately for us, to neglect or overlook a small snippet of information which did not seem important. It is important because it links the two men together just as closely as any major item of information.

The coincidence that Onias the Just and Jesus were deserted by their friends

Josephus tells us that, 'the principal men among the Jews left the country and fled into Egypt. Now there was one, whose name was Onias, a righteous man he was . . .'. The writing clearly, in my opinion, identifies Onias as being, originally, one of this group which went to hide in Egypt. It does not seem unreasonable to construe this as describing Onias being deserted by other members of his group.

In the same way, at the time of the arrest of Jesus, Matthew 26 : 56 records similar circumstances. It reads: 'Then all the disciples forsook him and fled'. The companions of Onias fled. The companions of Jesus fled.

This is another firm link, I believe, between the two men.

The coincidence of Onias the Just and Jesus both being 'beloved of God'

Josephus describes Onias the Just as being 'beloved of God'. So was Jesus. In Matthew 3 : 17 we are told that a voice came down from Heaven saying, 'This is my beloved son, with whom I am well pleased'.

No other men in the history of religion have been described thus.

Had the story of the Hyrcanus II/Aristobulus II dispute come down the line via historians, we could have expected the story of Onias the Just to have been ignored. He played no part in the political events developing in Judea at that time.

It is worth repeating that Josephus was reported to have been an Essene at some time or he had trained under an

Essene teacher. The religious line of transmission, particularly with it being Essene, has led to the story of Onias the Just, not simply an important figure for the Essenes but *the* figure, coming to Josephus in reasonably accurate form. I believe that the two accounts of Onias who was 'beloved' and Jesus who was 'beloved' can be traced back to their original source – the Dead Sea Scrolls and their account of the life of the Teacher of Righteousness. Here, we have evidence to merge all three men into one.

The coincidence that God punished the Jews for the deaths of both Onias the Just and Jesus

Josephus tells us that it was the belief of a number of Jews that because Onias the Just was stoned to death, God punished the Jews. His description reads, 'Nor did He (God) delay their punishment but sent a strong and vehement form of wind that destroyed the fruits of the whole country, till a modius of wheat was then bought for eleven drachmae'. God also punished the Jews for the death of Jesus. In Matthew 27 : 51 we are told of an earthquake, and in both Mark and Luke there is reference to 'darkness over the whole land'. This is discussed in more detail in Chapter 12, 'The Crucifixion, the Resurrection and Peter'. We have to decide whether it is simply coincidence that two apparently different priests, each being 'beloved of God' were killed at the time of the Passover whose treatment resulted in punishment from God. In my opinion, the uniqueness of the evidence leads to one conclusion only – that Onias and Jesus were the same man.

The coincidence that Onias the Just and Jesus make a similar speech

In the Gospel of John, almost the whole of chapter 17 is devoted to a speech made by Jesus immediately before his arrest. There are a number of instances in the Gospels where events are not in the correct chronological order, and I believe this is one of them. I think the speech was made after his arrest. If it is accepted that descriptions of events and speeches, transmitted over a period of 150 years or more, can become somewhat corrupted, I think there are reasons for

thinking that the Jesus speech compares with that given by
Onias. I give them below for comparison but have shortened
the one by Jesus in order to bring out the salient points.

Speech by Onias the Just	*Speech by Jesus*
O God, the king of the whole world, since these that stand with me now are thy people, and those that are besieged are also thy priests, I beseech thee that thou wilt neither hearken to the prayers of those that are against these, nor bring to effect what these pray against those.	. . . I am praying for them; I am not praying for the world but for those whom thou hast given me for they are thine; all mine are thine and thine are mine . . . (John 17 : 9–10) I do not pray for these only but also for those who believe in me through their word . . . (John 17 : 20–21)

The points to note are:

1. There are no other instances in the history of Christianity
   or of Judaism, wherein an accused priest prays to God on
   behalf of the people.
2. Both are prayers on behalf of the Jews – Onias for the
   Essenes both inside and outside the temple, Jesus for
   'those whom thou hast given me', whom I would identify
   as his supporters and disciples.
3. Onias refers to 'these' and 'those'; Jesus refers to 'these'
   and 'those'.

I suggest only that the similarities are there. When taken with
other evidence connecting the lives of Jesus and Onias, the
suspicion must be strong that the two speeches by two
apparently different men were, in fact, the same speech by
one man.

*The coincidence that a Roman leader was involved in the deaths of
Onias the Just and Jesus*
Theology tells us that Pontius Pilate was the Roman leader
involved in the death of Jesus. On the other hand, secular
history of those early years of the 1st century AD has no

knowledge of Pontius Pilate whatsoever.

As I have argued, the name is a corruption of the Roman leader who was involved in the war raging between Hyrcanus II and Aristobulus II in 63 BC.

The Roman general who captured Jerusalem was Pompeius Magnus and his ally was Hyrcanus II, the enemy of Onias the Just. His soldiers carried the Roman 'pilum', the javelin, and it is my belief that he was referred to as Pompeius Pilatus and that, with the passage of time, this became distorted to Pontius Pilate. Onias the Just and Jesus are therefore linked with the same man.

The coincidence that the High Priests involved in the persecution of Onias the Just and Jesus were related

According to the Gospels, Annas and Caiaphas, apparently High Priests together at the time of Jesus, were father-in-law and son-in-law respectively. The two High Priests involved with Onias the Just were the brothers Hyrcanus and Aristobulus and held office in the year that Onias was killed – 63 BC.

The coincidence that there was an earthquake when Onias the Just and Jesus were persecuted

In Matthew 27 : 51 the Gospel records that when Jesus died on the cross, 'the earth shook'. This was God expressing His anger at the Jews. Josephus tells us of circumstances which we could expect to follow an earthquake – God sent a vehement storm of wind which caused a famine. It is not unusual for dust clouds to follow earthquakes and for crops to be destroyed by the fall-out. Again, God was angered at the death of Onias. Now, apart from the Gospels, there is no record of an earthquake in AD 30, the supposed year when Jesus died, but there is a record of an earthquake in 64 BC.

The coincidence that there was an eclipse when Onias the Just and Jesus were persecuted

In Luke 23 : 45, we are told that following the death of Jesus, 'the sun's light failed'. There is no record of an eclipse in the year AD 30.

However, scientists can calculate when an eclipse would

have been seen in Jerusalem, and there was such an eclipse in 64 BC.

This is close to the year when Onias the Just was killed.

There was therefore an eclipse when both Jesus and Onias were persecuted.

Honi the Circle Drawer

'Honi' is another name for Onias the Just, both names having the same Hebrew root.

Tradition tells us that when Honi prayed for rain, he first drew a circle on the ground and placed himself within it. It is believed that the circle represented the universe and that Isaiah 40 : 22 with its allusion to God has some significance; it reads, 'It is he who sits above the circle of the earth . . . who stretches out the heavens like a curtain'.

It is not known if Honi frequently drew a circle on the ground, but there is a link with Jesus which is recorded in a text sometimes added at the beginning of John, chapter 8. In 8 : 6 it reads: 'Jesus bent down and wrote with his finger on the ground'.

We are not told precisely what he wrote on the ground, but taking into account all the evidence linking Onias and Jesus, the conclusion must be that he wrote not words, but a circle.

Another tradition associated with Honi is that he went to sleep at the time of the destruction of the first Temple and did not wake until after the building of the second Temple.

I think that this is a muddled tradition which may have confused a 'falling asleep and later awakening' with 'dying and a subsequent resurrection'.

Perhaps the most important tradition is that Honi was an Essene, was a scholar of repute with many pupils, and dealt with all questions which were put to him by Rabbis.

Everything we know about Honi, in fact, supports the contention that he was Onias the Just and the Jesus of the New Testament.

The lives of Jesus Christ and the Teacher of Righteousness compared – summary

Code: EWQ . . . *Essene Writings from Qumran* by Professor Dupont-Sommer

LF . . . Leaked fragment from the unpublished translations of the Scrolls

1. Teacher was described as Son of God and Son of the Most High (LF)

   Jesus was described as Son of God and Son of the Most High (Luke 1 : 32 and 35)

2. Reference to 'leader of a sect' being 'pierced' (LF)

   Jesus was the Christian leader and was 'pierced' (John 19 : 34)

3. Teacher received God's word from the prophets (EWQ)

   Jesus received God's word from the prophets (Matthew 17 : 1–13)

4. Teacher claims 'my being proceeds from Thee' (EWQ)

   Jesus claims to be God's son (Matthew 17 : 5)

5. Teacher expounded the Law of Moses (EWQ)

   Jesus expounded the Law of Moses (John 7 : 19)

6. Teacher's death involved Roman soldiers (EWQ)

   Death of Jesus involved Roman soldiers (John 11 : 48 and 19 : 23)

7. Teacher was hung on a tree to die (EWQ)

   Jesus was hung on a tree to die (Gal 3 : 13 1 Pet 2 : 24)

8. Teacher appeared after death (EWQ)

   Jesus appeared after death (John 20 : 19)

9. Teacher featured in Essene writings (EWQ)

   Jesus featured in Gospels

10. Teacher's death involved Pompeius Magnus (EWQ)

    Death of Jesus involved Pontius Pilate

11. Teacher required followers to sell their goods (EWQ)

    Jesus required followers to sell their goods (Luke 18 : 22)

12. Teacher's followers desert him (EWQ)	Followers of Jesus desert him (Matthew 26 : 56)
13. Teacher betrayed by 'Man of Lies' (EWQ)	Jesus betrayed by Judas (John 6 : 71)
14. Teacher harassed by authorities (EWQ)	Jesus harassed by authorities (Luke 20 : 19)
15. Teacher's followers 'murmured' at him (EWQ)	Disciples of Jesus 'murmured' at him (John 6 : 61)
16. Teacher killed in the year of two High Priests (EWQ)	Jesus killed in the year of two High Priests (Luke 3 : 2)
17. – who were related (EWQ)	– who were related (Luke 3 : 2)
18. Teacher's sect wrote in cryptic, veiled style (EWQ)	Followers of Jesus wrote in cryptic, veiled style (2 Cor 4 : 3)
19. Teacher's sect buried writings in earthenware jars (EWQ)	Followers of Jesus buried writings in earthenware vessels (2 Cor 4 : 7)
20. Teacher's sect used 'poor', 'perfect', 'elect' and 'saints' to describe themselves (EWQ)	Followers of Jesus used 'poor', 'perfect', 'elect' and 'saints' to describe themselves
21. Teacher associated with extreme illumination (EWQ)	Jesus associated with extreme illumination (Matthew 17 : 2)
22. Teacher's sect held their 'mysteries'	Followers of Jesus held their 'mysteries'

Is it really necessary to comment further? The sheer weight of evidence linking the two men, who have so much in common, permits no conclusion other than they were the same man.

The same exercise with a comparison of the lives of Onias the Just and Jesus ends with the same thought that these two must be the same Jewish Rabbi and, extending the comparison, that Onias the Just was the Teacher of Righteousness.

The lives of Onias the Just and Jesus compared – summary

Code: J . . . *Antiquities of the Jews* by Flavius Josephus
     TJE . . . *The Jewish Encyclopaedia*

1. Onias the Just was a Rabbi (J)

    Jesus was a Rabbi

2. Onias killed at the time of the Passover (J)

    Jesus killed at the time of the Passover

3. Onias was a miracle worker (J)

    Jesus was a miracle worker

4. Onias worked only one miracle (J)

    Jesus appears to claim only one 'deed'

5. Onias linked with prayer for rain (J)

    Jesus appears to describe a deed as involving the weather

6. Onias was judged before the High Priest (J)

    Jesus was judged before the High Priest

7. Onias lived in 1st century BC (J)

    Jesus linked with 1st century BC

8. Onias killed in the year of two High Priests (J)

    Jesus killed in the year of two High Priests

9. Onias described as 'righteous' (J)

    Jesus described as 'righteous'

10. Onias stoned to death (J)

    Jesus threatened with stoning

11. Onias 'judged' others (J)

    Jesus judged others

12. Onias linked with Nicodemus (J)

    Jesus linked with Nicodemus

13. Onias refused to speak (J)

    Jesus refused to speak

14. Onias deserted by friends (J)

    Jesus deserted by friends

15. Onias was 'beloved of God' (J)

    Jesus was also beloved of God

16. God punished the Jews for the death of Onias (J)

    God punished the Jews for the death of Jesus

17. Onias makes a speech (J)

    Jesus makes a similar speech

137

18. A Roman leader involved in death of Onias (J)	A Roman leader involved in the death of Jesus
19. High Priests who were involved in death of Onias were related (J)	High Priests who were involved in the death of Jesus were related
20. When Onias was crucified there was an earthquake (J)	When Jesus was crucified, there was an earthquake
21. When Onias was crucified, there was an eclipse (J)	When Jesus was crucified, there was an eclipse
22. Honi (identified as Onias the Just) drew circles on the ground (TJE)	Jesus reported to have written on the ground

Again, with so many incidents common to both lives, can there be any reasonable doubt that Onias the Just was the Jesus of the Gospels?

Josephus and his reference to Onias the Just

A reasonable question to ask is why Josephus did not identify Onias as Jesus or the Teacher of Righteousness.

Josephus certainly had some theological training with the Essenes, but in view of his short-lived membership it is unlikely that he was privy to Essene secrets and, in any case, he would be bound not to divulge them by an oath of secrecy. At the time that Josephus wrote his books, the Essene sect had been routed by the Romans, and he could well have thought that the sect was no longer operating. He probably recorded the death of Onias as an event which involved someone of special importance – Onias was beloved of God – never thinking that his reference would figure in the identification of a man who was to become the focal point of one of the major religions of the world, and one which, when Josephus wrote, had not even begun. Gentile Christianity developed after the death of Josephus.

As a writer, Josephus would almost certainly be a scribe within the community, but it is doubtful whether he would be allowed to deal with any writing which involved the secrets of the sect. This may explain his knowledge of some aspects of the life of Onias the Just but not the awareness that is displayed by those who compiled the Gospels.

Jesus and the references to him in the Rabbinical writings of the Jews

It is obvious from the number of references to Jesus, Mary Magdalene and 'a certain person' that Jesus had made a considerable impact on the Jews of his time – and of those of later. There is no other dissident who is featured to that extent in the Talmud.

Perhaps if he had been a lone figure whose influence made only a temporary impact on the Jewish community he might have been forgotten within a short period. Instead, his followers, in effect, formed a sect and developed writings which had Jesus as the focal point of their prayers and their teaching. Although dead, his influence continued through the presence of the Essene sect and was an ever present reminder to the Jewish community that there was a Jewish approach to the worship of God other than the traditional Pharasaic teaching.

It was important to the Jews to brand dissident teaching as the work of fools. This is why the derogatory writings about Jesus and his mother were carried down through the years by either the oral or written tradition, and were eventually included in the Talmud.

In this section, I will present evidence which:

1. Sets out certain references to Jesus in the Jewish Talmud.
2. Describes how these link up with each other, with Jesus, with Onias the Just and with the Teacher of Righteousness.

The information about the Talmudic references comes from a book by an English theologian, R. Travers Herford who, in his *Christianity in Talmud and Midrash*, also pays tribute to the help he received from research done by a German theologian, Heinrich Laible (who wrote *Jesus Christus im Talmud*). Travers Herford is an example of a theologian who is as modest as he is brilliant. He examines difficult Jewish texts and presents his conclusions with clarity and honesty. If he is not able to explain a problem, he says so and tells us the difficulties. Not for him the easy answer to impress the reader. The final sentence in his book probably explains why. It reads: '. . . I finish this book; and, in parting from it, take regretful leave of what has been to me a friend and companion through many years'. You treat a friend with respect, and he gives the Talmud this in full measure.

To be featured in the Talmud is rather like being in *Who's Who* – however much or little is said, the fact that there is an entry carries a message – here is someone of importance.

The Rabbinical writings were designed to give guidance to the Jews on how best they could love and serve their God. Jesus was one whose conduct should not be followed. They criticised him for being illegitimate, for being a fool, for being a deceiver and for leading Israel astray. He was a reminder to Jews of what could happen to those who broke away from traditional Jewish beliefs.

Here, then, is the evidence from the Talmud. I have not quoted chapter and verse or given actual quotations; to have done so would have required explanations which are best read in the original book. Those who wish to consider the detail may well be able to obtain a copy of the Travers Herford book through their local library.

As with a number of people in the ancient writings of the Jews, names can cause some confusion. There are a number of references to Jesus in the Rabbinical writings of the Jews. Some are misspellings, some are forms of ridicule and one – 'a certain person' – due to censorship where clear references to Jesus might have provoked reprisals from the gentiles. Here is a list:

1. Jeshu Ben Pandira (or Pentira or Pandera or Pentiri). Travers Herford regards this as a name given in order to mock Jesus. He discusses possible meanings of the name although he does not favour any particular one. I am inclined to his suggestion that the name indicates 'birth from a virgin' as perhaps a sneer that would find favour

with the Jews of the time. As we shall see, the contributors to the Talmud believed that Jesus was an illegitimate child.

2. Ben Stada. Travers Herford suggests that 'Stada' derives from 'Stath da', which means that the mother had 'gone aside from her husband'. Again, this reflects the belief that the mother was not married to the father of Jesus and had committed adultery.

3. Balaam. According to Numbers 22 : 32 the original Balaam led people astray and God told him that, 'your way is perverse before me', which was the charge levelled at Jesus.

4. Jeshu ha-Notzri. An alternative form of Jesus of Nazareth.

5. 'A certain person'. This has been explained above.

From the Talmud we learn certain facts about Jesus and these other named people which lead to some interesting conclusions. We find:

1. That in two different passages in the Talmud, dealing with the same matter, one refers to 'Jeshu' and the other to 'Ben Stada'. The conclusion is that Jeshu was Ben Stada.

2. That another passage tells us that Ben Stada was also 'Ben Pandira'. Travers Herford comments that 'Pandira' has been written 'Pandera, or Pantira or Pantiri'.

3. That Miriam (Mary is the equivalent) was a hairdresser and she was the mother of Ben Stada and Ben Pandira.

4. That another text tells us that Miriam (Mary) was the mother of Balaam.

5. That another passage records that Miriam (Mary) is also the mother of someone referred to as 'a certain person'.

6. That the following references in the Talmud (which actually name these 'alter egos') all point to Jesus being the man behind the names. Consider them:
   — 'people claiming to heal the sick in the name of Ben Pandira' (Ben Pandira);
   — 'in the beginning a prophet, in the end a deceiver . . .' (Balaam);
   — to being the son of a woman who 'played the harlot with carpenters' (Balaam);
   — to being repulsed in the time of Alexander Jannaeus

141

(104–78 BC) . . .' (Jeshu the Nazarene);
— to being 33 years old when he was killed (Balaam);
— to being stoned and hung on the eve of Passover (Ben Stada).

7. That the full reference in the Talmud is to 'Miriam m'gaddela nashaia'. The word 'm'gaddela', which means 'hairdresser', gives rise to the name 'Mary Magdalene'.

The conclusion must be that Jesus was Jeshu Ben Pandira, Ben Stada, Balaam, Jeshu the Nazarene/ Jeshu ha-Notzri and 'a certain person', and that Mary Magdalene was the mother of Jesus.

I discuss this later, in the chapter entitled 'Mary and the birth of Jesus'.

In the Talmudic passages we can see how information about Jesus and his alter egos connects with what we know about Onias the Just and the Teacher of Righteousness.

Ben Stada:
— brought magic spells out of Egypt (Onias the Just performed a miracle). It should be noted that M. Gaster, a contributor to *The Encyclopaedia of Religion and Ethics* (published by T & T Clark of Edinburgh) says of magicians that they were people who sought to 'Subvert the regular course of events – to obscure the sun and moon, to bring the dead to life and to do that which is contrary to the laws of nature'. I think a successful prayer for rain would come under this description;
— cut marks on his flesh (Honi the Circle Drawer). I think the reference to cutting flesh is a mistranslation. There is no such Jewish tradition. I think that what was meant described cutting or inscribing on the ground. There is a similarity between the Hebrew word 'flesh' and 'ground', providing a link with Honi/Onias, who, like Jesus (John 8 : 6), wrote or inscribed on the ground;
— was stoned (Onias the Just);
— was hung on a tree (the Teacher of Righteousness);
— was killed at the time of the Passover (Onias the Just and the Teacher of Righteousness).

Jeshu ha-Notzri:

— had five disciples. The important reference here is to 'disciples', a recognition that Jeshu had followers. Names of the disciples are given, four of which do not accord with the Gospel names. Travers Herford explains the names as being a sneer. I would liken it to a critic of Stalin, for example, commenting that he had five disciples – poverty, cruelty, inefficiency, persecution and dictatorship (Onias the Just and the Teacher of Righteousness had followers);

— deceived and led Israel astray (Jesus);

— practiced magic (Onias the Just performed a miracle).

The conclusion of this section of the chapter must be, I suggest, that there are clear Talmudic references to Jesus and his alter egos. Further, that these lead to the conclusion that the events and situations described add to the evidence linking Jesus, Onias the Just and the Teacher.

The coincidence factor

A coincidence is defined as 'circumstances without apparent causal connection'. Suppose two people meet and find that they share the same birth date; that would be a coincidence.

If they found that they were born in the same town, that too would be a coincidence, but a mite more unusual.

If they then found that their mothers both had the Christian name Helen, the surprise would begin to turn to a suspicion that there might be some factor other than coincidence involved in the unexpected links.

If they then found that the maiden name of their mothers was, for example, Jones, they would know that the coincidence was no coincidence and that there was now a reasonable certainty that they had the same mother and that they were twins.

One coincidence may raise a smile of surprise; a second may raise an eyebrow acknowledging an unusual situation; but then, as coincidence follows coincidence, the conviction grows that what is beginning to unfold is not sheer chance, but an underlying and so far unforeseen connection which has yet to be revealed.

This is, I suggest, the situation with Jesus and his alter egos.

I have deliberately headed each apparent linkage with a heading which begins 'The coincidence that . . .'. In this way I hope that each and every connection is not only spelled out in detail but that the reader is reminded each time of the growing enormity of the so-called coincidences.

As each circumstance and each incident involves Jesus and the Teacher, then Jesus and Onias the Just, and then Onias the Just and the Teacher, the mathematics of probability build up to a point where the chance of these men being three different people becomes mathematically monstrously high.

Take, for example, the twins referred to earlier.

The odds against two people having the same birthday would be 364 to 1.

The odds against them having the same year of birth would be, for a thirteen year old teenager, 12 to 1.

The odds against being born in a town of population 50,000, assuming a national population of 50,000,001, would be 1,000 to 1.

The odds against having a mother with the same Christian name – Helen – being one of, say, 51 likely names – would be 50 to 1.

At this stage, without even considering the surname, the odds against these coincidences involving two different mothers is 364 × 12 × 1,000 × 50: a total odds of 218,000,000 to 1.

This calculation completely ignores the coincidence of the same surname, where even a multiplying factor of 1,000 would take the odds to an almost astronomical level.

The brain, when learning of a series of coincidences, does not carry out mathematical calculations to give some sense of probability.

It does, however, allocate a degree of 'unusualness' to them, and instead of expressing odds of 218,000,000 to 1, judges the progression as being from 'unusual', 'surprising', 'unlikely' and finally, 'impossible'.

And that is precisely what I suggest is the case with Jesus, the Teacher of Righteousness and Onias the Just. As each coincidence is weighed, the three men draw closer so that within a span of no more than four coincidences, they are well and truly merged into one man.

But there are not just four coincidences; there are 22 linking Jesus with the Teacher of Righteousness and 22 connecting him with Onias the Just.

In addition to this, there are the multiplicity of links between the New Testament writings and the Dead Sea Scrolls. The evidence is as complete as it could be. It is more persuasive than a written admission – such a document could be forged, but not the wide-ranging evidence we get from different writers.

Conclusion

Jesus was Onias the Just, the Teacher of Righteousness of the Dead Sea Scroll sect, the Essenes. The mathematics of probability point unequivocally and unerringly to this truth.

CHAPTER TWELVE

The Crucifixion, the Resurrection and Peter

In this chapter I will present evidence that Peter was the principal betrayer of Jesus and that this was because he did not believe that Jesus had the support of God.

Further, that although Jesus was sentenced to death, he was rescued alive by Joseph of Arimathea. The unusual and impressive circumstances following the crucifixion persuaded Peter and the other disciples that Jesus had the support of God. This explains the change of heart which led to the detailed writings and organisation of the Essene sect.

Peter, the betrayer of Jesus

First the bad news, later the good.

The traditional teaching of the Christian Churches is that Peter was the close friend of Jesus Christ. After all, it was Simon who was to be called 'Cephas' (Peter), the rock on which the Church would be founded. Wherever Jesus was, there was Peter alongside him giving help. He was a supportive and loyal companion. However, as with the identity of Jesus, the Christian Churches have completely misunderstood, even deliberately ignored, the events so clearly set out in the Gospel accounts of the ministry of Jesus.

It is reasonably certain that early on in his leadership of the apostles, Jesus counted on the twelve as his friends. There are verses in the Gospels, however, which clearly describe discord, disbelief and doubt. If a leader presents ideas to his followers in terms which they do not understand, then they must begin to have doubts about his competence to lead the group. Take, for example, the verses Matthew 15 : 16 and 16: 9; Jesus complains that he is not understood.

Experience of life tells us that whenever there is a lack of understanding there is invariably argument and opposition. It was this that led to the rejection of Jesus by his apostles and to his eventual betrayal. And it was Peter, not Judas, who was the chief betrayer of Jesus. This will be made clear when the suppressed translations of the Dead Sea Scrolls are eventually published.

However, it is not necessary to await that eventful day; the evidence is there for all to read in the Gospel stories. There are a number of verses which have been ignored – even deliberately avoided – by theologians because they present problems which they cannot solve.

How is it possible to ignore the import of the words in Matthew 16 : 23? This reads: 'But he [Jesus] turned and said to Peter, "Get behind me, Satan. You are a hindrance to me; for you are not on the side of God, but of men"'.

This is no ordinary man being abusive to another. This, according to the Gospel, is the all-knowing, miracle-working and prophesying Son of God referring to his closest companion as Satan. This was no error of translation; the words which follow – 'hindrance' and 'you are not on the side of God', fully support the critical passage. No friendship here; no regard for a loyal companion; just clearly expressed hatred. If words mean what the dictionary says they mean, then here is a passage which should be regarded by theologians as one which it is their duty to explain to the non-experts, the laity. Peake's *Commentary on the Bible*, which analyses the Bible in detail for the benefit of lay people, does not comment on this verse.

This verse is just one of a number which point to Peter being not only the enemy and betrayer, but also the tempter of Jesus.

It might be thought that the incident recorded in Matthew 16 : 23 which I have quoted above is quite different from the 'temptation of Jesus' which is described earlier in Matthew 4: 1–11. In my opinion, they both relate to the same incident for the following reasons:

147

1. In Chapter 8, 'The Gospels', I give a number of examples of the duplication and even triplication of verses. Matthew obviously used at least two different copies of the Essene 'Gospel of Jesus' when compiling his own Gospel. He did not realise that verses he copied from two copies of the Essene Gospel were the same incident. The abuse of Peter in chapter 16 referred to above and the 'temptation of Jesus' in chapter 4 is another example.

2. It is, I think, more than coincidence that Jesus uses a very similar wording in the fourth chapter ('Begone, Satan') and the 16th chapter ('Get thee behind me Satan') when rebuking his challenger. The likelihood of two different incidents being terminated by almost the same wording seems, to me, remote.

3. If the words in Matthew 16 : 21–23 are examined closely, they present what to me is an unreal situation. Abbreviated, they read:
   a) Jesus said that he 'must suffer many things ... be killed ... and raised'.
   b) 'Peter ... began to rebuke him saying, "God forbid, Lord"'. Now, these words cannot be described as a rebuke. Peter seems to be doing no more than expressing hope that Jesus is mistaken. Further, and just as important, in no way did Peter's response merit the extreme abuse of him by Jesus.
   There is something wrong with the account as presented by Matthew in these verses.

4. Note closely the words of Jesus in 16 : 23, '. . . for you are not on the side of God, but of men'. He is saying to Peter that he is not thinking of Godly values but of selfish human desires. It is almost as if Peter had said to Jesus, 'Look, if you really are what you claim to be, why not use these powers to enjoy the wealth and attractions of the kingdoms of the world?'. These are the sort of words which a tempter would use. They would then justify the charge made by Jesus that '. . . you are not on the side of God, but of men'.

   Let us now look at Matthew 4 : 1–11. In these verses, the tempter – and that specific word is used as well as the words 'devil' and 'Satan' – points down from the heights and suggests to Jesus that the kingdoms of the world could be his. Now, it seems to me that the verses we find in Matthew 4 : 1–11 and the circumstances they describe are just the ones which would naturally end with the critical words of Jesus found later in the 16th chapter, which read: '. . . you are not on the side of God, but of men'.

5. I do not accept the existence of 'Satan'. If God created the universe then, as the all-powerful Designer, it seems a nonsense to suggest that a rogue or fallen angel, or a Satanic force, would be permitted to oppose Him.

We do not need to invent Satan in order to explain the many problems and unhappinesses of the world. In the final chapter, I explain why I think that the problems and conflict evident in the world are to be welcomed, because they are the basis of an interesting life. The very idea, therefore, of Jesus being tempted by a devil is one that I simply do not accept.

For these reasons, I believe that the 'temptation of Jesus' was actually a confrontation with Peter. It was an expression of Peter's lack of confidence in Jesus and his disbelief that Jesus was what he claimed to be – the Son of God. Rather than an actual temptation, it is likely that Peter was merely taunting Jesus and challenging him to prove his claims. It is possible that this was the incident which led to the break between Jesus and Peter, and which culminated in the desertion of the disciples and the betrayal by Peter and Judas.

We see exactly the same circumstances described in the Dead Sea Scrolls wherein the Teacher of Righteousness (Jesus) is betrayed by the 'Man of Lies' (Peter). This is all part of the evidence which connects Jesus with the Essene Teacher of Righteousness. The fact that they were both killed at the time of the Passover (hung on a tree to die) but reappeared after 'death', together with a host of other connections which are described in Chapter 11, prove them to be the same man.

As for Peter, there are other verses which are critical of him which theologians conveniently ignore and which lay-readers overlook because they appear in the Gospels in situations which seem to describe friendly normality. These verses are deceptive. But this is precisely what the bland, covert style of writing adopted by the Essenes was intended to be.

Their writings were not intended to inform the reader. They were to serve as a background for the 'Men of Knowledge' who would explain the full significance of the passage to whoever was authorised by the sect to have that information. For those who might accidentally have access to their scrolls and who were not entitled to have the Essene 'gnosis', the texts would describe in the most casual terms happenings which, in fact, were of extreme importance to the sect. I think the examples which follow fully support my contention.

In John 13 : 10–11, talking to Peter, Jesus says: '"He who has bathed does not need to wash . . . and you are clean, but not all of you." For he knew who was to betray him; that is why he said "you are not all clean"'. Now, does 'you' refer to Peter, or is it the plural 'you' referring to the twelve disciples? It is easy for the actual meaning to be confused, and we could only be certain if we knew the original source of Matthew's information. Nevertheless, the evidence already presented here, and that which is to come, makes it reasonably clear that he was referring to either Peter or to Peter and Judas.

Other verses in Luke's Gospel (22 : 31–32) repeat the Satanic connection and the denial of Jesus which was to come. These verses read: 'Simon, Simon, behold Satan demanded to have you that he might sift you like wheat . . .', and Jesus continues, prophesying that Peter would deny him three times.

These verses describe Jesus telling Peter that he knows that he is in the hands of Satan and will be operating on his behalf. In what way, then, can Peter be regarded as the friend of Jesus? The average layman, reading these words in isolation, unaccompanied by any reference to a quarrel or argument, may assume that they were more of a casual comment made to Peter and that the friendship continued. However, not only do they make clear the alliance with Satan, they refer to a denial which is of extreme seriousness.

Again, the wording and presentation of the Gospels is

deceptive. By using the word 'deny' the Gospel writer is enabled to portray Peter's action as simply pretending that he did not know the accused man – a lapse, perhaps, but not too important. The denials were, however, of the utmost importance, leading, as we shall see, to Peter actually 'invoking a curse upon himself'.

In John 8 : 44 we have a very interesting verse in which, although hitherto having been addressing 'the Jews', Jesus appears to be speaking to and about one particular man. It reads:

> You are of your father the devil and your will is to do your father's desires. He was a murderer from the beginning and has nothing to do with the truth because there is no truth in him. When he lies he speaks according to his own nature, for he is a liar and the father of lies.

Names are not given, but taking all the other verses into consideration in the Gospels, the Old Testament and the Dead Sea Scrolls, there is a coming together of accusations of Satanic connections and of lying that can only have Peter at the centre.

The previous reference in Matthew 16 : 23 to him being on the side of men, and the above strong descriptions of Peter as, like his father, having 'no truth in him' and being 'a liar and the father of lies', link very clearly with the Dead Sea Scrolls. In the Scrolls, the betrayer of the Teacher of Righteousness is the 'Man of Lies', and there can be no doubt that Peter was that man.

The sheer wretchedness of the betrayal of Jesus is made clear in Mark 14 : 71. We read that after Peter had denied Jesus three times he 'began to invoke a curse upon himself'. This sets the record straight. It indicates the gravity with which the act of betrayal was viewed by the writers of the Scrolls. Friends of Jesus, those who love God, do not invoke curses upon themselves.

Some translations of the Bible unintentionally divert attention away from the curse that was on Peter by translating the words to mean that Peter 'began to curse and swear' or that Peter actually 'asked for a curse to be placed on himself'.

They are ingenious, but unhappily are corruptions of the truth. The evidence in this chapter proves, beyond any doubt I think, that the curse upon Peter was fully justified.

There is further evidence, and the Dead Sea Scrolls, the Old Testament and the Gospels provide it in some detail. It is spelled out blandly but leads to the conclusion that Peter was the betrayer of Jesus and Judas was an accomplice. It has to be understood that Jesus was accused of apostasy – of being a deceiver, of wanting to change the religion and of tempting others to change. As far as Judaism was concerned, it was the most heinous of crimes. For anyone so accused, Judaic law required certain conditions to be fulfilled. It is not clear from the Gemaras, Rabbinical writings of extreme importance to the Jews, whether this law had been used before the trial of Jesus or whether the procedures used with the Jesus trial became the standard for all such future trials. However, what the law required was:

1. Two witnesses who were able to see the accused and hear his voice.
2. Light to be provided so that the witnesses could see the accused.
3. That the witnesses be hidden from the accused. (It is interesting that the Palestinian Gemara requires witnesses in an inner chamber whereas the Babylonian Gemara placed them in the outer chamber. I think the Babylonian is the correct version.)

In Matthew 26 : 58 we read that Peter followed Jesus into the courtyard of the High Priest. It is necessary to ask why Peter should follow Jesus. If, as we are asked to believe, he was the friend of Jesus, then he would be in considerable danger. The other disciples recognised the situation – in Matthew 26 : 56 it reads: '. . . then all the disciples forsook him and fled'. For Peter to follow Jesus was to risk being arrested and, like his leader, accused of apostasy. If that really were the situation, it would have been an outrageously reckless act. Peter, however, must have known that he was acceptable to the authorities. We read in Luke 22 : 55 that 'Peter sat among them'. Note that he sat with 'them' (the word 'them' can only mean the leaders of the Jews). Peter did not sit with 'him' – Jesus was alone; there was no one to sit with him.

Now, two witnesses were required to testify against Jesus, and in John 18 : 15 we read that Peter was followed into the courtyard by another disciple who was known to the High Priest. This tells us clearly of the treacherous partnership of Peter and Judas. Condition 1 had been met. In Luke 22 : 55 it reads, '. . . and when they kindled a fire in the middle of the courtyard, Peter sat among them'. Mark's Gospel suggests that the fire was to provide warmth, but this shows his misunderstanding of the reason for kindling the fire – the fire was to meet Condition 2 (to provide light by which witnesses could see the accused). Mark 14 : 30 tells us that the trial was at night. Finally, in Matthew 26 : 69 we are told that Peter was sitting outside in the courtyard – hence, with the fire in the inner yard and Peter in the outer yard with a wall separating the accused and witnesses, Condition 3 had been met.

When the trial of Jesus started, we find false witnesses giving evidence against him, but then the Gospel focuses on two others where, in Matthew 26 : 60–61 it reads: 'At last two witnesses came forward and testified against Jesus saying, "This fellow said 'I am able to destroy the temple of God and build it in three days'"'. There can be little doubt that Peter and Judas were the two referred to; they were present when Jesus made the claim in John 2 : 19, 'Destroy this temple and in three days I will raise it up'.

Some critics of Christianity have suggested that the Gospels are a fabricated account of the life of a man who never lived. The critical verses in the Gospels, relating to Peter and to Jesus, are proof if it were needed that the New Testament records the life of a man who was very much involved with the religious life of his times. No one wishing to persuade people to believe in Peter's friendship would write the clear and unambiguously damning verses which I have quoted.

There are passages in the Old Testament which support the Gospel accounts of a righteous man betrayed by a friend and persecuted by his enemies. Consider these:

Psalms 41 : 7 and 9	All who hate me whisper together about me ... even my bosom friend in whom I trusted, who ate my bread, has lifted his heel against me.
Psalms 55 : 12–14	It is not an enemy who taunts me ... not an adversary ... it is you, my equal, my companion, my familiar friend ...
Psalms 55 : 20	My companion stretched out his hand against his friends.

In the Gospels, the verses clearly brand Peter as the traitor. The covert references to the one who betrayed being a close friend are support evidence from Psalms consistent with Peter being the betrayer.

There is one final point which might be relevant to the betrayal of Jesus. In his Letter to the Corinthians, Clement of Rome writes, '. . . Peter . . . after thus giving testimony . . .'. The Greek word used was one which conveyed the concept of 'sealing one's testimony in blood'. Was the testimony that given by Peter at the trial of Jesus, and was the blood that of Jesus? If it was, then it would be consistent with the evidence given in this chapter.

The repentance of Peter

Can there be any doubt that Peter was the prime betrayer of Jesus? If that is the bad news for Christians then, fortunately, there is good news to follow.

In Chapter 9, 'Peter, John and James', I explain why the Peter who was the companion of Jesus was not the Peter who is referred to in the New Testament letters. It is quite a coincidence that there should be two 'Peters' at the head of the sect in two different periods, and I believe that there is a sensible explanation for this. I think that the Essenes, when they developed the writings of the sect and set out the rules of conduct, laid down that the man at the head of the sect would, in order to maintain links with the originators of the sect, always be referred to as 'Cephas', which means Peter. If this is correct, then obviously the Essene opinion of Peter was not influenced by his treacherous behaviour leading to the arrest of Jesus. It follows, I think, that the Peter who was the companion of Jesus repented and returned to the Essene fold.

This seems to be the explanation of the verse in Luke 22 : 32 which describes Jesus saying, '. . . but I have prayed for you that your faith may not fail; and when you have turned again, strengthen your brethren'.

The words 'and when you have turned again' imply an original turning away from Jesus followed by a 'turning again' back to belief in Jesus.

When the so far unpublished translations of the Scrolls are examined, it is as certain as can be that this change of heart will be featured and reference made to Isaiah 57 : 17–19. This tells of the conflict and reformation of Peter in these words: 'Because of the iniquity of his covetousness, I was angry, I smote him, I hid my face and was angry . . . I have seen his ways but I will heal him; I will lead him and requite him with comfort'.

There is, however, one question which even the Scrolls may not answer. What was it that made Peter change from being the enemy of Jesus to one who was to return with his Essenes to Qumran, and to found a sect which was to develop into a world-wide religion?

The crucifixion and resurrection of Jesus

Research into the origins of Christianity leads to the conclusion that there is a considerable amount of truth in the Gospel accounts of the ministry of Jesus. There are inaccuracies, of course, and in the case of the crucifixion and resurrection of Jesus, it would be possible to write at some length about them. Perhaps one example will suffice – none of the Gospels agree on those who attended the sepulchre where Jesus had been laid. There are many more discrepancies.

Nevertheless, we know that Jesus was not a mythological figure, that he did live, albeit in the 1st century BC and not the 1st century AD, and that he was crucified in 63 BC and not 30 AD. Perhaps if we combine the account by Josephus of the death of Onias the Just (Jesus), the evidence from the Dead Sea Scrolls about the Teacher of Righteousness (Jesus) of the Essene sect, and the information contained in the Gospels, we can get near to the truth about the death of Jesus. He was, it would seem, hounded by the Pharisees, went into hiding, was found and arrested, betrayed by Peter and Judas, found guilty of apostasy, stoned and then hung on a tree to die.

But what happened afterwards?

The resurrection and subsequent appearance of Jesus are of critical importance because it was these that seemed to have persuaded Peter to believe once again in Jesus.

Peter's change of heart, from betrayer of Jesus to becoming the leader and founder of an organised Essene sect which had Jesus as the focus of their prayers, must have been due to some impressive display of power by God.

Peter had not been convinced that Jesus had a special relationship with God. He would, therefore, not be satisfied with an escape from death which was ordinary; only extraordinary circumstances would persuade him that Jesus really did have the protection of God. What happened to change his mind?

A scenario can be constructed which satisfies two essential requirements – that there were no miracles and that what happened would convince a previously sceptical Peter. It is, however, necessary to present in some detail the thinking which leads to the explanation of what are, in fact, quite complex circumstances.

It is necessary to understand:

1. The origins of certain Old Testament books.
2. The reality of the prophecies relating to Jesus.
3. The origins of the Gospel stories.
4. How certain 'core truths' about events in the life of Jesus have been distorted.

The origins of certain Old Testament books

I have already argued in Chapter 10, 'Miracles, Prophecies and the Old Testament' that certain parts of Psalms and

Isaiah, to name but two of the Old Testament books, have many verses in them which have been written by the Essenes. The 'Essene Connection' is an important part of an understanding of the origins of Christianity.

The reality of the prophecies in the Old Testament relating to Jesus

In the same chapter I argued that the prophecies of the Old Testament were written by the Essenes after the event – that they were a record of Essene history and not a prediction about the future. This should be understood because there are other verses in the Dead Sea Scrolls and in Psalms and Isaiah which throw an interesting light on the happenings of 2,000 years ago.

When a chapter or verse in Psalms or Isaiah, which I quote, appears to be a prophecy, it has been written by the Essenes. They wanted their followers to think that the Old Testament prophets actually foretold the life of Jesus, when in actuality the writers were looking back and writing of events which had already happened.

The origins of the Gospel stories

One theologian dates the writing of Mark's Gospel as AD 65, the Matthew and Luke Gospels as between AD 80–90 and John's Gospel at about AD 100. Other theologians give similar dates. They have, however, absolutely no evidence whatsoever which could justify these dates. They are guesses, pure and simple.

The Gospels were written by Essenes who thought that the teaching about Jesus should be taken to the gentiles; their activities followed the routing of the Essenes from their base at Qumran in AD 68. The most that can be said is that the Gospels were compiled sometime after AD 68.

There is much that we do not know about the early days of the developing gentile Church with its belief in the Essene Teacher of Righteousness (Jesus). What we can do is reason out some aspects of the Gospel stories which do not stretch belief.

How historical 'core truths' became distorted

The four Gospels, particularly the Synoptic Gospels of Matthew, Mark and Luke have much material in common. It is reasonable to conclude that they were using one particular source. For example, some of the wording in one Gospel verse is precisely, word for word, that used in another Gospel. Sometimes the wording differs, and' sometimes incidents in one Gospel appear earlier or later in the ministry of Jesus than recorded in another Gospel. Nevertheless, there is a common thread connecting the four Gospels, but the discrepancies and differences need to be explained.

Now, it was the practice of the Jews to commit large tracts of Rabbinical writings to memory. However, in order to commit them to memory there must be some standard written form to memorise. This leads to the conclusion that somewhere, perhaps among the so far unpublished Dead Sea Scrolls, there is a Gospel of Jesus.

Papias, a 2nd century Bishop of Hierapolis, has some interesting information which probably explains the errors and discrepancies between the Gospels.

Papias said that Matthew 'collected the oracles in the Hebrew language and each interpreted them as best he could'. If only we knew what 'interpreted them as best he could' meant.

Was it interpreting Hebrew into Greek?

Was it interpreting the deliberately secretive Dead Sea Scrolls' material?

The passage clearly indicates some uncertainty about the meaning of some parts of the oracles.

Papias also said that, 'Mark, who had been the interpreter of Peter, wrote accurately, as far as he remembered them, the things said and done by the Lord but not, however, in order'. When Papias said that Mark remembered as best he could the teaching of Peter, we tend to picture Mark trying to recall the sermons as preached by Peter. Now there is absolutely no way that a remembrance of Peter's varying sermons could result in the almost identical wordings found in Mark and the other Gospels. What Papias meant, I think, was that Mark had memorised the gospel and although he had forgotten parts, set out what he had remembered as best he could.

We have, therefore, some understanding of how errors crept into the Gospels – a combination of translation and memory problems together with, perhaps, damaged scrolls leading to an incorrect reading.

This has affected our understanding of the Gospels.

Take, for example, verses Mark 13 : 20 and Matthew 24 : 22 where there are references to God 'shortening the days for the elect'. This really has no meaning unless one understands the Essene origins of the Gospel material. The 'elect' was how the Essenes referred to themselves, and in the already published Dead Sea Scrolls, we read that in the final battle between the forces of Light – the Essenes – and the forces of Darkness, God would 'lengthen the days'. This was to enable the Essenes to pursue the enemy to their destruction. Obviously, the Gospel compilers knew that it was an expectation that God would change the length of the day in some way. A faulty memory, or perhaps a damaged scroll, resulted in a lengthening of the day being recorded in the Gospels as a shortening of the day.

Another example is to be found in Mark 14 : 47 which reads: 'But one of those who stood by drew his sword and struck the slave of the High Priest and cut off his ear'. It would be an eccentric writer indeed who invented a verse which describes the loss of an ear – an arm, perhaps, or a severe injury to the body or head, but not an ear. There is, however, some truth in this inaccurate verse.

We know from the writing of Josephus that:

1. At the time of Jesus's arrest (63 BC) Aristobulus II was the High Priest but his right to this office was disputed by his brother, Hyrcanus II, who also claimed the High Priesthood.
2. Hyrcanus II eventually won the contested office, but in 40 BC the man who deposed him, Antigonus, 'himself tore off Hyrcanus's ears with his teeth', thus ensuring that Hyrcanus II would never again hold office. It was a requirement that the holder of the High Priesthood should be free of bodily blemish.

Now, the written word in both Hebrew and Aramaic for 'brother' is very similar to the word for 'slave'.

What has happened is that the Gospel compiler has read, perhaps from a damaged scroll, that an ear had been lost by the slave or brother of the High Priest. Looking back to AD 30, the time when he thought Jesus had lived, he would have found that the High Priest did not have a brother. Had he researched back to the time of 63 BC, he would have found that the High Priest did, in fact, have a brother – Hyrcanus II and Aristobulus II were brothers. However, unable to find a brother for the High Priest in AD 30, he would assume that the correct reading of the damaged scroll was 'slave'.

Further, even if the tradition came down to the compiler correctly that the loss of the ear was due to it being bitten off, he would probably have doubted it. It seems so unlikely. It is understandable that he attributed the loss of the ear to a blow from a sword, and this is how it was written into the Gospel account.

This is how a 'core truth' can be corrupted; a half-remembered verse or a damaged scroll is rationalised so that the account makes sense.

This is the explanation of how the true story of Antigonus biting off the ear of Hyrcanus II became transmuted into the loss of an ear by a slave of the High Priest from a sword blow.

It is the eager efforts of the Gospel writers/compilers that have caused so much trouble. Only one miracle is associated with Onias the Just (Jesus) and that had to do with a successful prayer for rain. Once one miracle is accepted, however, the miracle barrier has been broken and miracles then become the norm on the principle that if one, then why not many?

They are used as a tool for making the simple actions of a man into those of a miracle worker.

One can almost hear an informant saying, or imagine a manuscript reading, 'Jesus spoke to the blind and they saw the light', meaning that they had heard and understood his teaching. It is understandable that this might be interpreted as the blind seeing, not the truth, but the light of day and that their blindness had been cured. In a similar way, references to the laying of hands on people and cleansing of their sins could be taken a stage further and be recorded as Jesus having cleansed them of disease. It is important to understand how misinterpretations and misunderstandings, together with over-enthusiastic scribes wanting to impress readers with miracles, have influenced our appreciation of the Gospels.

What, then, are the core truths in the Gospels which enable us to construct a scenario, with much logic to it, which explains the unique circumstances surrounding the crucifixion and resurrection of Jesus? It is these, I think, that changed Peter's mind.

We tend to think of plots, conspiracies and the like to be the preserve of the 20th century. There seems so much more to intrigue about today. However, we have no reason for thinking that 2,000 years ago people were very much different from those of today. The problems we face may be more complex, but the human response to the things that agitate us must be very much the same as those of the people of yesteryear. Faced with a problem, they probably assessed the situation and then tried to find a way of dealing with it.

The scenario is this: A rich supporter wanted to rescue Jesus. He bribed soldiers not to break his bones. When Jesus was taken from the cross, he was probably unconscious, but alive.

If it seems outrageous to propose that Jesus was rescued from the cross alive, rather like the hero of a movie, then it must be said that there is much evidence to support the theory, both from the Dead Sea Scrolls and the Old Testament.

Joseph of Arimathea

Joseph is the key to the scenario. The information we have about Joseph in the Gospels and about the betrayal of Jesus tells us that:

1. Joseph was a rich man. I think the word 'rich' is important. In Essene writings there is usually a word or phrase which acts as a trigger and enables the 'Man of Knowledge' of the sect to introduce the 'pesher' or explanation of the word or phrase. 'Rich', in this case, would explain how

Joseph could afford to bribe the Roman soldiers. The word 'rich' is used again in Isaiah 53 : 9, and I explain at the end of this section why I think this refers to the burial, much later, of Jesus with Joseph.

2. Luke 23 : 50 tells us that Joseph was '. . . a member of the council, a good and righteous man who had not consented to their purpose and deed'.

3. In the Dead Sea Scroll Biblical Commentaries, we are told that Jesus was chastised in front of the council.

4. Putting 2 and 3 together, we can conclude that the deed, the betrayal of Jesus, was opposed by Joseph – that he was still a friend and supporter of Jesus.

5. It would be consistent with these facts if Joseph were to express his support in practical terms by trying to rescue Jesus alive.

6. In Mark 15 : 43 we learn that Joseph 'took courage and asked for the body of Jesus'. Now, why should Joseph risk his life if all he wanted to do was to bury Jesus? Identifying himself as a supporter of Jesus could be dangerous, but still justified if, having bribed the centurion and the soldiers, he knew that he would be able to take Jesus from the cross alive.

To develop the last point a little further, I do not know what arrangements were normally made for the burial of people who had been found guilty of a serious crime and put to death. It would not be unreasonable to think that the authorities would let the family of the deceased make arrangements for the burial. The likelihood was, therefore, that the family of Jesus would receive his body in any case. Why should Joseph short-circuit the system by arranging to take the body from the cross instead of waiting for the body to be handed over? I think the reason is this: that if an unfriendly Jew or Roman soldier had taken down the body, it would have been obvious that Jesus was not dead.

In order for a rescue plan to succeed, Joseph had to:

1. Ensure that the soldiers did not carry out the normal check of breaking the bones of Jesus, a routine designed to verify the death of the victim.

2. Ensure that he, Joseph, and not some unfriendly Jew or unfriendly soldier took down the body of the unconscious Jesus.
3. Ensure that the authorities were told that Jesus was dead.
4. Ensure that key soldiers accepted bribe money.

Only when these conditions were satisfied would Joseph, I think, take the risk of asking for the body of Jesus. This is precisely what happened.

The following explains, in my opinion, why Jesus was rescued by careful planning and not by accident.

The breaking of bones

In John 19 : 31 it reads: 'In order to prevent the bodies from remaining on the cross on the Sabbath the Jews asked Pilate that their legs may be broken and that they might be taken away. So the soldiers came and broke the legs of the first and the other who had been crucified with him; but when they came to Jesus and saw that he was already dead, they did not break his legs'.

The writers have misunderstood the reason for breaking bones (sometimes by 'bones' a writer may be referring to the 'body'). In either case, there is a reason for abusing the bones or body. No sustained bleeding when the bones were broken would indicate death. A steady flow of blood would be a sign that the heart was still beating and that there was still life within the body. As soldiers acquainted with death, they would be well aware that a still body was not a certain way of identifying death. The victim could be unconscious, and if that was the case, then they could deliver a final blow. The fact that Jesus appeared to be dead made it all the more necessary for them to break his bones. Why did the soldiers act contrary to their instructions, breaking the bones of two but sparing the most important member of the trio? In fact, if John 19 : 34 is correct ('But one of the soldiers pierced his side and at once there came out blood and water'), then there was a clear sign that Jesus was not dead and that his heart was still pumping blood. Despite this, they still did not break his bones.

163

There is support for the belief that Jesus cheated death on the cross in the Old Testament in a passage which, as we have seen, is not a prophecy but a record of an actual event. In Psalms 34 : 17–20 it reads: 'When the righteous cry for help [as Jesus did in Mark 15 : 34, 'My God, my God, why hast thou forsaken me?'] the Lord hears and delivers them out of their troubles . . . He keeps all his bones, not one of them is broken . . . the Lord redeems the life of his servants'.

Again, in Psalms 33 : 18–19 it reads: 'Behold the eye of the Lord is on those who fear him . . . that he may deliver their soul from death and keep them alive in the famine'. (As we shall see, there was a famine following the death of Onias the Just (Jesus) according to Josephus.)

However, if my contention that these Old Testament verses were written after the event and were a record of what had happened is correct, then Psalms 34 : 17–20, quoted above, is as clear an indication as one could get that Jesus was redeemed – taken from the cross alive – and so escaped death.

There is significant support from various sources that God did not allow Jesus to die, quite apart from the two passages from Psalms already quoted. For example:

Isaiah 51 : 14	He who is bowed down shall speedily be released. He shall not die and go down the Pit neither shall his bread fail.
Hebrews 5 : 7	In the days of his flesh, Jesus offered up prayers and supplications with loud cries and tears, to him who was able to save him from death and he was heard for his godly fear.
Psalms 22 : 24	. . . he has not despised or abhorred the affliction of the afflicted . . . but has heard, when he cried to him.
Dead Sea Scrolls Thanksgiving Hymn D	Thou hast redeemed the soul of the poor one whom they planned to remove by shedding his blood . . . .

Psalms 37 : 32   The wicked watches the righteous
                  and seeks to slay him. The Lord will
                  not abandon him to his power or let
                  him be condemned when he is
                  brought to trial.

Here are verses which specifically describe the wicked
'seeking', but not succeeding in their effort, to slay the
righteous man. This last verse is one which the Essene
Biblical Commentaries use when alluding to the threat to
their Teacher of Righteousness. They comment, again, that
the Wicked Priest tried to put to death the Teacher of
Righteousness, and by using the word 'tried' indicate that the
attempt was unsuccessful.

All this evidence points clearly, in my opinion, to Jesus
escaping death on the cross.

The core truth about the soldiers, led by the centurion, is
that whilst breaking the bones of the two who were alongside
Jesus, they refrained from doing so to Jesus. In the following
section I suggest the reason for their disobedience.

The bribe

There is a curious story in the Gospels regarding the
mysterious disappearance of Jesus from the sepulchre.

Matthew 28 : 11–15 reads: '. . . some of the guard went
into the city and told the Chief Priests all that had taken place.
And when they had assembled with the elders and taken
counsel, they gave a sum of money to the soldiers and said
"tell people His disciples came by night and stole Him away
while we were asleep" . . . so they took the money'.

There was, therefore, a bribe involving the soldiers.

However, the story as presented to us in Matthew's Gospel
offends reason.

1. At the request of Joseph of Arimathea, the body of Jesus
   had already been handed over to the followers of Jesus.
2. Therefore neither the Romans nor the Chief Priests had
   any further interest in or responsibility for the body.
3. The followers of Jesus, having taken the body, could make
   whatever claims they liked, but who would believe them?

After all, the disciples and the Pharisees had never acted as though Jesus was a miracle worker and they were not expecting him to return after his apparent death.

4. Having handed over the body and not expecting a miraculous resurrection, there was absolutely no point in soldiers guarding the sepulchre.

5. Having been given the body, there was no reason for the followers of Jesus to steal the body and no need for soldiers to guard the sepulchre.

6. In other words, if the account of Joseph being given the body (Matthew 27 : 57) is correct, then the verses given later in 28 : 11–15 do not make sense.

7. In these circumstances, why should the soldiers be bribed?

What has happened here, I suspect, is that there is a 'core truth' which has come down to the compiler of Matthew's Gospel which was so slender that he developed it as best he could.

He had probably heard that soldiers had been bribed and that the body of Jesus had been taken. He assumed this to have been from the sepulchre rather than the cross. He therefore formed a story which included these elements.

The core truth is that the soldiers were bribed not to break the bones of Jesus, thus ensuring a successful escape from the cross. Curiously, there appears in *Antiquities of the Jews* by Josephus, a verse which is consistent with the soldiers having been bribed. In Book 13 : 3 : 2 he tells us that there 'came ambassadors again to him, Antipater from Hyrcanus and Nicodemus from Aristobulus; which last also accused such as had taken bribes, first Gabinius and then Scaurus, the one 300 talents and the other 400'. Now, John's Gospel tells us that Nicodemus assisted Joseph of Arimathea with the body of Jesus and, therefore, of his involvement in the plot. As a leader of the Jews, he would bring considerable influence as well as Joseph's money to the discussions with the Roman leaders.

There was, therefore, bribery of the leading Roman soldiers and although the precise circumstances have not been revealed, I think the circumstantial evidence links the bribery to the rescue of Jesus.

Further, the well informed Josephus has provided us with another interesting link between the Nicodemus of 63 BC and the Nicodemus of the Gospels purportedly of AD 30.

Now, we are told in Mark 15 : 45 that the centurion had confirmed to Pilate that Jesus was dead. The centurion could not have been telling the truth because neither he nor his soldiers had broken the bones of Jesus in order to confirm the death.

When we find:
— Joseph of Arimathea risking his life by asking for the body of Jesus;
— soldiers disobeying orders by not breaking the bones of Jesus;
— the centurion falsely claiming Jesus to be dead when a check had not been made;
— bribe money being paid to soldiers;
— that verses in Psalms, Isaiah, the Dead Sea Scrolls and the Letter to the Hebrews confirm that Jesus was rescued from death;

there is a coming together of evidence which points to a 'core truth' – that bribe money was paid out by Joseph of Arimathea to spare the life of Jesus, who was then taken from the cross unconscious but alive.

I suspect that when the suppressed Dead Sea Scroll translations are published we shall recognise that the Essene writers referred in their typical covert style, in Isaiah 57 : 1, to the rescue of Jesus from the cross. It reads:

The righteous man perishes, and no one lays it to heart; devout men are taken away, while no one understands. For the righteous man is taken away from calamity, he enters into peace. They rest in their beds who walk in their uprightness.	My interpretation is that apparently Jesus dies but no one seems to worry. This is because Jesus is rescued from the cross unknown to the Pharisees. He is taken from the cross and escapes death. He recuperates as befits one who is righteous.

167

The appearance of Jesus

The Gospel accounts of the appearance of Jesus all differ in the detail of their stories. Mark, Luke and John agree, however, that when first seen, Jesus was not recognised.

There is no explanation for his change of form and there seems no reason why God should arrange for Jesus to change his looks if it was His intention that the disciples should heed the words of the risen Jesus. There is no suggestion that it was a 'spiritual' appearance, and the Dead Sea Scrolls also make it clear that when the Teacher of Righteousness 'appeared' to his followers after death (using Professor Dupont-Sommer's translations), the form of the Teacher was a normal bodily appearance and not spiritual. The disciples do not recognise him and even Mary Magdalene, whom I identify as the mother of Jesus, did not know him. Puzzling though it might be, the story makes sense if the miraculousness and the 'religiousness' of the circumstances are stripped away.

There is a core truth here which is not stated but is there nevertheless. We all know that a man can change his appearance by simply shaving off his moustache. How much more would his facial looks change if he were to shave off his beard? We do not know if Jesus had a beard, of course, but in the absence of the sort of shaving devices that we have today, the growth of facial hair would seem to be the norm with a simple daily trimming to keep it neat. It would be reasonable to think that he had a beard and moustache.

With Joseph of Arimathea now responsible for the welfare of Jesus, it would be necessary to ensure that Jesus was not recognised by the Pharisees or the local population. As a well-known figure, word would quickly reach the authorities and Jesus, together with Joseph, would be re-arrested.

It would be understandable, therefore, if Jesus was shaved. The failure of the disciples and Mary Magdalene immediately to recognise Jesus, shaven and almost certainly looking gaunt from his experience on the cross, is perhaps understandable. There are two quotations which appear in the Old Testament which seem to apply to Jesus.

| Isaiah 52 : 13 and 14 | Behold, my servant shall prosper, he shall be exhalted and lifted up . . . as many were astonished at him his appearance so marred beyond human semblance and his form beyond that of the sons of men – so shall he startle many nations. |

The reader will recognise the expression 'as many were astonished' as referring to the Essenes; 'many' was one of the words they used to describe themselves. This leads to the suspicion – and perhaps the truth may be revealed by the unpublished Dead Sea Scrolls – that the assertion in 1 Corinthians 15 : 6 that Jesus appeared to more than 'five hundred brethren' could be true. There must have been a number of followers who would wish to see Jesus. They may not have been able to recognise him immediately, but, like the disciples, they would know his voice. We may never know the facts here, particularly if there is no confirmation from the Scrolls. Nevertheless, a return to Qumran to see his followers there would seem a reasonable thing to do. Well away from Jerusalem, he would be safe from the authorities. I do not think, therefore, that we should reject the idea out of hand.

The second quotation, from Psalms, which confirms the escape from death reads:

| Psalms 41: 1–3 | The Lord delivers him in his day of trouble; the Lord protects him and keeps him alive . . . the Lord sustains him on his sickbed; in his illness thou healest all his infirmities. |

There are others, such as those in Psalms 116 : 6 and 118 : 5 – the clear and unambiguous message they give is that Jesus did not die on the cross.

I do not think there can be any doubt that the Gospel accounts of the appearance of Jesus and of him not being recognised are true. Like so many incidents in the life of Jesus, there is usually a 'core truth', possibly distorted but substantial enough for us to relate it to other Essene writings to enable the actual happening to be discerned.

What happened to Jesus afterwards?

I have no doubts whatsoever that the following verse from Isaiah had some significance for the Essenes.

Isaiah 53 : 9: 'And they made his grave with the wicked and with the rich man in his death although he had done no violence . . .'.

Now Ephraim was a place which had a reputation for wickedness. It was near to the Sea of Galilee. In the Gospels Jesus is said to have arranged to meet the disciples in Galilee. I assume that the 'rich' man was Joseph of Arimathea.

Perhaps the story behind these bland words is this: that Joseph took Jesus to Ephraim to recuperate and to live away from danger. Presumably Joseph died first, and later, Jesus. Jesus was, therefore, buried with a rich man and with the wicked – the dead of Ephraim.

All the indications we have, after analysing the Gospel accounts of the crucifixion and resurrection of Jesus, point to incidents happening at the direction of humans rather than due to the intervention of God.

Why Peter changed his beliefs about Jesus

If there was no miraculous resurrection of Jesus, then Peter would be well aware of the circumstances. We are, then, back to the basic problem of identifying the happenings which persuaded Peter that Jesus was, if not the Son of God, then at the very least a very special protégé of God.

It is possible to explain his conversion. As a lead into the explanation it is necessary to show that:

1. Dates quoted by historians may be inaccurate.
2. There is historical backing for an earthquake around the time of the crucifixion of Jesus.
3. There is scientific support that there was an eclipse around the time of the crucifixion of Jesus.
4. There is support for there being a famine.

Dates
The dates for the events recorded in the Gospels and in the

writings made in both the 1st centuries BC and AD may be slightly inaccurate. Obviously, those I have quoted herein are generally accepted to be correct. However, when Josephus was writing his *Antiquities of the Jews* and *The Jewish Wars* he was looking back over a period of years when there were no calendars. Our present calendar started with Julius Caesar in 46 BC, and was changed by Pope Gregory in 1582 before being finally adopted by Britain in 1751. For those years in which we are primarily interested – 63 BC and thereabouts – there was no calendar. Josephus would be reliant on informants who may well have passed on details of events in the wrong chronological order. I think we must accept that a little latitude should be allowed when dealing with the dates around the time of Jesus.

Earthquakes and famines
It may surprise many people to learn that the Dead Sea area of Israel is on a fault line, and that earthquakes have caused damage to Jerusalem in the past.

In Matthew 27 : 51 we are told that at the crucifixion of Jesus, 'the earth shook and the rocks were split . . .'. In Psalms, we get support from verses 60 : 2, 'Thou hast made the land to quake, thou hast rent it open', and 5, '. . . thou hast set up a banner for those that fear Thee . . . that thy beloved may be delivered'.

Amos Nur, when a chairman of the Department of Geophysics at Stanford University in California, quoted 64 BC as a year when there was an earthquake in Jerusalem.

He also recorded an earthquake in AD 30, but this is information which has been provided by the Gospels. I have shown that the death of Jesus was in 63 BC, so the AD 30 earthquake can be disregarded. The date 64 BC is so near to the date quoted for the death of Jesus that a margin of error might be allowed here for the reasons stated above.

The Gospels tell of the earth shaking at the time of the crucifixion; history seems to support the Gospel story. Now, it is known from recent experience with an earthquake in California that these violent eruptions of the earth can cause clouds of dust which affect crops grown for both human and livestock consumption. In those days, such a happening could lead to a famine as replacement foodstuffs would not be as readily available from other countries as they are today. In Josephus's book *Antiquities of the Jews* we read that God was so angered at the death of Onias the Just (Jesus) in 63 BC that he punished Israel by sending a vehement wind which caused a famine. History confirms the Gospel story.

Eclipses

No matter how unusual might be the information required, it is surprising to find that someone, somewhere has either written a book or an article which satisfies the need. We are fortunate that two geophysicists, Hermann Mucke and Jean Meeus, have taken the trouble to calculate the eclipses of the sun which have occurred from 2003 BC right through to those which will be seen up to the year AD 2526.

On the 28th May 64 BC and the 18th May 63 BC there were eclipses, minor in magnitude, but eclipses nevertheless, which were visible in Jerusalem. The Passover, the festival associated with the death of Jesus, is usually celebrated in April or May. There is scientific support, therefore, for the Gospel reference in Luke 23 : 45, '. . . and the sun's light failed'. For those who support the belief that Jesus was killed in the 1st century AD, there is no record of an eclipse in AD 30, although there was one on the 12th September AD 33. It was not at the time of the Passover nor was it in the year traditionally associated with the death of Jesus.

The curtain of the Temple

There is a reference in Mark 15 : 38 to the curtain of the Temple being torn in two, from top to bottom. This was another sign of God's anger. It is impossible to get confirmation of this from any non-Gospel source. However, we know that earthquakes have damaged the Temple area in Jerusalem; moreover, the Gospels were correct about the earthquake and the eclipse, and in these circumstances it does not seem unreasonable to suppose they were correct about the Temple curtain.

We are seeking an explanation for Peter's conversion back to a belief that Jesus had a special relationship with God. How would Peter regard the conjunction of an earthquake, an eclipse, damage to the Temple and an amazing rescue enabling Jesus to escape from the cross with his life? It would not be surprising if Peter, considering the circumstances, concluded that the natural disasters were a show of God's anger at the treatment of Jesus.

In his *Antiquities of the Jews* Josephus tells how God punished the Jews for their treatment of Onias the Just (Jesus). This was how it was seen by those whose story came to Josephus. It would not be surprising if Peter viewed the unhappy circumstances in the same light.

Conclusion

I conclude that Jesus was rescued from the cross alive and that the impressive display of God's anger persuaded Peter to return to the fold. He founded a sect which, in its influence on the world of religion, on the lives of literally billions of people, and on the standards of conduct governing relationships with one's fellow humans, is quite unparalleled for such a small and little-known group.

CHAPTER THIRTEEN

Mary and the Birth of Jesus

In this chapter I hope to satisfy the reader that evidence from a range of sources points clearly to Mary Magdalene being the mother of Jesus and to his birth being the result of an adulterous relationship.

There are a number of reasons for thinking that the story of the birth of Jesus is, to a large extent, a fabricated account:

1. It is a miracle story and, *vide* Chapter 10, miracles are not a part of today's life and nor were they 2,000 years ago. If this is accepted, then it must be a fabricated story.

2. There are no references to the virgin birth of Jesus in either the Gospel of Mark or the Gospel of John. The special relationship between God and Jesus was at the very heart of Christian teaching. In what circumstances, therefore, could Mark and John not report, not know and not even be reminded by God, of the miraculous birth so that it could be recorded by all four Gospel writers?

3. It is not mentioned by Paul writing either during the period AD 54–64 (the traditional dating) or in the 2nd century AD (my dating), nor by any writer before Ignatius (who was active early in the 2nd century AD).

4. There are many discrepancies between the accounts of Matthew and Luke. For example, according to Matthew, Joseph is visited by the angel and baby Jesus receives his first adoration from the Magi, whereas Luke has the angel visiting Mary and shepherds adoring Jesus. There are many more, and the reader might refer to *The Jesus of the*

Early Christians by Professor G.A. Wells for a detailed list.
5. There are no references to a virgin birth in the Dead Sea
   Scrolls.

Having taken into account information from various sources,
including the Dead Sea Scrolls, and the Old as well as the
New Testaments, I conclude that if the miracles are taken out
of the story, there are certain 'core truths' which enable us to
understand the actual circumstances surrounding the birth of
Jesus Christ.

These 'core truths' will become apparent when I discuss
certain aspects of the birth of Jesus under the following
headings:

1. That Mary Magdalene was the mother of Jesus.
2. The cover-up.
3. The problem of names in the Talmud.
4. Evidence from the Talmud.
5. Miriam, the dresser of women's hair.
6. Mary Magdalene – harlot?
7. Mary and the birth of Jesus.
8. The census and the birth of Jesus.
9. That Joseph deserted Mary: Jesus was adopted by the
   Essenes: the Three Wise Men.
10. Jesus and his courtly connections.
11. The Star of Bethlehem.
12. The dishonesty of the Essenes.

That Mary Magdalene was the mother of Jesus

In the Gospels, there are references to 'Mary', 'Mary, the
mother of Jesus', or just the 'mother of Jesus' and also to
'Mary Magdalene', but, with one exception, never in the same
context. In other words, there would be no conflict with the
text if all the references to 'Mary' and 'the mother of Jesus'
were replaced with the words 'Mary Magdalene'.

The one exception is to be found in John 19 : 25–26 where
both Mary Magdalene and the mother of Jesus are described
as standing by the cross. There are two reasons for thinking
that these two verses are unreliable.

175

1. No other Gospel places the Virgin Mary by the cross, nor at the sepulchre. However, Mary Magdalene is named, whenever names are given, by all the Gospel writers, both at the cross and at the sepulchre. She is also the first to see Jesus after the resurrection. In other words, Mary Magdalene is present at all the important events in the life of Jesus and, by being there, is behaving as one would expect of a loyal and loving mother.

2. The verses John 19 : 25–26 include an order from Jesus to 'the disciple who Jesus loved' to take care of his mother. Now, in Chapter 8, The Gospels, dealing with the problem of the 'disciple who Jesus loved' I explain why this is an interpolation by a late writer who wanted the readers of the Gospel of John to think that it had actually been written by this disciple – Lazarus.

Now, the 21st chapter of John's Gospel is regarded as a late addition to the Gospel because there are copies of the Gospel which do not include this chapter. If the 21st chapter has been specially written by an interpolater to prove that this Gospel had been written by a man who had been resurrected, then other references to 'the disciple' in earlier verses of the Gospel are similarly suspect. Now, John 19 : 25–26 are such verses. They include the reference to the beloved disciple and they are also the ones which place both the Virgin Mary and Mary Magdalene together at the cross. We can therefore regard the reference to both Mary Magdalene and the Virgin Mary as unreliable. It was a late addition by a writer who did not understand that Mary Magdalene was the mother of Jesus. The evidence from the Gospels does not, therefore, conflict with my contention that Mary Magdalene was the mother of Jesus.

It may come as a surprise to many lay people that Mary Magdalene might be the mother of Jesus. This is because the Church makes sure that the evidence to support the belief is never discussed in public and, as far as those writing on behalf of the Church are concerned, never published in matter likely to be read by the general public. There is considerable evidence and the Church has tried to cover it up.

The cover-up

The Rabbinical writings of the Jews provide very interesting evidence regarding both Jesus and Mary Magdalene. This testimony is very important. The Jews of 2,000 years ago were not writing to influence the gentile population. As far as they were aware, the handwritten work in which they recorded their beliefs and their history was never likely to be read by gentiles. The language was foreign, their history was of no interest to the gentiles and gentile Christianity was at a stage of development which presented no threat to Judaism. These Rabbinical writings were for Jewish consumption only. What is recorded, therefore, can be taken as what the Jews knew about and thought about Jesus and Mary Magdalene in those early years of the 1st century BC. No one at that time would ever expect Jesus and Mary, his mother, to become such important figures in a religion of world-wide importance.

In some extracts from the Rabbinical writings the wording is not always clear, and sometimes Jesus and Mary Magdalene are not named. In these cases I will explain why I believe the references are to them. The overwhelming evidence from the Rabbis provides confirmatory support for information we get from other sources.

The evidence for a cover-up by theologians is embarrassingly clear. On the shelves of all the main libraries in the country, there are reference books which give a brief description of people and events who feature in the Bible. The titles tell us that they are 'A Dictionary' or 'An Encyclopaedia' of the Bible or New Testament or of people who feature in the Bible. The contributions are made by theologians who are experts in their particular field of Bible study. Usually, they provide a list of books from which the reader can obtain further detailed information should they so desire.

In six encyclopaedias I could name, the expert contributor does not give the Talmud as a source of further information about either Mary Magdalene or Jesus. Readers, keen to know more about these two important people, would thus be deliberately denied the sources which would take their enquiries a critical stage further. Moreover, nothing is said from the pulpit or in radio or television broadcasts which might inform the laity on a matter which would be of interest to them. This cannot be accidental. It is a deliberate concealment of information.

Many people, if asked what they know about Mary Magdalene, might reply that they think she was a prostitute. Few know the original source of this information.

Revealing texts in the Jewish Talmud, which I quote later, might give that impression, but of perhaps greater import as far as the Church is concerned is the identification of Mary Magdalene as the mother of Jesus. Even worse, perhaps, readers would find that the traditional beliefs among learned Rabbis of the time of Jesus and later, was that he was an illegitimate child.

Again, bearing in mind that the Jews were writing for their own benefit, and never expected gentiles to read their treasured Talmud, we can look on them as an unbiased source of information.

The problems of the names used in the Talmud

May I remind readers that individuals are often referred to by different names, sometimes their real names, and sometimes by nicknames which are either derogatory or complimentary. Jesus was no exception. It is necessary to set these names out, because they cross-reference with each other to show that it was the belief of contributors to the Talmud that Mary Magdalene was the mother of Jesus.

Before the Talmudic texts are examined for references to Jesus, therefore, it may be helpful to remind readers why different names are used when mention is made of him. This has been covered in more detail in Chapter 11 – 'Jesus Identified'.

| Ben Stada | This could be a corruption of 'Stath-da' which means in Hebrew 'gone away from her husband'. In other words, it is a sneer at Jesus for being the son of a woman who |

	had deserted her husband for another, he, Jesus, being the result of the liaison.
Ben Pandira	This could be derived from the Greek meaning 'born of a virgin' which would be another sneer at Jesus, knowing the physical impossibility of such a conception.
Jeshu and Jeshu the Nazarene	These words are an obvious naming of Jesus.
'A certain person'	There are two Talmuds, a Palestinian and a Babylonian version. In parallel texts, where in one a reference is made to Jesus, the other refers to 'a certain person'. The change was due to gentiles taking offence at references to Jesus. To avoid further persecution the name was changed and the pseudonym substituted.
Balaam	In Numbers, chapters 22, 23 and 24, there are references to a man called 'Balaam' who, allegedly, led Israel astray. What the Talmud is saying is that 'as Balaam did, so did Jesus'. This allusion is confirmed in a passage about Balaam where reference is made to his mother 'who played the harlot with carpenters'.

Evidence from the Talmud

The Palestinian Talmud dates from about AD 300 and the Babylonian Talmud from approximately AD 400. From texts in these books, we get information about different men. Cross-checking enables us to recognise them as the same man:

1. In two different manuscripts, describing the hanging of a man on the eve of the Passover, one gives his name as Jeshu and the other as Ben Stada. Jeshu is, therefore, Ben Stada.
2. Miriam (Mary) is named as the mother of Ben Stada and Ben Pandira.
3. Miriam is the mother of Balaam: this is the conclusion to be drawn from a passage dealing with Balaam. It describes the mother of someone who was 'in the beginning a prophet, in the end a deceiver' as being 'a descendant of princes and rulers, she played the harlot with carpenter(s)'.
4. Balaam was 33 to 34 years of age when he died.
5. Jeshu the Nazarene 'practiced magic and deceived Israel'.
6. 'A certain person' was illegitimate.
7. Miriam was the mother of 'a certain person'.

Taking these together, there can be no doubt that Jesus was Ben Stada, Ben Pandira, Balaam, 'a certain person' and Jeshu the Nazarene, and that he was an illegitimate child. Further, that Mary Magdalene was his mother.

Miriam, the dresser of women's hair

Mary Magdalene (Miriam is the equivalent name) is very much associated with the town of Magdala, and few question this because the town name is very similar to Mary's name. For the record, the place name is also referred to as Magadan and is now known as Medjdel.

In fact, according to the Talmud, she was known as Miriam m'gaddela nashaia which means Miriam, women's hairdresser, the 'hairdresser' being translated from the word 'm'gaddela'. Her name is not therefore a corruption of 'Magdala'.

It is important that we understand how Mary got her name, and that there were not two women but one. Evidence from the Talmud clearly points to Mary the hairdresser being the mother of the men named above.

First, there is no evidence whatsoever that Mary was from Magdala. Her name as given in the Talmud makes it quite clear that the reference was to Mary being a hairdresser.

Second, if an identifying name were to be given, it would make sense for it to describe the occupation she had rather than her town of birth.

One particular Talmudic passage makes this reasonably clear by describing a situation where Miriam the children's nurse is called for and Miriam the hairdresser is sent. Here, the identifying word describes the trade, not the town. Further, it makes sense too; people are wanted for their trade not for their origins. Asking for Miriam the hairdresser would make clear immediately who and why a particular person was wanted.

There can be no doubt that according to Talmudic tradition, Mary Magdalene was the mother of Jesus. Further, that considering the absence of reference to a virgin birth in the Gospels of Mark and John and the New Testament epistles, and noting the contradictory evidence from Matthew and Luke, the identity of the mother of Jesus as Mary Magdalene is revealed as convincingly as can be. Many books have been written about the Virgin Mary and, based as they are on a mere handful of appearances in the Gospel, they are testimony to the inventiveness of writers, both then and now.

The Church, ably supported by the theologians, steadfastly maintains the myth that the Virgin Mary was the mother of Jesus. The truth is that it has become such a focal point of Christian beliefs that no one wants to – or even dares to – reveal what the Church has known for hundreds of years.

There can be few readers who, now aware of what has been written about Jesus and Mary Magdalene, will not have connected the allegations with the Gospels of Matthew and Luke who describe the miraculous birth of Jesus. Many have commented that the Gospel stories could be construed as describing the birth of a child out of wedlock, with the miraculous intervention of the Holy Ghost providing a cover story for what could be an embarrassing truth. The Talmud provides ample evidence to support this view.

I will quote certain passages from the Talmud. I must repeat my indebtedness to an English theologian, R. Travers Herford, and his book *Christianity in Talmud and Midrash*. As a theologian, he is almost unique. He is so refreshingly honest and frank that his book stands out as an example of first class scholarship and a model for all theologians to emulate.

Mary Magdalene – harlot?

In a Talmudic passage referring to Balaam it says of his mother that, 'She was the descendant of princes and rulers, she played the harlot with carpenters'. In another text, the singular 'carpenter' is used. The tradition, as it came down from those early years of the 1st century BC, was that Mary Magdalene had an affair with a carpenter, as a result of which an illegitimate child – Jesus – was born.

May I repeat that the Jews were not writing for the benefit of the gentiles. They never expected their religious tracts to be available to others so there can be no question about their genuine belief that Mary Magdalene had committed adultery with a carpenter. Had they wished to damn Jesus even further, they could have incorporated far more derogatory statements about both Jesus and Mary. Instead, they make a rather harsh, but still technically true statement, that Mary, though not a harlot, 'played the harlot' with one man.

Mary was, therefore, not a harlot. Hers was an experience not uncommon for those whose marriages have soured – of falling in love and having an adulterous relationship leading to the birth of a baby. At a time when the Western world is seeing, despite the availability of contraception facilities, an increase in the number of illegitimate births, perhaps we can now look on the circumstances with a little more sympathy.

It can happen to the lowest and to the highest born of women. Curiously, in the light of the modesty of his place of birth – a manger – and the royal links of his mother, Jesus seems to span the two extremes of social life.

Mary and the birth of Jesus

There is evidence from the Dead Sea Scrolls and both the Old and New Testaments that points to Jesus being an illegitimate child.

The Dead Sea Scrolls were written in a vague and cryptic style which concealed secrets known only to the 'Men of

Knowledge' of the sect. When the text, though vague, seems to have a relevance to the Teacher or the sect, the Essene-watcher stops, and examines it again. What, he wants to know, is the reason for the verse and how would it be explained by the Men of Knowledge?

Such a verse is found in Hymn P of the Thanksgiving Hymns. This reads: 'And Thou hast comforted me in my confusion and in pardon I delight; and I was comforted for the original sin'. Five lines later there is: 'Can human born of human be righteous . . . can flesh born of the guilty inclination be glorious?'.

Professor Dupont-Sommer notes that the 'original sin' is the coming together of Adam and Eve in the Garden of Eden. I doubt it.

In my opinion – and the reader makes his own judgement – the introduction of a sinful conception is a reference to the writer's own situation. Why should he – the Teacher of Righteousness (Jesus) is obviously the writer – worry about Adam and Eve to the point where he needed God to comfort him? Knowing the circumstances of his own birth he might well have thought that his illegitimacy might disqualify him from receiving God's support. The reference to 'guilty inclination' suggests that the conception was not in the marriage bed. His thoughts are obviously on the human who was born – Jesus – and whether that person could possibly achieve 'righteousness'.

The writers of the Talmud certainly regarded Jesus as having been born out of wedlock. There are verses in the Bible which also lead to this conclusion.

In Chapter 10, 'Miracles, Prophecies and the Old Testament', I argue that many chapters in Psalms and Isaiah and other books of the Old Testament, were written by the Essenes. It was, as I have said, their intention that they should be looked on as being prophecies involving their Teacher of Righteousness (Jesus) and, in fact, the Christian Churches quote them as such.

In Isaiah 7 : 14 there is a verse which reads, '. . . the Lord himself will give you a sign. Behold, a young virgin shall conceive and bear a son'. It seems to be a prophecy about the birth of Jesus. It is acknowledged, however, that the Greek word could be translated as either 'virgin' or 'young woman'.

In support of the traditional belief that Jesus was born to the Virgin Mary, there are other verses which do not specifically claim an immaculate conception, but could be interpreted as such by those who wish to believe them. For example, in Isaiah 44 : 2 it reads: 'The Lord formed thee from the womb', and in Psalms 22 : 9 there is the comment: 'Yet Thou art he who took me from the womb'. They are, however, not specifically stating as a fact that the actual conception was from God, and it should be made quite clear that there are none that do so. The Essenes were not a sect which believed in miracles, except for the questionable miracle performed by Onias the Just. There is nothing in the Dead Sea Scrolls which might be interpreted as describing an immaculate conception by a virgin.

The Essenes were quite definitely the writers of the verses given above, and they inserted the verses in Psalms and Isaiah to make it clear that their Teacher, Jesus, was the figure prophecied and that his 'being proceeded from Thee [God]'.

In these circumstances, I am reasonably certain that the correct translation from the Hebrew was 'young woman' and not 'virgin'. The verses that the Essenes used were quite adequate to convey the uniqueness of Jesus without resorting to a miraculous conception.

The Talmud is quite clear on the subject. Mary had an adulterous relationship with a carpenter and, as a result, the illegitimate Jesus was born. There is support from the Gospels that this is what the Jewish Pharisees believed. In John 8 : 41 the Jews say to Jesus: 'We were not born of fornication . . .', and the implication is clear – we were not, but you were.

One particular Talmud text (b. Kallah 51a) ties up with verses in the Gospels. The actual passage tells of a Rabbi seeing a boy in the street and saying to his mother: 'Your son, what kind is he?'. She replies: 'When I entered the marriage chamber, I was having a period and my husband kept away from me. But the best man came to me. For this reason this boy is both a bastard and the son of a menstruous woman'.

184

Travers Herford doubts whether this has anything to do with the legendary Jesus, but on this point I disagree with him. Both Jesus and Mary are specifically referred to in the Talmud. No other mother/son relationship is covered by the Rabbis. In my opinion, it simply must refer to Jesus and his mother.

There is an account in chapter 9 of John's Gospel which is relevant; the verses describe a beggar who has been cured of blindness by Jesus and, after being challenged by the Jews, the beggar replies: '"If this man were not from God he could do nothing". They answered him, "... You were born in utter sin and would teach us?" ... And they cast him out'. These words seem to have been spoken to the beggar.

Now, being blind was not a sin. There is nothing in Judaic writings which would brand a blind man as a sinner. It is my contention that the reference to being born 'in utter sin' was said to Jesus. Now, it was not a sin for an unmarried girl to have a baby. However, it was a sin for a married woman to conceive in adultery, which was the case with Mary Magdalene. The distinction between the two cases was that the unmarried mother had made no promise to God whereas the married woman was one who at the marriage ceremony had pledged faithfulness in the presence of God.

She had sinned by breaking that promise. Further, it was against the law to have sexual intercourse with a menstruating woman, so that the conception of Jesus was a double sin. This would surely qualify for the description 'utter sin'.

There is a verse in Psalms 51 : 5 which I identify as having been written by the Essenes (see Chapter 10), which supports the 'double sin' and which certainly confirms the illegitimacy of Jesus. It reads: 'Behold I was brought forth in iniquity and in sin did my mother conceive me'. If the writer was deliberately differentiating between an iniquity (a moral offence) and a sin (an offence against God) then this is a further link with the Talmudic text.

Although there are more texts from the Talmud which refer to Jesus, I think the evidence I have produced so far leads to the conclusion that:

1. Mary Magdalene was the mother of Jesus.
2. Jesus was her illegitimate son.
3. Jesus was sometimes referred to as 'Ben Stada', sometimes as 'Ben Pandira' and sometimes as 'a certain person'. In addition to these names, he was also referred to as 'Onias the Just' by Josephus, 'the Teacher of Righteousness' in the Dead Sea Scrolls, 'Honi the Circle Drawer' in Rabbinical writings and Jesus Christ in the New Testament.
4. Theologians have deliberately and knowingly withheld this information from the public in general and their own lay Church members in particular. How surprising that a Church, committed to truthfulness and righteousness should so disregard them. For make no mistake, what I know and have recorded, they know too. But suppose they had referred their readers to the Talmud for further information; suppose that they might have given in their pen-pictures an inkling of what might be found in the Talmud.

Questions might have been asked and a debate started which could have led to a collapse of confidence in Christian beliefs. The same thinking is behind the suppression (so far (1992)) in the publication of certain translations of the Dead Sea Scrolls which some suspect will make it quite clear that Jesus was the Essene Teacher of Righteousness.

The census and the birth of Jesus

In Luke 2 : 1 there is reference to a decree issued by Augustus Caesar, '. . . that all the world should be enrolled'. It was because of this decree that Joseph and Mary went from Nazareth to Bethlehem 'to be enrolled'. This has been a source of controversy because:

1. There is no evidence that Augustus Caesar asked for or carried out a census over the Roman Empire in the year of Jesus's birth.
2. There is no evidence of a local Judean census around this time – AD 1.
3. There is no record of a census under Herod, who died in 4 BC.

4. Josephus mentions a census in AD 6 under Quirinius and he describes this as the first such census. This, however, conflicts with Luke's assertion that the enrolment happened at the time of Herod and in the year that Jesus was born.
5. Some have called into question Luke 2 : 3 which reads: 'And all went to be enrolled, each to his own city'. It was, after all, a property and income tax. Why should anyone from Nazareth, whose property was there, go to Bethlehem simply because that was his birthplace? It does not make sense.
6. For these reasons, Luke's evidence is unreliable.

The Greek word used designates the 'numbering of people' and it is no coincidence, I suggest, that the Essenes had a system which numbered their members.

The Scroll of the Rule required each member to be examined 'according to his understanding and his works with regard to the Law'. The Essenes aspired to perfection so that they might righteously represent the forces of Light in the final confrontation with the forces of Evil. The examiners were then to 'inscribe them in order, one before the other, according to their intelligence and works, that they may obey each other, the lower obeying the higher'.

This examination was to be repeated each year in order to 'promote each man according to his understanding'.

Where were the members to be inscribed? Obviously, it was a written record and the reference in Philippians 4 : 3, 'the rest of my fellow workers, whose names are in the book of life', explains a situation where members are numbered each year and then named in the book of life. This is what is meant in Acts 1 : 17 which reads, 'For he was numbered among us and was allotted his share in this ministry', and in Romans 12 : 3 which refers to the 'measure of faith which God has assigned to him'.

The Essene 'numbering of people' was, therefore, a census in every sense of the word but dealt, not with physical wealth and property, but with the more important spiritual qualities of the members.

Why did Luke introduce the census into his Gospel?

There was no Essene census at the time of the birth of Jesus – approximately 93 BC.

There was no Roman census in Judea at that time because Roman influence started 30 years later with their invasion in 63 BC.

I think that the most likely explanation is this:

1. That Joseph and Mary were lovers and driven from home; they sought shelter in faraway Bethlehem.
2. Essene traditions which came down to Luke described a journey and the birth in a manger. Luke felt he had to explain the journey.
3. That writing around AD 100 and looking back, he knew of a census around AD 1, the year he believed Jesus to have been born.
4. He used the Roman census to explain the journey.
5. It is not known when the Essene Dead Sea Scrolls were written, but it is likely that the rules for the sect were devised sometime after 40 BC when Hyrcanus II, the 'Wicked Priest' of the Scrolls, was replaced as High Priest. It could be that Essene membership was initially limited to the community at Qumran but that in order to reach the figure of 7,000 – the unbowed remnant of 1 Kings 19 : 18 – they began to recruit members in Judea and the Middle East Jewish communities.
6. In order to know how membership numbers compared with the target of 7,000 they would need to introduce a numbering system, perhaps between 20 BC and AD 20.
7. When Luke writes in 2 : 2 that, 'This was the first enrolment . . .', he could be referring to a newly introduced Essene system of checking Essene membership. Perhaps the tradition referred to the Essene census, but Luke misunderstood and assumed it to mean the Roman census.

That Joseph deserted Mary: that Jesus was adopted by the Essenes: the Three Wise Men

It was the practice of the Essenes to adopt young or baby male

188

children. According to Josephus the Essenes 'disdain marriage themselves but adopt the children of others at a tender age in order to instruct them; they regard them as belonging to them by kinship and condition them to conform to their own customs'. I doubt whether the Essene organisation would have been sufficiently organised in 96 BC to running such a system; it may be that Jesus was the first child taken in, and the success with his adoption led to it being introduced for others later on. If an adoption were made, it would almost certainly be the three Elders who would make the decision. These 'Men of Knowledge' of the sect could be described as 'Wise Men' and I suspect that when the suppressed Dead Sea Scroll translations are published, they will support this theory.

There is credible evidence that an adoption was made.

In Chapter 8, 'The Gospels', I set out a number of verses in Luke's Gospel which have been duplicated. I put forward the conclusion that Luke had used two or more copies of the Essene 'Gospel of Jesus' when compiling his Gospel. Carelessly, he included the same verses twice. There is what I consider to be another duplication in Luke which is relevant to my contention that Jesus was adopted.

In Luke 1 : 80, referring to John the Baptist, it reads: 'And the child grew and became strong in spirit and he was in the wilderness till the day of his manifestation to Israel'.

Luke 2 : 40 refers to Jesus and reads: '. . . and the child grew and became strong, filled with wisdom; and the favour of the Lord was upon him'.

The following are the reasons for thinking this to be a duplication and one which originally referred to Jesus:

1. There is a correspondence between the words used and the sense they convey.
2. John the Baptist had no 'manifestation' as such. He appeared on, and quickly disappeared from the scene and little is said of him in either the Gospels or the Epistles.
3. There is no reference to John the Baptist in the Dead Sea Scrolls either by actual name or, as far as it is possible to tell, by code name.

4. Jesus was the man upon whom the writing of the Scrolls –
   and hence the Gospels – was focused.
5. The verse has an Essene 'feel' to it, in the sense that it only
   gives some information and that it was in need of 'pesher'
   – an explanation of its meaning.

For these reasons I think that Luke had pages or fragments
each of which included this verse referring to Jesus. He
decided to allocate one to John the Baptist and the other to
Jesus.

I think that the meaning of this verse is that Jesus was
adopted by the pre-Essene group and taken out to Qumran.
There is support for this theory in the Dead Sea Scrolls and
Psalms.

Here is what they say:

Dead Sea Scrolls Thanksgiving Hymn V	Blessed art thou, O Lord thou hast not abandoned the orphan.
Dead Sea Scrolls Thanksgiving Hymn IX	Until I am old, Thou wilt care for me, for my father knew me not, and my mother abandoned me to Thee.
Psalms 10 : 14	The hapless commit himself to Thee, thou hast been the helper to the fatherless.

These words have to be explained in some way and I do not
think there is any alternative but to take them as describing a
father having deserted his child and the mother giving up the
child to God – in the sense that he was handed over to the
instrument of God, the Essene sect.

There is very little information in the Gospels about the
childhood of Jesus. In fact the only story we have is one which
is almost unbelievable, but which might have within it a 'core
truth' which would not be inconsistent with Jesus being with
the Essenes – or a pre-Essene group – as an adopted child.

In Luke 2 : 41 there is an account of Jesus, aged 12, going
with his parents to Jerusalem. On the return journey, Mary
and Joseph were a day's travelling away from Jerusalem before

they realised that Jesus was not with them. When they returned, after three day's searching, they found him in the Temple. In response to their strictures, Jesus replied: ' ". . . did you not know that I must be in my Father's house?" And they did not understand the saying'. Now, how can two members of a party of three, even when travelling with others, be unaware for a day that the third member is missing?

Why did Mary not understand Jesus? She had been visited by the angel Gabriel and the special position of Jesus had been explained to her, so she should have known. It is an unusual story, of no special theological value, but one which seems in need of an explanation. I suspect that there might be a core truth at the heart of the account.

It would be consistent with the adoption theory if his parents had visited Jerusalem in order to see their adopted child and found him – not in the sense that he was lost, but meaning that he was seen – in the Temple, learning with the Rabbis. I think it likely that if and when the full corpus of Dead Sea Scrolls is available, this reference to Jesus learning in the Temple will be featured in some way.

Jesus and his courtly connections

The Talmud alleges that Mary Magdalene 'was a descendant of rulers and princes and played the harlot with carpenter(s)'. The royal connection must be true. Had they wished to blacken the character of Mary, the writers could have included another derogatory comment. Instead, they include a compliment. The royal connection, therefore, in my opinion, is true. Is there any other evidence?

Verses in the Gospels seem to point to Jesus having connections at a very high level, and I think they resulted from family links through his mother. The Gospels tell of Elizabeth, a kinswoman of Mary, who was to be the mother of John the Baptist. Elizabeth was 'of the daughters of Aaron' and therefore linked with the priestly Levi tribe. On this evidence, Mary was born into a family which had influence in the community.

The Talmud does not tell us how close she was to 'princes and rulers', but it records that Jesus was said to be 'near to the kingdom'. This could be interpreted as being 'near to God's kingdom' or it could mean 'near to the kingship' i.e. the Government. There is support for the latter interpretation, because the same words were applied to the patriarch Gamliel II and in his case it meant that he had influence at court. Some have noted the reluctance of Pontius Pilate to condemn Jesus and have speculated that this may be explained by the high-level contacts of Jesus.

Now Josephus, when describing events around the time of the death of Jesus in 63 BC, tells of Nicodemus being sent by Aristobulus II to negotiate as his ambassador. In his capacity as an extremely important associate of Aristobulus II, Nicodemus could be described as one of the rulers of the Jews. Now, the Gospels tell us in John 3 : 2 that a man called Nicodemus, 'a ruler of the Jews . . . came to Jesus by night'. It is unlikely, I think, that there could be two different men who were named Nicodemus and were highly ranked leaders of the Jews. Nicodemus was the man who later helped Joseph of Arimathea after he had claimed the body of Jesus. Jesus did, therefore, have contacts at high level.

All the evidence clearly points to contact between Jesus and those at court due, almost certainly, to his family connection through Mary. We can only hope that the unpublished translations of the Dead Sea Scrolls, or further new finds, may reveal the truth of the situation.

There is one final thought on this point – Jesus, Mary, Nicodemus and Joseph of Arimathea are inextricably linked together in the Gospel stories. Could, therefore, Joseph of Arimathea be the Joseph who was the father of Jesus? If, as I have suggested earlier, Jesus and Joseph were buried together, then this would not be inconsistent with them being related.

The Star of Bethlehem

The very idea that a shining star can guide people, coming from afar, to a specific location – a manger in a small town – cannot be taken seriously.

It is part of the Jesus story, attractive but quite unreal.

This is another instance of a core truth being

misunderstood by a writer and leading him to change reality into the delightfully fanciful.

In order to verify the story, astrologers have examined the conjunctions of shining stars and have considered the possibility of Halley's Comet being the vision seen in the sky. However, the problem remains unsolved. Halley's Comet appeared in 12 BC, and there were no major conjunctions of stars which might explain the Gospel story.

It will come as no surprise to learn that the Teacher of Righteousness of the Essenes was referred to as 'the Star'. It is another link with Jesus, who was also described as a 'star'. Compare these two quotations:

Revelations 22 : 16	*Dead Sea Scrolls – Damascus Document*
I Jesus, have sent my angel to you with this testimony for the churches. I am the root and offspring of David, the bright morning star.	And the Star is the Seeker of the Law who came to Damascus; as it is written a star has journeyed out of Jacob and a sceptre is risen out of Israel.

The Seeker of the Law was the Teacher of Righteousness, so that both he and Jesus were described as a star. The important point is to appreciate that the 'star' was a reference to a person and not to a celestial body. The story of the guiding star was probably some scribe's way of explaining a tradition, either written or oral, which had been received by him. A distortion which changed Jesus from 'being the star' to 'at the time of Jesus there was a morning star' probably accounts for the legend. The Essenes, of course, rose at daybreak and offered prayers at the time of the morning star, which they looked upon as a manifestation of God – as was Jesus.

The dishonesty of the Essenes

Two of the lines in the above quotation from the Damascus Document are actually taken from Numbers, chapter 24. The reference to a star and sceptre are preceded in Numbers 24 : 17 by the words: 'I see him, but not now, I behold him, but not nigh . . .'.

193

Obviously, it is saying that, not now but later, there will appear a star and sceptre in Israel.

Now, in Chapter 10, 'Miracles, Prophecies and the Old Testament', I argue that many chapters and verses were actually written by the Essenes and that by accident or design they found their way into the Old Testament scriptures. The book of Numbers was written about 900 years before the Romans invaded Judea in 63 BC, and yet these verses refer to the Romans using precisely the same word used by the Essenes – the 'Kittim'. There can be no doubt – these are Essene verses.

There is also a typically bland Essene reference to a person who is to 'come to destruction'. The 'Kittim' in Essene writings were the Romans who, under the command of Pompey, the Roman general, invaded Israel and were responsible for damage to the Temple in Jerusalem. Pompey's invasion coincided with the arrest of Onias the Just (Jesus), so that in my opinion the 'prophecy' indicated the appearance of the 'Star' at the same time as the coming of the Kittim. If this is correct then the one who has to 'come to destruction' would be Pompey himself, who was murdered in Egypt.

These verses were, I am certain, written by the Essenes who then, when the books of the Old Testament were being copied by hand, inserted them to give the impression that 900 years earlier, the Teacher of Righteousness, the Romans and Pompey were the subject of this prophecy. The righteous Essenes could, when it suited their purpose, be quite deceitful.

Conclusion

I think that the evidence quoted from various sources leads to the conclusion that Mary Magdalene was the mother of Jesus, that Jesus was an illegitimate child and that he was the Teacher of Righteousness of the Essenes.

Further, it might be recognised that, until now, the Church has successfully protected the traditional beliefs about the birth of Jesus by that most effective of weapons – silence.

CHAPTER FOURTEEN

Paul and the New Testament Letters

In this chapter I aim to satisfy the reader that theologians have misunderstood both Paul the man and the various letters attributed to him. Further, that he and his associates were Essenes, that he lived over 150 years after the death of Jesus Christ and that some of the letters attributed to him include parts of letters from other writers.

The evidence presented in this book identifies Jesus as the Essene Teacher of Righteousness who lived in the first half of the 1st century BC. If the life of Jesus has been placed in the wrong time-slot, then obviously the dating of the ministry of Paul is brought into question.

Now, the New Testament letters have been examined in detail. Estimates have been made and three journeys have been identified, with dates, which were undertaken by Paul during the period AD 46 to 61. This is quite wrong.

Paul was active during a period following the routing of the Essene camp at Qumran in AD 68. Paul took his beliefs to the gentiles between this date and approximately AD 150 – it is impossible to be precise. The evidence for this is:

1. During the late 1st century AD and the 2nd century AD, a number of letters were written by known early Christian leaders – Ignatius, Polycarp, Clement of Rome and Theophilus. Sometime during the 2nd century AD someone collected the various letters from different Churches in the Middle East and put them together as best he could. Perhaps the rather stylised script of Greek

and Hebrew deceived him, but it is apparent that pages from the letters of one writer have been included in letters attributed to another writer. To complicate matters further, letters were sometimes physically written by a junior member of the Church, perhaps at the direction of Paul or other leaders, because they were not familiar with the Greek or Hebrew. Others may have been written by these junior members on their own initiative. A number of these composite letters were then attributed to Paul.

2. The traditional belief is that Paul was active only a matter of some 16 years after the death of Jesus. If this were true, then it is reasonable to assume that Paul – or the various writers of the letters – when referring to Jesus, would make clear a recent association with either Jesus or those who knew him. There are verses in the Pauline letters, however, which suggest that Jesus lived many, many years before the writer.

Take the following examples:

Colossians 1 : 26 ... this mystery hidden for ages ...
and 27 the mystery which is Christ in you ...

Could a period of 16 years – from AD 30 to AD 46 – really be described as 'ages'? It must indicate a period stretching way back over a number of years, far beyond the understanding of the writer.

2 Tim 1 : 9 and the grace which he gave us in Christ Jesus ages ago.

Again, the writer refers to a vague period which goes back to a time which is beyond his comprehension.

2 Thess 2 : 15 So then, brethren, stand firm and hold to the traditions which you were taught.

The definition of a 'tradition' is 'teaching transmitted from age to age'. The question is, therefore, can teachings which have come from a mere 16 years ago be fairly described as traditions? I think not.

However, the chronology of Christianity which I have proposed certainly fits the description 'ages ago'. If Jesus was killed in 63 BC and the letters were written in, for example, AD 100, then 163 years could be, to the people of that time, fairly described as 'ages' ago.

3. If Jesus and Paul had lived during the first half of the 1st century AD then it could be reasonably expected that Paul would have spoken to many who had seen Jesus, had witnessed his miracles and who had other experiences which they would relate to any who wished to hear. The fact is that those who contributed to the Pauline letters seem to have very little knowledge of Jesus. There are no references to Mary and Joseph, none to the virgin birth nor any to the circumstances of the birth. The miracles of Jesus are not mentioned, nor is the denial by Peter, the place of the crucifixion or the gospel teachings of Jesus. John the Baptist does not appear. There are claims in 1 Corinthians and Galatians to Jesus having appeared to the writer, but this seems to have been a spiritual revelation rather than a physical contact.

The conclusion I reach is that relatively little was known of the detail of Jesus's life and this is why the various writers enjoin their readers to 'have faith'. Now faith could be described as belief unsubstantiated by evidence and this is, I suggest, precisely what we find when analysing the letters.

An examination of the New Testament letters

All the evidence, therefore, conflicts with the traditional belief that Paul was active only a few years after the death of Jesus. As we shall see when the New Testament letters are examined, they reveal that they were written by men who lived towards the end of the 1st century AD and the first half of the 2nd century AD.

It would be a monumental task to try and identify every part of a letter and allocate it to a particular writer, even assuming that it would be possible to do so. What I will do is to deal with certain aspects of the letters under the following headings:

1. The New Testament letters and their links with the Essenes.

2. The Essene characteristics of the letters.
3. Paul and the Essenes.
4. Repetitions, contradictions and abrupt changes of subject.
5. Writers who have contributed to the New Testament letters.

The New Testament letters and their links with the Essenes

The 'mystery' of Esseneism and Christianity

There are 17 references to 'mystery' in the New Testament correspondence, and the initial reaction is to assume that they are casual references to the unknown aspects of Jesus and God. For example, Ephesians 1 : 9 says: 'For he has made known to us in all wisdom and insight the mystery of his will . . .', and in 1 Timothy 3 : 9 the writer enjoins deacons to: '. . . hold the mystery of the faith with a clear conscience'.

For the Essenes, the 'mystery' of the truth about Jesus was very much part of the secrecy of the sect. In the Dead Sea Hymn Scroll, there is this reference to the Teacher of Righteousness: 'And he who causes the Shoot of Holiness to grow into the planting of truth has remained hidden with none to consider him, and his Mystery has been sealed with none to know it'. None, that is, except the Men of Knowledge who were privy to the secrets of the sect.

In their writings the Essenes compared the birth and life of their Teacher to a planting by God – a shoot, 'an everlasting planting' which 'shall take root and provide growth and all the winged birds shall use its branches'.

This last reference almost certainly is the inspiration for the verses in Matthew 13 : 31–32: 'The kingdom of heaven is like a grain of mustard . . . when it has grown . . . it is the greatest of shrubs . . . so that the birds of the air come and make nests in the branches'.

The Dead Sea Scrolls and the New Testament letters

In 2 Corinthians, there are verses in which the writer makes the Essene/Christian link as clear as it is possible to be. Referring to the 'knowledge of the glory of God in the face of Christ', 4 : 7 reads: 'But we have this treasure in earthen

198

vessels . . .'. The Essenes also stored their scrolls in earthen-ware jars.

Earlier, verse 3 refers to the secretive style of writing adopted by the Christians. It reads, 'And even if our gospel is veiled, it is veiled only to those who are perishing'. Again, this is how the Essenes wrote – in a cryptic, covert style. Here we have evidence that the Christians practiced precisely the same Essene method of writing and then concealing their manu-scripts. There are no references to these so-called Christian practices in any of the commentaries on the New Testament by theologians. To do this would be to bring Essenes and Christians alongside each other, shoulder to shoulder. They remain there, however, testimony not only to the link between the two sects but also to the deliberate refusal of theologians to publicise that link to the laity.

In Romans 16 : 25 and 26 there are verses which refer to the 'mystery' of the last paragraph, the secrets of this section and the 'ages' mentioned earlier. They read, '. . . the preaching of Jesus Christ, according to the revelation of the mystery, which was kept secret for long ages but is now disclosed . . .'. These two verses identify as clearly as it is possible to do so the Essene affiliations of the writer.

The Christian and Essene dislike of the rich

It is no coincidence that both Christian and Essene writings speak ill of the rich. The Essene member gave his wealth to the Essenes so that it should be 'held in common'. Whilst the sect was rich the individual members were poor, and the references in the Gospels and the letters to 'the poor' invariably meant not the general public who had little money, but the Essene members. This, too, was a Christian practice, for it was Jesus who told the young man who wished to join him to first of all sell his goods. The Essene dislike of the rich is carried through into the New Testament letters. In the letter of James 1 : 9 it reads: 'Let the lowly brother boast in his exultation and the rich in his humiliation . . . so will the rich man fade away . . .'. Later, in 5 : 1 there begins a diatribe against the rich which begins: 'Come now, you rich, weep and howl for the miseries that are coming to you'.

The morning star

It was the Essene practice to rise early in the morning and say prayers to the sun, which they regarded as a wonderful example of God's work.

They referred to the Teacher of Righteousness as the 'Star' and Jesus too, in Revelations 22 : 16, is described in exactly the same way. It reads, 'I Jesus . . . am the root . . . the bright morning star'. Again, as with the Essenes, so with the Christians.

The evening supper

At the evening supper, there was a meeting of members. It was a feature of Essene life and was patterned on the messianic meal which was to take place at the very end of time.

The Essene Rule Annexe lays down that before eating the Priest must 'bless the first fruits of the bread and wine'. This is clearly the ritual which was carried forward into the practices of gentile Christianity; in 1 Cor 10 : 16 it reads: 'The cup of blessing which we bless . . . and the bread which we break is it not a participation in the body of Christ?'.

The Way

The 'Way' was how the Essenes described the lifestyle which led to God and goodness. In the Scroll of the Rule, referring to the need to keep the secrets of the sect, each member is required to 'keep true Knowledge and the right justice for them that have chosen the Way'.

There are a number of references to the word 'way' where it is used in this sense. For example, in 1 Thess 3 : 11 it reads: 'Now may our God and Father himself, and our Lord Jesus direct our way to you', and in 2 Peter 2 : 2 '. . . and because of them, the way of truth will be reviled'. In Acts 24 : 14 the connection is explicit. Paul says, 'I admit to you that according to the Way which they call a sect, I worship the God of our fathers'.

Lightness and darkness

It was the Essene belief that, in the final confrontation, the forces of the Prince of Darkness would be defeated by the forces (the Essenes) of the Prince of Light. References to lightness and darkness, and to light and dark, feature noticeably in the New Testament letters. In Ephesians 5 : 8 there is reference to the recipients having been 'darkness but now you are light in the Lord; walk as the children of light', and in Colossians 1 : 12 it reads, 'giving thanks to the Father who has qualified us to share in the inheritance of the saints in light. He has delivered us from the dominion of darkness . . .'.

There are many other such references, and all go to support the contention that the thinking of the Essenes and the early Christians was the same – because Christianity was simply Esseneism passed on to gentiles by some routed, but still very enthusiastic, Essenes following the Jewish Wars of the 1st and 2nd centuries AD.

The requirement to sell their possessions

On joining the sect, all Essenes were required to give all their wealth to the Council of the Community. The individual members were, therefore, without goods of any kind, and that is why they referred to themselves as the 'poor'. This explains the various references to the 'poor' in the New Testament letters; for example, in Romans 15 : 26 it reads: 'Macedonia and Achaia have been pleased to make some contribution for the poor among the saints in Jerusalem', and in James 2 : 5, '. . . has not God chosen those who are poor in the world to be rich in faith?'.

This practice also explains the verses in Philippians 3 : 7 and 8 where the writer refers to his donation to the sect in this way: 'But whatever gain I had, I counted as a loss for the sake of Christ. Indeed I count everything as loss because of the surpassing worth of knowing Christ Jesus, my Lord'.

In the Gospels, too, we find the same injunction to the people to rid themselves of wealth. In Luke 12 : 33 Jesus says, 'Sell your possessions', and in Matthew 19 : 21 he tells a young man, 'If you would be perfect, sell what you possess and give to the poor . . .'.

The use of 'perfect' is, like 'poor', an Essene word used to describe themselves.

Evidence that Essenes and not Christians were persecuted

There is another link between the Essenes and the New Testament letters. There are references in the letters to the writers being oppressed; for example, in 2 Corinthians 1: 6–10 it refers to 'the afflictions we experienced in Asia . . . we were so utterly, unbearably crushed that we despaired of life itself', and to 'God who . . . delivered us from so deadly a peril . . .'.

Now, there are no reports from secular sources of Christians being persecuted in the Asian area at any time during the 1st century AD. There would be no particular reason to persecute anyone who behaved as Christians were expected to conduct themselves – with love for all and malice to none.

My contention is, of course, that the worshippers of Jesus Christ – the so-called Christians – were the Essenes.

The only group which was militant and likely to become involved in confrontations with the Romans was the Essene sect. Although history ascribes the responsibility for the conflicts to the orthodox Jews, there are reasons for thinking that there was some Essene involvement in the revolts which took place in AD 66–70, in AD 116 and in AD 130:

1. In the revolt of AD 66–70, John the Essene was a noted Jewish general.

2. In AD 116 there were revolts at communities in Mesopotamia, Cyrene, Cyprus and Alexandria. If it had been a national Jewish revolt, then one would have expected all areas in Judea to have been involved. The limited number of areas would be consistent with dissatisfaction by people in different parts, but linked by a common political or religious protest. The most sensitive and militant group among the Jews was the Essenes, and the likelihood is that they were responsible for the revolt.

3. The revolt in AD 130 ended with the death of Simon bar Kokhba who was an Essene. I suspect that the 'afflictions' referred to in 2 Corinthians 1 : 6–10 is the revolt of AD 130 because I identify this particular passage as one written by a man involved in the Church during that period.

Quite apart from the words and thoughts expressed in the epistles of Paul, there is evidence that he trained as an Essene.

The Essene characteristics of the letters

If the reader were asked to identify the subject matter of a book which contained references to 'bits', 'bytes', 'central processing units' and 'programs', he would recognise it as covering something to do with computers. To those who have read through the Dead Sea Scrolls, there are words used by the Essenes which are exclusive to them. The wide useage of these words in the New Testament identifies the writers as being Essenes. Below, I give a list of Essene words and where they appear in the New Testament letters (including those believed to have been written by Paul):

'Elect': Rom 8: 33, Col 3: 12, 1 Tim 5: 21, 2 Tim 2: 10, Titus 1: 1 and more.
'Perfect': Phil 3: 15, Col 1: 28, 2 Tim 3: 17, Heb 10: 1, Heb 12: 23 and more.
'Way': 1 Cor 12: 31, 1 Thess 3: 11, Heb 9: 8, 10: 20, 2 Pet 2: 2 and more.
'Many': 1 Cor 10: 17, 2 Cor 2: 6, Heb 9: 28 and more.
'Poor': Rom 15: 26, 2 Cor 6: 10, Gal 2: 10, Jas 2: 5 and more.
'Saints': Phil 1: 1, Col 1: 2, 1 Thess 3: 13, 2 Thess 1: 10 and more.

The use of one or two words in the corpus of letters could be regarded as coincidence; the consistent use of particular words in conjunction with other identifying words cannot simply be chance. There can, I think, be little doubt that the writers of all the New Testament letters, and the Gospels too, were Essenes.

Paul and the Essenes

In Galatians, there are fairly clear indications that the writer had joined the Essenes. After saying that he was a persecutor of the Church he tells of his conversion; he continues in Galatians 1 : 17–24 and 2 : 1 as follows: 'Nor did I go up to Jerusalem to those who were apostles before me, but I went away to Arabia; and again I returned to Damascus. Then after three years I went up to Jerusalem to visit Cephas, and remained with him 15 days. But I saw none of the other apostles except James the Lord's brother. (In what I am writing to you before God, I do not lie.) Then I went into the regions of Syria and Cilecia. And I was still not known by sight to the Churches of Christ in Judea; they only heard it said "he who once persecuted us is now preaching the faith he once tried to destroy". And they glorified God because of me. Then after 14 years I went up to Jerusalem with Barnabus, taking Titus along with me.'

Note that he went first to Arabia, returned to Damascus and then, after three years, went to Jerusalem. The duration of his stay in Damascus is important because three years was the period which a newcomer was required to spend in a commune (first as a postulant then as a noviate) before being accepted into an Essene community.

In Philippians 3 : 8, there is supporting evidence for the belief that the writer joined the Essenes, because he says, 'Indeed I count everything as loss because of the surpassing worth of knowing Christ Jesus my Lord. For his sake I have suffered the loss of all things . . .'. The verses immediately preceding this tell us that the writer was a persecutor of the Church, so that they could have been written by Paul. The 'loss of everything' could be a reference to the Essene practice of handing over all possessions to the community after the three years initial probationary period had been served.

This is the evidence linking the writer with the Essenes. The whole of the Pauline and pastoral correspondence amply confirms that these were letters to, from and about Essenes and the faith and the problems they were still facing under persecution.

I am not able to identify the writer(s) of the verses I have quoted. They may have been written by Paul, but it is unlikely. What is important, however, is that the passages are recognised as having all the characteristics of someone who was explaining his Essene credentials.

The Essene teaching, which was attractive in so many ways, may have struck a sour note with Paul because it discriminated against the gentiles. He would reason that a God who had created both Jew and gentile would love both equally well and would not arbitrarily destroy the gentiles without giving them the chance to espouse the faith.

Opening the door to the gentiles meant that some key Jewish shibboleths would have to go. No longer would circumcision be compulsory nor would all foods need to be regarded as clean. Both traditions were incorporated into Jewish life in order to promote health and cleanliness, but circumcision became much more than a health requirement. It became the mark of the Jew, and the word was used to indicate the Jewishness of a belief or practice – for example, the injunction to 'circumcise your heart' simply meant to change one's thinking to true Jewish thinking. It was to be a constant source of trouble between the Jews and gentiles.

The New Testament letters frequently urge members of a Church to avoid the disputes which were arising between the Jews and gentiles. Food, circumcision, beliefs about Jesus and the interpretation of the Law (of Moses) were all contentious.

If all the letters attributed to Paul had actually been written by him, or at his direction, then we could expect consistency of advice; moreover, having dealt with a particular issue in one part of a letter, we would not expect it to be dealt with again later in the same letter.

The fact that individual letters repeat advice on the same topic and contradict rulings given in other letters, is a pointer to the letters being a mixture of pages from different writers.

I think the following extracts from the New Testament letters support my contention.

Repetitions, contradictions and abrupt changes of subject

In a letter it is customary to deal with a particular topic and then move on to some other subject. Everything which needs to be said should be included in the first reference to the subject, rather than returning to the same topic time and time again.

In the New Testament correspondence, there are verses

which repeat an idea which has been expressed earlier in similar wording. This points clearly to a duplication due to an extract from one letter being incorporated into the pages of another letter. There are also verses in the epistles which contradict ideas expressed either earlier in the letter or verses in another letter supposedly by the same writer. Again, this points to there being a mix-up leading to pages from the letter of one writer being added to a letter from another evangelist. Abrupt changes of subject are another sign of misplaced pages.

The following is not a complete list, but I think that there are enough examples to make the point clearly and convincingly.

Repetitions
Take, for example, the following verses from 1 Corinthians. They express the same idea yet are separated by only 30 verses:

1 : 12–13	*3 : 4–5*
What I mean is that each one of you says 'I belong to Paul' or 'I belong to Apollos' or 'I belong to Cephas' or 'I belong to Christ'. Is Christ divided? Was Paul crucified for you?	For when one says 'I belong to Paul' and another 'I belong to Apollos' are you not merely men? What then is Apollos? What is Paul? Servants through whom you believed . . .

It is reasonably certain that both parts have been written by the same man, but that he has used the same idea in different letters. The same explanation probably applies to the following extracts from 1 Corinthians:

1 : 17	*2 : 4*
For Christ did not send me to baptise but to preach the gospel, and not with eloquent wisdom lest the cross of Christ be emptied of its power.	. . . and my speech and my message were not in plausible words of wisdom but in demonstration of the Spirit and power that your faith might not rest in the wisdom of men but in the power of God.

Here are more examples which require no explanation:

3 : 16

Do you not know that you are God's temple and that God's Spirit dwells within you? If anyone destroys God's temple, God will destroy him. For God's temple is holy, and that temple you are.

6 : 19

Do you not know that your body is a temple of the Holy Spirit within you, which you have from God? You are not your own; you were bought with a price. So glorify God in your body.

6 : 12

All things are lawful for me but not all things are helpful.

10 : 23

All things are lawful but not all things are helpful.

The following verses are from 2 Corinthians and are further examples of repetitions. The writer is asking the Corinthians for money. In the verses from chapter 8 he makes his points tellingly and finishes off in verse 24 in a manner which clearly closes the subject. However, in chapter 9, he introduces the subject of money in a way which suggests that this is his opening reference to it:

8 : 3–4 and 24

For they gave according to their means, of their own free will, begging us earnestly for the favour of taking part in the relief of the saints . . .

So give proof, before the churches, of your love and of our boasting about you to these men.

9 : 1 and 11

Now it is superfluous for me to write to you about the offering for the saints.

You will be enriched in every way for great generosity which through us will produce thanksgiving to God.

What has happened here, I think, is that pages from an early letter have been included with pages from a later letter. Another example of this is given below, where the repeated reference to a third visit indicates that the verses are from two different letters.

12 : 14	13 : 1
Here for the third time I am ready to come to you . . .	This is the third time I am coming to you.

What is particularly interesting here is that the verses which follow on from those quoted above seem to have been written by quite different personalities. In verses 15–21 the writer appears weak, on the defensive and lacking any authority whatsoever. In the whole of the 13th chapter, however, there can be no doubt that here is a leader of men. Here, then, we have an instance of not only repetition within a letter, but what appears to be extracts from letters originating from different writers.

Contradictions

If one verse contradicts another, it must surely point not to one man having two opinions, but to two men expressing differing ideas on the same subject. Referring back to 1 Corinthians again, consider the following:

1 : 4–5 and 7	3 : 3
I give thanks to God always for you because of the grace of God which was given to you in Jesus Christ that in every way you were enriched in him . . .	. . . for you are still of the flesh. For while there is jealousy and strife among you, are you not of the flesh and behaving like ordinary men?
. . . so that you were not lacking in any spiritual gift as you wait for the revealing of our Lord Jesus Christ.	

The compliments of the opening verses contrast sharply with the criticism of the second passage. These verses cannot be from the same letter and it is unlikely that they are even from the same writer (unless a considerable span of time separates the two letters).

The adoption of certain Jewish practices presented problems to those converts to the early Church. Consider the contrasting advice given from the following verses in 1 Corinthians:

8 : 4 and 8	*10 : 20–21*
Hence, as to the eating of food offered to idols, we know that 'an idol has no real existence' and that 'there is no God but one . . .'	. . . I imply that what pagans sacrifice they offer to demons and not to God. I do not want you to be partners with demons. You cannot drink the cup of the Lord and the cup of demons.
. . . Food will not commend us to God. We are no worse off if we do not eat and no better off if we do . . .	

In the chapter 8 verses the writer expresses no undue concern about the eating of food offered to demons, whereas the verses from chapter 10 are strongly against any such tainted food.

In 1 Corinthians again, there is a clear contradiction which occurs within a mere 23 verses.

1 Cor 7 : 2	*1 Cor 7 : 25 and 26*
But because of the temptation to immorality each man should have his own wife.	Now concerning the unmarried . . . I think in view of the impending distress it is well for a person to remain as he is.

In the first quotation the writer gives a clear reason in favour of marriage – temptation.

In the second, he writes unambiguously against marriage – there is an impending distress.

The writer could not have changed his mind between writing verse 2 and verse 25; the different injunctions only make sense if a page from one letter has become connected with pages from another, perhaps from a different writer.

According to theologians, the Letters to the Romans and those to the Corinthians were written by Paul or, if not by him personally, then by scribes who wrote as he dictated to them. Consider, then, the contrast between the following verses:

Letter to the Romans 12 : 17–19	*1 Corinthians 5 : 1–5*
Repay no one evil for evil . . . never avenge yourselves but leave it to the wrath of God . . . if your enemy is hungry, feed him; if he is thirsty, give him drink.	. . . there is immorality among you . . . let him who has done this be removed from among you . . . you are to deliver this man to Satan . . .

This is another example of contradictions which clearly, in my opinion, point to different men having written these passages. In fact, the verses in the Letter to the Romans are some which I have identified as having been written by Clement of Rome. He displays the same warmth, generosity of spirit and concern for those guilty of moral lapses as can be seen in his other writings. I cannot identify the writer of the Corinthian verses but, unlike Clement, he comes across as a cold, perhaps harsh, authoritarian who sees life in black and white terms.

Abrupt changes of subject

An abrupt change of subject in a letter – that is, a change which interrupts the continuity of a particular line of thought – is another indication that there may have been some manipulation of the original letter. Sometimes it is difficult to explain such changes. In the following example, however, the violent change in thought from one sentence to another is so clear that one wonders why the compiler linked them together.

In the 15th chapter of 1 Corinthians, the writer deals with death and resurrection. He continues with this theme into verse 29 which reads:

15 : 29	. . . if the dead are not raised at all, why are people baptised on their behalf?	Deals with death and resurrection.
15 : 30, 31 32 (part)	Why am I in peril every hour? I protest, brethren, by my pride in you which I have in Christ Jesus our Lord. I die every day. What do I gain, if, humanly speaking, I fought with beasts at Ephesus?	Refers to a personal problem.

15 : 32 (part)	If the dead are not raised let us eat and drink for tomorrow, we die.	Return to subject of death.
15 : 33 and 34	Do not be deceived; bad company ruins good morals. Come to your right mind and sin no more. For some have no knowledge of God. I say this to your shame.	Introduces another new topic – morals.
15 : 35	But some will ask how the dead are raised . . .	Return to the subject of death and resurrection.

Another example of an abrupt change of subject can be found earlier in 1 Corinthians. In a series of verses, chapter 14 deals with prophesying and continues:

14 : 32 and 33	and the spirits of the prophets are subject to prophets. For God is not a God of confusion but of peace.
14 : 34 – 36	As in all the churches of the saints the women should keep silence in the churches. For they are not permitted to speak . . . for it is shameful for a woman to speak in church . . .
14 : 37 – 40	If anyone thinks that he is a prophet, or spiritual . . . earnestly desire to prophesy . . . but all things should be done decently and in order.

The verses which refer to women speaking in the church are obviously out of place. If the reader cares to turn to 1 Corinthians 11 : 16, the writer is dealing with the duties of women in church, and the verses 14 : 34–36 would not be out of place there.

One further example from the same epistle can be found in chapter 5.

1 Cor 5 : 5	. . . you are to deliver this man to Satan for the destruction of the flesh, that his spirit may be saved in the day of the Lord Jesus. (Commenting on an immoral man.)

| 6, 7 and 8 | Your boasting is not good. Do you not know that a little leaven leavens the whole lump . . . Let us celebrate the festival, not with the old leaven . . . but with the unleavened bread of sincerity and truth. (Exhorts them to be sincere and truthful.) |
| 9 | I wrote to you in my letter not to associate with immoral men . . . (This and the following verse tells them to avoid immoral men.) |

This sequence of verses appears to have had perhaps a page of writing containing verses 6, 7 and 8 interrupting what seems to be a natural flow of words from verse 5 to verse 9.

I do not think that any of the examples I have given are interpolations. The particular 'out of place' verses are not critical as far as beliefs are concerned, and if the compiler had intended to insert writing to influence readers to his way of thinking there are better places in the epistle for this to have been done.

It is surprising that theologians and contributors to authoritative works of reference do not seem to have identified some of the problem areas to be found in the New Testament epistles. Perhaps they feel that the writers of the Bible have been influenced by God and that they should be wary of being over-critical.

Writers who have contributed to the New Testament letters

I have covered some, but not all, of the duplications, unexpected changes of subject matter and contradictions which indicate that more than one writer's work has been accidentally included in the so-called Pauline epistles. I think that the evidence of Essene words, expressions and thinking quoted, clearly show the link with this amazing sect.

The language and expressions enable us to identify Essenes as being responsible for the New Testament writings. Particular styles of writing enable the identification to be carried further so that individuals can be recognised as the writers of certain passages.

The final five chapters in Paul's Letter to the Romans provide an interesting exercise in examining the text for clues which will lead us to the writer of passages in a letter supposedly written by Paul.

The Tertius letter

Paul's Letter to the Romans is, so the received wisdom tells us, the very essence of Paul's feelings, thoughts and religious teaching. The reader may find it useful to see how I analyse the last five chapters of the letter, and it is worth noting that three different versions of the 'Romans' letter have been found – one ends at 14 : 23, another at 15 : 13 and the third at 16 : 27.

1. Verses 16 : 16 to 16 : 23 seem to be from Tertius – he signs it in verse 22.
2. In 16 : 17 he writes: 'I appeal to you, brethren . . .'.
3. Working backwards, we find the same phrase used in 15 : 30, so it seems reasonably certain that verses 15 : 30 to 15 : 33 are also by Tertius. The presence of 'Amen' in the final verse (15 : 33) seems to be the end of that section, so that we cannot be sure that the following verses – 16 : 1 to 16 : 16 – are from the same letter or have been written by Tertius.
4. If we drop back even further to chapter 12 we find 'I appeal to you, therefore, brethren' used again, indicating that this is another passage written by Tertius, which seems to end at 12 : 8. There is a change of subject here, because whereas the question of 'gifts' has been the topic, it changes at 12 : 9 to love and relationships. Later in this Chapter, I identify the passage 12 : 9 to 15 : 13 as having been written by Clement of Rome.
5. In the Tertius passage 12 : 5, another phrase is used by him which reads, 'For by the grace given to me . . .'. This also appears in a passage which follows the 'Clement of Rome' text. It is reasonable to conclude therefore that verses 15: 14–29 are by Tertius, and that they continue into the 15: 30 section already identified as having been written by Tertius.
6. At the end of Romans Tertius mentions Timothy and

other companions, but there is no mention of Paul. If this were material written by Tertius on behalf of Paul we could expect Paul to be mentioned at the end of the letter. The conclusion I reach is that those parts of the letter I have referred to were written by Tertius and that Paul was in no way involved.

7. I later identify Theophilus as the writer of another considerable part of the Letter to the Romans. This letter, regarded as the very personification of Paul's character and thinking, has been made up of parts of letters from three different writers. The following summarises the position as far as the last five chapters are concerned:

Romans	12 : 1 to 12 : 8	Written by Tertius.
	12 : 9 to 15 : 13	Written by Clement of Rome.
	15 : 14 to 15 : 33	Written by Tertius.
	16 : 1 to 16 : 16	Possibly written by Tertius.
	16 : 17 to 16 : 23	Written by Tertius.
	16 : 25 to 16 : 27	Possibly written by Tertius.

This gives the reader some idea of the complexity of the New Testament letters.

When analysing the various letters written by the early Christian leaders I have tried to avoid the natural pitfalls which are ever present when comparing styles of writing.

It has to be recognised that any religious or secular organisation, particularly political parties, for example, develop certain phrases or clichés which are an easy and accepted way of conveying an idea. In the case of the Essenes, who placed some importance on prophecies, the references in the New Testament letters to the Old Testament books were often preceded by the words: 'as it is written' and 'the saying is sure . . .'. It could be that only one writer used those particular terms, but it is impossible to be certain. Analogies are made with soldiers and wars, with athletes and with the importance of all parts of the body. Again, it could be that the same writer is using these, and that where texts correspond then that single writer is responsible. I feel, however, that if a neat phrase or analogy is used, and found to be an attractive way of projecting a concept, others will take up the idea and it will quickly become part of the organisation's terminology.

It is necessary to be cautious, therefore, whenever these expressions appear in a text.

There are three other writers who can be identified as having contributed to the New Testament letters.

Clement of Rome

Clement is supposed to have died around AD 96 and is reported to have been a Bishop of Rome. There are two letters attributed to him which have been melded into one long letter. His style of writing is such that it is possible to identify, with a reasonable degree of certainty, certain parts of Paul's letters which, by error, include some written by Clement. These stylistic features are:

1. In the whole of his letter, he never once refers to himself as 'I'. He always hides behind the plural 'we', which he uses to refer either to himself and the sect or himself and the recipients of the letter. This is unusual; we would expect a man who held the office of Bishop to be more authoritative. It is a style which suggests a lack of confidence in himself.

2. As a consequence, he makes much use of an expression which enjoins his readers to do as he suggests. The two words 'Let us' are frequently used, as is the word 'therefore', and sometimes he combines the two. He also invites his readers to 'consider' certain aspects of belief.

3. He frequently makes use of Old Testament quotations and never knows which book he is quoting. Invariably, he glosses over this by writing 'The Scripture says', but on five occasions he blythely admits his ignorance by writing 'Somewhere it is said . . .'.

Whenever one of these features is noticeable in a passage, there must be a suspicion that Clement is the writer. When more than one feature is used then the warning signals should be hoisted even higher.

Here are some examples from Clement's Letter to the Corinthians together with examples from Paul's Letter to the Romans and also the Letter to the Hebrews.

Chapter 5	Let us take the noble examples . . .
	Let us pass in review . . .
Chapter 7	Let us, then, give up those empty and futile aspirations . . .
	Let us attend to what is noble . . .
	Let us fix our gaze . . .
	Let us pass in review . . .
Chapter 9	Therefore, let us comply . . .
	. . . let us crave his mercy . . .
	Let us take Enoch . . .
Chapter 13	Let us, therefore, brethren . . .
Chapter 14	Let us be kind to one another.
Chapter 15	Therefore, let us associate . . .
	For somewhere it is said . . .
Chapter 21	For somewhere it is said . . .
Chapter 24	Let us consider, beloved . . .
	Let us consider, beloved . . .
Chapter 25	Let us consider the strange . . .
Chapter 26	Do we, then, consider it a great . . .

Romans 12 : 9	Let love be genuine . . .
13 : 1	Let every person . . .
2	Therefore he who resists
5	Therefore one must be . . .
12	Let us then cast off . . .
13	Let us conduct . . .
14 : 3	Let not him who eats . . .
13	Then let us no more . . .
19	Let us then pursue . . .
15 : 2	Let each of us . . .
Hebrews 2 : 6	It has been testified somewhere . . .
4 : 2	Let us fear . . .
4 : 4	For he has somewhere spoken . . .
4 : 11	Let us therefore . . .
16	Let us then . . .
12 : 1	Let us also lay aside . . . let us run . . .
3	Consider him who . . .
13 : 1	Let brotherly love . . .
17	Let them do this . . .

                    For somewhere it
                    is said . . .
Chapter 28   For somewhere the
                    Writing says . . .
Chapter 42   For somewhere it
                    says . . .

The whole of the Letter to the Hebrews exhibits such clear
literary links with Clement's letter that there must be the
strongest suspicion that he wrote the Letter to the Hebrews.

Quite apart from the stylistic similarities between the
Clement letter and the New Testament letters quoted,
Clement uses references to Old Testament figures to support
his preaching, and the same figures appear in the Letter to the
Hebrews.

Consider these examples:

Clement's Letter to the Corinthians   *Letter to the Hebrews*

Chapter 4   And God looked   11 : 4   By faith, Abel offered to
                    kindly on   God a more acceptable
                    Abel . . . but   sacrifice than Cain . . .
                    paid no
                    attention to
                    Cain . . .

Chapter 43   Moses, the faithful   3 : 2   . . . Moses was faithful
                    servant in all the   in God's house . . .
                    house . . .

Chapter 12   . . . faith were the   11 : 31 By faith, Rahab the
                    reasons why the   harlot did not perish . .
                    harlot Rahab was
                    saved . . .

There are more examples to be found in the references to
Abraham (Hebrews 11 : 17 and Clement chapter 10), Enoch
(Hebrews 11 : 5 and Clement chapter 9), Noah (Hebrews 11 :
7 and Clement chapter 9) and David (Hebrews 11 : 32 and
Clement chapter 52).

The link between Clement and the Letter to the Hebrews
is strengthened by the following extracts from the letters,
showing a clear correspondence of thinking between the two.

Chapter 17	those who . . . dressed in sheepskins and goatskins . . . men of attested merit . . .	11 : 37	. . . they went . . . in skins of sheep and goats . . . and all well attested
Chapter 19	. . . we are allowed to profit by so many glorious examples . . .	12 : 1	. . . since we are surrounded by so great a cloud of witnesses, let us . . .
Chapter 21	. . . For a searcher is He of thoughts and designs . . .	4 : 12	. . . the word of God is . . . discerning the thoughts and intentions of the heart . . .

These, together with the Old Testament personalities and the stylistic features common to the two letters surely point to a common hand, and to Clement of Rome having made what are, so far, unrecognised contributions to the New Testament letters. What is also interesting from an examination of his Letter to the Corinthians is that pages of a letter from Theophilus have been accidentally included. Chapter 45 has all the hallmarks of a Theophilus letter; the questions, the degree of harshness, the expression 'What shall we say, brethren?' and his response to his own question, 'Let no such thing be said', all point to the hand of Theophilus.

I think the analysis of the Letter to the Hebrews shows beyond any reasonable doubt that Clement of Rome was the writer. However, not everyone agrees. A Scottish theologian has commented that the Letter to the Hebrews is 'quoted by Clement of Rome who, if he had any idea of its authorship, gives no hint of it'.

Obviously, he never considered the possibility that Clement himself had written the letter.

Paul the apostle

'Religiousese' is a word I have coined to describe the rather fawning way in which theologians refer to important personalities in the New Testament. For example, one comments that Mark's Gospel is short, written in a no-nonsense style and is commended for its brevity. If, like Luke's Gospel, it is regarded as an extended version of Mark's account, then Luke is complimented for taking Mark's brief sketch and painting in the detail and colour. No matter whether short or long, it is admired.

The same is done when describing the letters of Paul, even when those attributed to him are sometimes muddled, repetitive and contradictory. For the majority of theologians, Paul is above criticism and, of course, this means that his letters do not receive the close examination they deserve.

The New Testament letters are, as we have seen, a mixture of different letters. One of the problems is that of knowing precisely who wrote which particular part of each letter.

Although there are thirteen letters in the New Testament attributed to Paul, the fact that an epistle opens – or closes – with a verse which suggests that Paul is the writer cannot be conclusive evidence of authorship. For example, it could be:

1. That Paul could not write Greek or Hebrew and required a scribe. In these circumstances he would probably indicate the main points to be covered by the letter.
2. That a junior member had written to a Church in order to promote his own ideas under the name of Paul.
3. That opponents of Paul wrote letters bearing Paul's name in order to give their beliefs the authority of Paul. In 2 Thess 2 : 2 the text warns the reader against being 'shaken in mind or excited, either by spirit or by word, or by letters purporting to be from us'.
4. That the compiler of the letters, thinking that Paul was the writer, wrote an introductory tag to that effect.

There is, however, one letter in the New Testament which seems to have been written by Paul. First, it is a personal letter to a friend. Because he is a friend, it could be that he spoke the same language as Paul and that Paul would therefore not require a scribe to write on his behalf. Second, it is a letter written with all the skill and authority of a leader, with acceptance taken for granted.

Here, and Paul clearly identifies himself as the writer, he can be seen pleading the case for the unwanted Onesimus to be accepted back by Philemon. Here are the salient points:

Verse 7

For I have derived much joy and comfort from your love . . . the hearts of the saints have been refreshed by you.

First, the flattery. Philemon is given to realise that he has certain high standards, respected by others, which they expect him to maintain . . . particularly in the following case.

Verse 8

. . . though I am bold enough to command you to do what is required, yet for love's sake I prefer to appeal to you – I, Paul . . .

Although I can pull rank, says Paul, I know I can rely on your love, friendship and goodwill, noted in verse 7.

Verse 12

I am sending him back to you, sending my very heart.

If you send Onesimus back, you send my heart back – and that would be very unfriendly, implies Paul.

Verse 14

. . . but I preferred to do nothing without your consent in order that your goodness might not be by compulsion but of your own free will.

But Paul *is* sending him back – see verse 12 above. Paul does not have Philemon's approval, but skilfully heads off a protest by attributing an acceptance to Philemon's natural goodness – but with a reminder that compulsion could be used.

Verse 15

Perhaps that is why he was parted from you . . . that you might have him back forever.

Another reason for not refusing – he was destined to be with you and, hopefully, will stay because we don't want him back here.

Confident of your obedience I
write to you knowing that you
will do even more than I say.

In case you still thought you had
a choice, says Paul – you
haven't. I expect obedience.
Further, he implies, you
should do more, but having
him back is the very least that
is expected of you.

In the Philemon letter, Paul writes so cleverly that even if
Philemon refused to have Onesimus back into the fold, he,
Paul, would not lose face. Although carrying the stick of
authority behind his back, he only brings it out to remind
Philemon that it is there. In the event of a refusal he could
claim that it was not his authority which had been rejected,
but his friendly request. He was not only a religious leader but
also a skilled politician.

This is not Paul's only contribution to the New Testament
letters. In the second letter to the Corinthians, we find the
same clever approach. In this letter we see how skilfully he
tackles the problem of relieving the unfortunate Corinthians
of their money. It is the way of the natural salesman, the
persuader, and wherever in the Biblical letters this trait is
recognised, then there we probably have Paul making his
contribution. In today's society he would be a director of a
fund-raising company or would have his own public relations
firm.

In 2 Corinthians (8 : 1–15) he generates interest and
excitement in his first line: 'We must tell you friends, how
gracious God has been to our congregation in Macedonia'.
What, the Corinthians would ask themselves, is this
generosity which the Macedonians have received from God,
but which hasn't reached us yet? Well, according to Paul, it is
that they have been so exuberantly happy that they have
shown themselves lavishly open-handed. All this was even
from 'the depths of their poverty', he says, tellingly, making
the point well in advance that they are even poorer than you
Corinthians, so you can't use that as an excuse. It was such
fun, he continues, that they begged to be allowed to share in

this generous service.

The whole thing has been such an outstanding success, he writes, that he has asked Titus to visit the Corinthians.

At no time has the offensive word 'money' been mentioned. Paul cleverly describes the collection of the money as completing 'this work of generosity'. He goes on to flatter and cajole and to remind those who might waver that, 'At the moment your surplus meets their needs, but one day your need may be met from their surplus'.

It is a brilliant letter; he does not order, does not try to wheedle and presents his case so cleverly that he is able to steer a neat course through that problem-infested water – the request for money.

Chapter 9 is again concerned with the raising of funds for the saints in Jerusalem, but is actually from a different letter – but from the same writer. Having dealt with the subject of money in chapter 8, it does not make sense that he continues with the subject in chapter 9. It seems to be a later letter because in 9 : 5 he writes that he is sending brethren to arrange 'in advance for this gift you have promised'. In other words, chapter 8 was successful in gaining a promise of money, and chapter 9 is Paul's letter telling them that he is arranging for the fund to be collected. It is written with the same skill evident in the previous chapter, with a mixture of flattery, hints of embarrassment to all concerned if they are not found to be forthcoming, and a final flourish of originality designed to prise open the tightest wallet. In verse 7, he writes: 'Each one must do as he has made up his mind, not reluctantly or under compulsion, for God loves a cheerful giver. And God is able to provide you with every blessing in abundance, so that you may always have enough of everything . . .'.

He is also seen in action earlier in 2 Corinthians where, in 7 : 8–16, it is apparent that he has sent a letter which has caused some offence. The recipient of the letter is annoyed and has protested because he, the recipient, has been accused of something of which he is quite innocent.

Paul is quite undaunted and does not feel the need to fight back with harsh words as a leader could have done. With the skill that we might expect of him, and pausing only to sharpen his quill, he neatly turns the whole thing round proving that far from being the villain, he is the hero. Abbreviated, his reply is:

'I did wound you but I am not sorry [shocked surprise of the recipient].
I am happy [even more surprise].
Not that your feelings were wounded [relief].
But that the wound led to a change of heart.
You bore the wound as I know God would have you do [both me and God approve].
And see the results.
How your longings for me awoke.
How eager you were to get justice done.
And you have. My concern was to make it plain in the sight of God that you were innocent'.

Paul does not apologise but boldly takes the offensive and, with a chutzpah that many might envy, claims that he wrote the letter in order to force the recipient to prove his innocence. In other words, you didn't realise it at the time, but I was doing you a favour.

These are the only passages in the New Testament letters which could be attributed to Paul with a reasonable degree of confidence.

Finally, we come to the man who has written most of Romans (the letter most closely associated with Paul) and who links the New Testament letters closely with the 2nd century AD.

Theophilus of Antioch
Theophilus was an enthusiastic convert to the developing gentile Christianity, and a number of pages from his letters are included in the Letter to the Romans. So that the reader can better understand the chronology of the early Christian years, the following might be helpful:

Traditional belief		Correct chronology	
AD 30	Jesus crucified.	63 BC	Jesus crucified. Followers flee to Egypt.
AD 54	Paul active around the Middle East.	30 BC or later	Followers return to Qumran and develop their organisation and writings.
		AD 68	Qumran overrun and Essenes scattered.
		c. AD 140	Theophilus converted and takes his simplified Essene beliefs to the gentiles.

Theophilus is the writer of *Ad Autolycus* and from it we learn some facts about the man. He:

— was brought up to speak Greek;
— was probably married;
— became a Christian;
— was familiar with the Greek Old Testament;
— was thought to be acquainted with Luke's Gospel.

On the last point, it is worth recording that in the opening verses to this Gospel it reads: 'It seemed good to me ... to write an orderly account for you, most excellent Theophilus'. In other words, Theophilus was a recipient of the Gospel. No theologian has, to my knowledge, ever related the 'Theophilus' in Luke's Gospel to the 'Theophilus' who wrote *Ad Autolycus*, simply because they thought that Luke's Gospel was written many years before in the first century AD. It seemed to theologians – and still does – that because the Theophilus of *Ad Autolycus* lived well into the 2nd century AD, he could not be the man referred to by the compiler of Luke's Gospel.

The Theophilus who lived in the 2nd century AD is the only man bearing that name who was active in the Christian movement. There can be little doubt that he was the same

Theophilus who is referred to in Luke's Gospel.

Theophilus has certain characteristics which no other known writer of that period exhibits. For example:

— he uses certain expressions frequently;
— he bombards his reader with questions;
— he argues his case in such complex detail that the reader becomes almost bemused by the flow of ideas;
— he argues the same theological points as can be found in some of the Pauline epistles;
— with his reference to the reader as 'O man' he seems to regard his reader with contempt.

Consider, first, the expressions he uses. On one side of the page I detail extracts from a letter written by Theophilus to Autolycus, on the other comparative examples from the Pauline epistles. These, I think, demonstrate as conclusively as it is possible to do so that these were written by the same man.

Autolycus		*New Testament*	
Chapter 3	You will say to me since . . . O man	Romans 9 : 19	You will say to me then . . .
		Romans 11 : 19	You will say
Chapter 3	You will say to me then, 'Is God angry?' certainly.	Galatians 2 : 17	. . . agent of sin? certainly not.
		Romans 2 : 1	. . . O man . . .
		Romans 2 : 3	. . . O man . . .
Chapter 11	You will say to me . . .	1 Cor 15 : 36	You foolish man . . .
Chapter 11	You will say . . . certainly. Again, you will say . . . certainly not.	Galatians 3 : 1	O foolish Galatians . . .
Chapter 2	So you also, O man . . .		
Chapter 3	Hear me, O man . . .		
		Romans 2 : 4	Do you not know . . .
Chapter 6	Consider his works, O man . . .	Romans 6 : 16	Do you not know . . .

Chapter 7	You speak of him, O man . . .	Romans 7 : 1	Do you not know . . .
		1 Cor 6 : 9	Do you not know . . .
Chapter 7	If you know these things, O man . . .	1 Cor 6 : 15	Do you not know . . .
Chapter 8	Do you not know . . .	1 Cor 6 : 16	Do you not know . . .

It is my contention that these expressions identify the writing of Theophilus almost as does a fingerprint. No other writer uses these expressions coupled with such an aggressive style of writing.

Theophilus has the typical rhetorician's style – he asks questions, not because he is interested in his opponent's answer, but simply to advance his own argument. In the list above I have quoted expressions which are, word for word, used in both the letter to Autolycus and those epistles attributed to Paul.

There are, in fact, many expressions used in *Autolycus* which could be described as derivatives. For example, the following have the familiar rhetorical flavour, and although they do not have their specific counterpart in the Pauline epistles, I do not think it unfair to suggest that they come from the same hand as the other expressions given above, and which appear Romans, Corinthians and Galatians:

Chapter 2: But if you should say 'Show me your God', I may reply to you . . .

Chapter 10: I shall enquire of you, O man . . .

Chapter 10: And if you should mention . . .

Chapter 10: Will you say he went to Crete? Yes . . .

These various expressions occur singly and also together in different parts of the Pauline letters, so that it is possible to identify, with almost complete certainty, those passages which have been written by Theophilus.

It is understandable that a writer who corresponds with different Churches will use the same or similar concepts. The following are examples of similar ideas being expressed in both *Autolycus* and the Pauline letters.

Theophilus	*Paul*
Chapter 14 . . . rewarding each one in accordance with what he deserves. To those who with endurance seek imperishability through good works he will give eternal life . . .	Romans 2 : 6 For he will render to every man according to his works Romans 2 : 7 To those who by patience in well-doing seek for glory and honour and immortality, he will give eternal life.
Chapter 14 But to the unbelieving who despise and disobey the truth but obey unrighteousness . . . and lawless idolatry there will come wrath and anger, tribulation and anguish.	Romans 2 : 8 But for those who are factious and do not obey the truth, but obey wickedness, there will be wrath and fury.

The following quotations from *Ad Autolycus* show how a writer can display characteristics which help to identify him. In this case, Theophilus exhibits a tendency for repetition. It is the hallmark of a forceful writer. Not content with one example, he supplies a number which help him to emphasise his point.

So show yourself to me. Are you not an adulterer? a fornicator? a thief? a swindler? a robber? a pederast? insolent? a reviler? quick-tempered? envious? a braggart? disdainful? a bully? avaricious? disobedient to parents? one who sells children? (Chapter 2.)

For if I call him Light, I speak of his creature; if I call him Logos, I speak of his beginning; if I call him Mind, I speak of his intelligence; if I call him Spirit, I speak of his breath; if I call him Sophia (Wisdom), I speak of his offspring; if I call him Strength, I speak of his might; if I call him Power, I speak of his energy; if I call him Providence, I speak of his goodness; if I call him Kingdom, I speak of his glory; if I call him Lord, I speak of him as judge; if I call him Judge, I speak of him as just; if I call him Father, I speak of him as all things; if I call him Fire, I speak of him as wrath. (Chapter 3.)

227

Compare these texts with Romans 1: 29–31:

> They were filled with all manner of wickedness, evil, covetousness, malice. Full of envy, murder, strife, deceit, malignity, they are gossips, slanderers, haters of God, insolent, haughty, boastful, inventors of evil, disobedient to their parents, foolish, faithless, heartless, ruthless.

Not only does the Romans text include some of the sins evident in the *Ad Autolycus* chapter 2 quotation, it uses the same 'disobedient to parents' criticism, which is itself an unusual imperfection to include.

This is another piece of evidence pointing to Theophilus being the writer of much of the Epistle to the Romans.

The fact that Theophilus has contributed a number of chapters to the Letter to the Romans does not mean that he was Paul. The letter has been attributed to Paul, not unreasonably, because Paul's name appears at the beginning of the letter. However, the fact that the letter can be seen to incorporate pages from other letters leads to the conclusion that no reliance can be placed on the opening verse.

There can be little doubt that Theophilus was a fanatic. Everything he has written, both in the New Testament and in his *Autolycus* is testimony to the amount of thought he has given to the Essene/Christian theology. It is almost as though it has taken a hold of him completely. He writes expansively, at such length, in such detail and with such complex and difficult to understand arguments that one cannot but associate him with another fanatic of that period called Marcion.

Having two or more names was not unusual amongst the religious men of those times. Ignatius was also known as 'Theophorus', Jesus was known as Onias the Just and as 'Honi the Circle Drawer', Peter was known as 'Cephas', and none of these were real names. Theophilus was almost certainly not a real name, so that different names, Marcion and Theophilus, do not exclude them from being the same man.

Unfortunately, the writings of Marcion, who was a very influential figure in the developing Christian movement, are not available to us. They have been lost. Or have they? Could it be that in *Ad Autolycus* and the contribution of Theophilus to the New Testament letters, mistakenly attributed to Paul, we have the thoughts of Marcion?

It must remain pure speculation.

What we can do now is to look at the Letter to the Romans and see what contribution has been made by Paul:

1: 1 to 1: 25	Unidentifiable
1: 26 to 11: 36	Written by Theophilus.
12: 1 to 12: 8	Written by Tertius.
12: 9 to 15: 13	Written by Clement of Rome.
15: 14 to 15: 33	Written by Tertius.
16: 1 to 16: 16	Possibly written by Tertius.
16: 17 to 16: 23	Written by Tertius.
16: 24 to 16: 27	Possibly written by Tertius.

Within the sections I have attributed to Theophilus, Clement of Rome and Tertius are the expressions which I associate with these writers.

If my analysis is correct, then there is not one word which has been written by Paul.

The other New Testament letters

Some of the other letters in the New Testament have all the appearance of being composites made up of pages from the letters of two or more writers. For example, Theophilus is the writer of 1 Corinthians 6 : 1 to 6 : 20 – the 'Do you not know' phrases identify him, in my opinion, beyond question. Theophilus is again seen in Galatians 2 : 15 to 4 : 11 where his expressions 'Certainly not . . .' and 'O foolish Galatians', together with his complex arguments, identify him clearly.

The sheer weight of questions can also be a clue to the hand of Theophilus. In 1 Corinthians 9 : 1 – 9 : 12, where a later 'Do you not know . . .' phrase provides the clue, Theophilus manages to pepper his bemused readers with 16 questions. It is an awesome performance.

It is, however, impossible to analyse all the New Testament letters, particularly when the signposts do not point to any writer and where the breaks between pages from one letter and another are not sufficiently defined.

For these reasons, I have confined my efforts to Romans and Hebrews.

Finally, there are letters from Ignatius and Polycarp which deserve a mention.

Evidence that some Pauline letters contain pages written by Ignatius

I return to the self-effacing, almost self-abasing, passages in the Ignatius letters because they have their counterparts in the Pauline letters. These lead to the suspicion that the writer of the weak sentences in the Ignatius letters has also had pages from his letters incorporated into the so-called Pauline letters. Compare these passages:

1 Cor 9 : 1	*From the Ignatius correspondence*
If to others I am not an apostle, at least, I am to you . . .	Indeed, I am now but being initiated into discipleship and I address you as my fellow disciples. (Ephesians – chapter 3.)

1 Cor 15 : 9	
Last of all, as to one untimely born he appeared also to me. For I am the least of the apostles, unfit to be called an apostle.	For myself, I am ashamed to be counted as one of her members. I certainly do not deserve to be one, being the least of them and one that came to birth unexpectedly. (Romans – chapter 9.)

Philippians 3 : 12
Not that I have already obtained this or am already perfect; but I press on to make it my own.

1 Cor 3 : 1

But I, brethren, could not address you as spiritual men . . . but as babes in Christ.

. . . but I fear to inflict harm on you who are mere babes . . . (Trallians – chapter 5.)

1 Peter 2 : 2

Like newborn babes, long for the spiritual milk.

I think these passages support my contention.

When I originally began investigating the evidence for the life of Jesus, it had not been my intention to examine the Ignatius/Polycarp correspondence. However, I found myself thrust into it for this reason – if Jesus lived in the 1st century BC then Paul, too, may have been inadvertently placed in the wrong time-slot.

The evidence for the letters attributed to Paul and others having been mixed up by some compiler is quite comprehensive. Interestingly, in his letter to the Philippians, Polycarp writes: 'The Epistles of Ignatius which were sent to us by him and such others as we have in our possession, we send to you, as requested'. So, it seems that Polycarp collected some of the letters and sent them to someone at Philippi. Whether the sorting of the pages was done by Polycarp or the recipient is not known. The responsibility for the Pauline mélange lies with one or the other.

Ignatius and Polycarp

It is not my intention to write at length about the letters attributed to two of the early Christian fathers – Ignatius, Bishop of Antioch, and Polycarp, Bishop of Smyrna. What I would like the reader to understand, however, is that these letters, like the New Testament letters, are not single letters but composites which include some pages from other writers. It is all part of what might be described as the Biblical Letters Problem. The difficulties I have with them are outlined below.

Evidence that Polycarp's letter includes an extract from a Clement of Rome letter

Clement wrote in the first person plural – we – and made great use of the injunctions 'Let us, therefore . . .' and 'Therefore . . .'. In Polycarp's letter to the Philippians, there are three paragraphs, commencing 'Wherefore forsaking . . .', 'Let us, therefore . . .' and 'Let us therefore . . .' again, which are in sharp contrast to the rest of the letter. The words 'us' and 'we' are used, never the word 'I'. For these reasons, I think it likely that a page or pages from a Clement letter have been included by accident in the Polycarp letter.

Evidence that the Ignatius letters include pages from other writers

Ignatius wrote one letter to Polycarp and six letters to different Churches in the Middle East. There are some aspects of these letters which present problems for me.

In the Ignatius letter to the Ephesians, chapter 10 displays the hand of Clement, with the injunctions 'Let us . . .' and the plural 'we'. It also neither follows on from chapter 9 nor does it continue naturally into chapter 11. I would make the same comments about chapter 15, which again has the characteristics of Clement's hand and neither follows on from chapter 14 nor continues into chapter 16.

I find some difficulty, too, when comparing the letter to Polycarp with the other six letters. The letter to Polycarp has all the stamp of someone who has position and authority. Although both are bishops, Ignatius writes as though Polycarp was a junior. He gives advice and orders, for example:

'Do justice to your office . . .';

'Stand firm, like an anvil . . .';

'After the Lord, you must be their guardian . . .'.

In chapter 6, the letter starts, 'Heed the bishop that God may heed you too . . .' and raises the suspicion that this chapter is from a letter addressed to the community in general. After all, when writing to the bishop himself, Ignatius is unlikely to tell him to 'Heed the bishop . . .'.

Apart from this, the letter seems to be a genuine letter to Polycarp. However, when this is compared with the six other letters which are also attributed to Ignatius, there are significant differences in tone which raise doubts about some parts, if not all, of these letters. The authoritative and confident tone of the letter to Polycarp is often missing from these other letters. The following are examples of an unexpected weakness, if in fact the writer was Ignatius. For example:

'I give you no orders as though I were somebody...' (Ephesians, chapter 3).

'I am now but being initiated into discipleship and I address you as my fellow disciples ...' (Ephesians, chapter 3).

'Pray for the Church in Syria ... though I am the least of the faithful there ...' (Ephesians, chapter 21).

'Not like Peter and Paul do I issue orders to you. They were Apostles ... At last I am on the way to being a disciple ...' (Romans, chapters 4 and 5).

It could be, of course, that the weak letters, or parts of them, were written by Ignatius when he was in a junior position. However, I doubt it, because the man of authority, even when in a junior position, would not write in that self-abasing way.

There seems, therefore, to be two writers who have unwittingly contributed to the Ignatius letters, the real Ignatius being the stronger, authoritative writer.

The average reader may not be over-interested in the New Testament letters. I have analysed them at some length in order to demonstrate that obvious evidence has been overlooked by theologians. This is because they have been so overawed by the thoughts of Paul, as set out in the letters believed to have been written by him, that they have carried out only a surface examination of the letters. They were more interested in the message, even though sometimes it was self-contradictory, than in examining the letters critically for what lies behind them.

From the evidence I have given, I do not think there can be any doubt that the writers of the letters were Essenes, and that Paul and the other writers were taking Essene beliefs about Jesus, the Essene Teacher, to the gentiles.

Some parts of the letters could quite easily have been

written by the Essene leadership during the time when the Essene sect was still a quite influential force in Judaic culture, prior to the rout of AD 68. For the reasons I have given, however, I am certain that most of the writing, perhaps all, originated in that period AD 68 to roughly AD 150, when the displaced Essenes were adjusting to their new situation.

What must be said about the writers, I think, is that they were men of outstanding character. At a time when the standard of living was low, the harshness of life may have made people look out for their own interests rather than those of their fellow men. This was not the Essene way.

Their motivation sprang from the belief that in order to represent God in the final conflict, the soldiers of God had to be perfect and without sin. It was a standard which put one's fellow man first and oneself second. It was a concept which led to the very highest standards. Even if involved in a quarrel with a fellow member, forgiveness must be immediate. When they enjoined the brethren to 'not let the sun go down on your anger', the injunction meant precisely that. To have delayed forgiveness would have been to let the emotions fester with sin. Although it is clear from the letters that there were many who fell from grace, it was not due to any lack of leadership.

Their thoughts and their standards were wholly admirable.

There can be no other judgement on the men represented by the writer who contributed to Philippians 4 : 8:

'. . . whatsoever is true, whatever is honourable, whatever is just, whatever is pure, whatever is lovely, whatever is gracious, if there is any excellence, think about these things'.

What fine men they were.

Conclusion

In my opinion the evidence is overwhelming. There are at least three identifiable men who have contributed to the Pauline letters, and the time-slot in which the letters were written was between AD 68 and the middle years of the 2nd century AD.

CHAPTER FIFTEEN

The New Christianity?

In this chapter I set out the reasons for believing in God and how I think the Church will develop in the future.

Surveys have shown that in the educated West there has been a consistent fall over the years in the numbers of people who believe in a personal God. It points clearly to the average man and woman rejecting the teachings of the Church, and there are now theologians who are beginning to doubt the existence of God. One recently defined God as the 'sum of our values who represents to us their ideal unity'.

I am in no doubt that what I call the 'coincidence factor' rules out any explanation for the Universe and the amazing life we find within it, other than a personal, loving and concerned God.

The coincidence factor

When we consider how the Universe came to be formed, we come across a theological brick wall. The choices are:

1. That the atoms from which the Universe is made have appeared out of nothing. The trouble with this theory is that it defies our experience of life. Everything, even the first atom, must have been subject to some influence which caused it to form. If, originally, there was a void where there were no temperature changes, no pressures and no factors which might have caused the first atom to form, then there seems no convincing explanation for the proposition that atoms could appear out of nothing.

2. That the atoms have always been in existence – they never had a beginning. Again, it really does not make sense to suppose that the vast number of atoms which make up our Universe were here all the time. Our experience tells us that everything must have a beginning.

3. That God created the Universe. The trouble with this theory, as with the previous one, is that it raises the question: even God must have had a beginning, so where did God come from?

Strangely enough, the three objections given could be used to prove that there is no Universe and that we – me, the writer and you, the reader – are not and cannot be here. And yet, against all the theory, we are here.

To be an agnostic is not the answer; it is the theological cop-out. It is obvious that there is something which we do not understand, and in order to reach some conclusion about the beginning of the Universe, perhaps a different approach is called for. I call it the coincidence factor.

When coincidence follows coincidence and they continue, one can be reasonably certain that what we are witnessing is a series not of coincidences but the revelation of some truth which was not previously apparent.

Consider these:

1. When matter was first created, was it coincidence that of all the atom designs which might have been developed, the particular design which did materialise was one of such breathtaking uniqueness and perfection?

2. Was it a coincidence that the design was such that the basic atom design could incorporate an extra charge to change it from a hydrogen atom into a different element, and that the design allows for further additional charges to be incorporated to give a range of over 100 different elements?

3. Was it coincidence in the original design which allowed the different atomic elements to combine into molecules and then to form more complex compounds?

4. When the mass of molecular compounds was flung in all directions at the time of the Big Bang, was it coincidence

that the mass had the characteristics to form into stars and galaxies?

5. Was it yet another outrageous accident that the original design of the atom allowed, when the conditions were just right, for inert matter to change into life-forming structures on at least one planet?

6. Was it another prodigious coincidence that when life developed, the original design of the atom was just the correct design which allowed the life-forms to reproduce themselves?

7. Further, can coincidence take credit for the most amazing development of all – that the original atomic design enabled life to develop into an intelligent form of immense complexity which can think, reason, invent and do all the things which a creator, God, would have designed it to do?

8. It is one thing for life to appear suddenly, but quite another for it to prosper. We can be grateful that the original design of the atom permitted the right cocktail of chemical compounds to be generated in the air and ground for human and plant life to thrive.

9. Basic to life is an abundance of water, and associated with it a climatic system which ensures a self-cleansed, recycled and widely distributed supply for most of the world; again, we have to thank that original design.

10. What good fortune, too, that plant life and the water we drink provides the sustenance needed by human and animal life. What might have followed had the atom design been different and water had been poisonous?

11. But this is only the beginning. So that man could exploit the resources of the world it would be essential that he had specific in-built characteristics:
   — a memory so that he could learn from experience – and he has;
   — curiosity about his environment, for without it the secrets of the world would remain hidden – and he has;
   — logic and intelligence in order to exploit his curiosity – and he has;

> — an in-built desire to reproduce, without which the species would become extinct – and he has.

Is it coincidence that we have these and many other qualities without which our advancement would have been significantly impaired, and probably made impossible?

12. Further, at a material level, is it by accident that the minerals necessary for civilisation to prosper are available in abundance?

Without fossil fuels, laid down millions of years ago and now on-stream in the form of oil to lubricate and fuel machines, the industrialisation of the world may well have been made impossible.

Without metals, the development of electrically-operated appliances might never have taken place.

The list of natural resources without which civilisation would have been still-born could be extended considerably.

By accident, it appears, we have all that we need for an interesting and fascinating life. Is this sheer chance?

Do we really appreciate how well designed the world is? Unfortunately, familiarity breeds contempt. We accept the amazing complexity of life without too much thought. That is the way life has worked out, we say, with a dismissive shrug of the shoulders and without considering the theoretical impossibility of it happening at all.

What a miraculous and outrageous extravaganza is this life and the Universe we see around us.

Surely it is not the believer in God but the unbeliever who has some explaining to do.

We might ask ourselves, what would have been the effect on the Universe if a different design of atom had been originally formed?

Would it have led to the creation of new elements, compounds and masses from which planets, stars and galaxies developed?

Could life have self-generated?

Would it have been intelligent life?

Would it have been a life in which, from a very primitive

understanding of nature, there was at first puzzlement, and then interest and excitement as the secrets were unravelled, so that life was eventful, sometimes for good sometimes for ill, but always interesting?

Our science fiction writers use their vivid imaginations to describe forms of life and civilisations on other stars and planets. Despite their talent for invention, none has ever described a form of intelligent life which is basically very different from life here on earth. The characters depicted seem to have the same emotions – hate, love, aggression, timidity, cruelty and kindness, and forms which can be wounded and killed. They have heads to contain the brain, legs to give mobility, and arms and hands to aid manipulation. Even our ingenious writers have not come up with a completely new form of life which might have sprung from another design of atom.

Is there anything missing from the life we have which results from the atom we have?

We enjoy love, thrills, excitement, pleasure, affection, friendliness and many more emotions. If there are any new, previously unexperienced emotions then I cannot think what they might be.

There is, of course, the other side of the coin. We might prefer life without the hatred, cruelty and sometimes barbarism which we know all too well is part of life today. Nevertheless, as I argue later, even the unpleasant emotions can sometimes play a part helpful to society.

How is it, then, that the right design of atom came into being? Why not the wrong type? We know the facts; we consider them and then make a decision. We can choose to think that it was coincidence, but in my opinion sheer chance has played no part whatsoever. We have, surely by design, everything needed to enable us to experience interesting and eventful lives.

Free will or predestination?

Free will
The concept of 'free will' was inspired by a wish to justify the

appearance on earth of Jesus Christ. Man was sinful; he had the freedom to choose between good and evil and was rejecting Godly virtues. Hence, God sent Jesus Christ as our Saviour, and the teaching of the Church is that those who follow Jesus will have everlasting life. Teaching changes, and although those who reject Jesus were thought at one time to face being cast into the everlasting fires of Hell, the Church seems to have modified its position. The future fate of non-believers now varies according to the speaker.

The portrayal of God is muddled. It asks us to accept that God created mankind with a predilection for sin, and then blamed mankind for its behaviour. We are, after all, as He designed us.

Why should a creator, who made us as we are, warts and all, need to send His son to save us? The only one who would punish us if we failed to follow the righteous life, would be God himself. Instead of sending His son to die on the cross, all He need do is to refrain from punishing us or, alternatively, to change the mould and make us righteous in the first place.

There is another aspect to the theory of free will which I find unconvincing. How can an all-knowing God not know what is to happen in the future?

God created the atoms which make up the stars, galaxies and mankind.

He had total control and He achieved his plan of life as we live it upon this earth, because the atoms performed as they were intended to do.

God is 'all-knowing' because the Universe is His design. If God knows what is to happen therefore, how can there be 'free will'?

Predestination

There is a natural order at even the lowest levels of life which point to a predestined programming of behaviour as part of the Grand Design.

In Matthew 6 : 26 Jesus says: 'Look at the birds of the air; they neither sow nor reap nor gather into barns and yet your heavenly Father feeds them'.

Birds, and every other living species, have specific control mechanisms built into the brain. The cuckoo does not know why it lays its eggs in the nests of other birds, but each and every cuckoo behaves that way. The cuckoo chick, barely out of its own shell, does not know why it pushes the host eggs out of the nest. This predestined pattern of behaviour, designed by God, thus ensures the continuance of the cuckoo species.

What would happen if the life of the cuckoo were not predestined and it did not follow the normal cuckoo mating rituals? There would be chaos. Out of the confusion which would surely follow, there would come comedy. The cuckoo might be attracted to a rabbit or a beaver. It might try to build a warren or a lodge. With all the other species acting independently, it is not too difficult to predict not only the disorder ahead, but the very extinction of life.

Consider the consequences of cuckoos being born without the predestined and natural attraction of one cuckoo for another.

Lacking direction, out of 400 cuckoos, only 10 per cent mate to produce 20 eggs. When the 400 die, leaving 20 chicks, only 10 per cent subsequently mate to produce 1 egg.

When the 20 die, the lone chick would have no potential mate.

Lack of in-built direction would also affect our plant life. The pollen-spreading activities of insects, now no longer programmed, would cease to be carried out efficiently. The same problems would affect invisible life as well as the visible. How could man plan any form of prevention against, or attack upon, germs and viruses if these were random in their behaviour?

Unorganised lifestyles might lead to the extinction of germs, and although this would be good for humanity, it could also lead to the extinction of man – we would be no less affected than the other forms of life.

I conclude that a laissez faire, non-programmed nature would lead to the extinction of life.

Further, that order enables life to flourish and that predestination is the only way the Great Designer can achieve control, not only of the present but also the future. Everything

241

I see about me reinforces my belief that there is an in-built direction to life.

I cannot believe, for example, that God would, with a twist of His finger, twirl the atoms around and, having seen them settled into stars and galaxies, wait to see what would happen to the life He had created.

What a complete waste of time it would have been if some action by a super-hydrogen bomb-owning dictator blew the Universe to smithereens. Would God hand over responsibility for the future of His creation to some irrational mortal? Designs are created for a specific purpose. Would a great architect order cement, timber, plumbing materials *et al.*, arrange for their delivery to a site and then wait to see what happens? There could be no circumstances which would lead to these materials moving methodically and logically into positions such as would produce a building of any sort, let alone one that would be to the architect's satisfaction.

The sensible architect produces a design, decides how best this can be achieved with the engagement of labour and materials, and finishes up with a building which will fulfil its design specification.

Would God do otherwise?

We can see that He has already done it.

Following their predetermined course, the atoms have formed into molecules and compounds.

The compounds formed masses which eventually spun forth into planets, stars and galaxies.

On one of these planets He took inert matter one stage further and created plant life.

Having predetermined every stage of the development of the Universe why should God stop when He created human life?

We may seem to have a free will to do as we wish, but if stars and galaxies function according to His design, why not people? The body, and the brain that motivates it, is no more than a complex chemical compound, and in our daily lives we are merely responding to other mobile chemical compounds. Having designed the atoms which make up the compounds, how could God be unaware of how His own atoms would behave relative to each other?

Worldly computers can perform their mind-blowing calculations in fractions of a second. Whilst human behaviour is infinitely complex, would the Divine computer have any problems in predicting the future progress of human atomic reactions?

The key to predestination is the original design of the atom. Once this was fixed, then the atoms could be relied upon to react to one another in predictable ways to give an equally predictable course of events, which will lead inevitably to an equally predictable conclusion.

If the starting-off point is fixed and the behaviour pattern also, then the outcome must also be fixed.

In these circumstances, how could God 'not know' about our individual futures?

In verses from Matthew, in fact, Jesus seems to be alluding to a predestination in chapter 10 : 29–31 which reads: 'Are not two sparrows sold for a penny? And not one of them will fall to the ground without your Father's will. But even the hairs on your head are numbered. Fear not, therefore; you are of more value than many sparrows'.

If we are to take these verses as expressing the word of God, then they clearly relate to a life controlled by God rather than one in which free will operates.

Given that life is fated to the nth degree, what sort of existence would we choose for ourselves if we were able to do so, and how would it compare with the life that God has given us?

What sort of life would we choose?

Revelations 21 : 4 reads: 'And God himself will be with them; he will wipe away every tear from their eyes and death shall be no more, neither shall there be mourning nor crying nor pain any more for the former things have passed away'.

Revelations seems to be describing perfection, and our natural reaction is to agree with the sentiments. But I am sure that if we experienced perfection for even a short time we would become so utterly and completely bored with life that we would yearn for the excitements and uncertainties of our normal lives.

Solitary confinement is not, I think, an unfair example of perfection.

There would be warmth and food.

There would be no personal relationship problems.

Finances would never be a worry.

A chair and bed would ensure no discomfort.

But the sheer complete and utter boredom of it all would quickly have us crying out for the life we have today – problems no doubt, but at least there would be incidents to lighten as well as darken the day, there would be interest, and our minds and energies would be engaged.

If this has been a fair description of perfection, then it must rate as the equivalent of being in Hell. The uncertainty of life, for all its difficulties would be, by comparison, Heaven.

We tend to accept the pictures painted by the Church of an after-life full of happiness. It is never explained what we are supposed to do; we are left to imagine tranquility and happiness, but with no clear indication from the Church which might help us to understand how we reach and maintain this contented state.

If God is to give us an existence, is it not reasonable to expect Him to give us the best life possible? If Heaven was the way to happiness should we not have been allowed to stay there? If living on earth is second best then why should a loving God treat us this way?

I think it is reasonable to conclude that the life we have been given is the superior existence – that Heavenly perfection is Hell and Hellish life on earth is Heaven.

We tend to look on conflict as a sinful activity, but when one examines it more closely, it seems to be one of the most important aspects of life. Certainly, in the way it is designed, conflict is an essential element in making life interesting. Most of the games we devise are based on conflict, albeit friendly.

Twenty-two soccer players attacking the same goal is boring.

Thirty racing cars going at the same speed is boring.

Two tennis players, each wanting to help the other score the point would be boring.

The games only become interesting when the twenty-two soccer players divide into two teams with two goals, the racing drivers each try to lead the field and the tennis players try to out-score their opponents.

Conflict creates interest.

It may also give rise to problems, but then solving these generates more interest. Consider this: God created three different ethnic groups – Caucasoids, Negroids and Mongoloids, none of whom are immediately attracted to one another. Within the ethnic groups, there are various racial groups which, again, are not naturally disposed to each other, and who occupy land whose borders are a constant source of friction.

Furthermore, as if to add to the problems, in civil wars, we fight among ourselves.

Finally, and this may be the coup-de-grâce, He created man and woman.

This is not a design for peace and tranquility. It brings into play powerful forces not only at a personal, but also at a national level, and has given us a world history of wars and conquests which continues to this day.

It is a life in which out of the bad qualities, good can come.

We tend to assume that certain attitudes to life – greed, ambition, disregard for others – are bad for mankind, but these and others equally unattractive can be factors in moving civilisation forward.

During the past centuries, explorers and adventurers, for their own gain, have unfairly dispossessed natives of land and assets which were not being used and then developed them to everyone's advantage.

Unbridled ambition may not be attractive, but the man who ruthlessly pushes others as well as himself may drive the company forward to greater success.

Captains of the early sailing ships disregarded the living conditions of the crews and in so doing, played a part in developing trade between nations.

I am not, of course, recommending greed and ruthlessness,

only asking for recognition of the fact that the impetus for change and improvement come from unlikely directions.

As the world moves forward we can see a gradual improvement in the standard of living for more and more people.

It may not make them any happier. Once we have an improvement, the higher standard becomes the norm and we then want more. But we never have to suffer the dullness of perfection.

If there is a meaning to life, I can only think that it is intended that life should be an adventure, a problem-solving and interesting life which we see through from beginning to end. One life seems pointless. If it is short, what experience can we gain from that?

But if we enjoy more than one life (but with no memory access to previous lives) then if one life is very short, or very troubled, then the likelihood is that the next – or the one after that – will be better.

Disasters involving perhaps thousands of people have been part of human experience since time immemorial. It is tragic, and we should do all we can to avoid repetitions of these calamities. Nevertheless, it is not one man losing his life a thousand times, but thousands losing their lives once. What might at first be seen as God's cruel world becomes a little less so if, in fact, there is a later rebirth for every victim.

One might think that those starving in Africa would willingly change places so that they might live in a perfect environment. I am sure that if problems create interest, they would claim that their lives had enough interesting problems to last them many lifetimes. Nevertheless, if we were given the choice of perfect surroundings or the risk of a life which may be good, bad or indifferent, we would choose to take our chance with the three variables. Anything would be an improvement on perpetual boredom. Long live imperfection.

Prayers

Can prayer help?

Does God answer prayers?

Most of us who have prayed, with only partial success, may have been satisfied, even though disappointed, with an explanation given by some genius who sought to absolve God from blame. God, he said, does answer all prayers, but sometimes He has to say 'no'. What a breathtakingly brilliant answer.

It neatly sidesteps the whole point of the prayer; we are not asking for a yes/no response; we want a 'yes'.

We might bear in mind that if God responded favourably to prayers, that someone's plus is almost certainly matched by another's minus. A favour for one is a disfavour for others.

You pray that you may get the advertised job – but then 20 other applicants fail.

You pray that you may win the girl's affection – but others are the losers.

For every winner, there is at least one loser.

As I argue shortly, I believe life to be fated, and in these circumstances there can be no question of prayers being answered.

The Great Play of Life

Shakespeare was very perceptive when he likened people to being actors on life's great stage.

If life is fated to the nth degree then we are indeed players in the Great Play of Life. The script has been written, the roles have been cast and, as in all well-crafted plays, every word, every action, by every character plays its part in taking the play from its beginning to the final curtain. The storyline has been written and cannot be changed. We are all essential. Without being aware of what influence we have in developing the story, it is there nevertheless. The best of us and the worst of us, the longest life to the shortest life, all direct the course of events in accordance with the Divine plot.

No one is more important than the other. Some may seem to enjoy the leading roles and the best speaking parts. But in a predestined life, no one is more important or less so than any other.

You, the reader, may think your life humdrum, that you are

undervalued by society and that due to circumstances beyond your control, you have not made any useful contribution to mankind. And yet you have. Your role is absolutely essential. You, modest by nature and humble in circumstance, are just as important to the unfolding plot of the Great Play as any of the great names that bestride world history.

Even the non-speaking roles are essential to the story.

The baby dies stillborn; the school-bound toddler is killed in an accident. The parents are heartbroken. They have lived good and honest lives and have done no one any wrong. They ask why God should have punished them in this way and why God should have ordained that the young life, so dear to them, should be extinguished so suddenly and so unnecessarily. But God designed laws governing the behaviour of the atom and once they have been brought into play, they grind inexorably on in accordance with the Great Design. There can be no exceptions; no special laws to operate where children are concerned and no hand of God to sweep down from Heaven to rescue those in danger.

The role of the child, sadly for those closest, has been written out. It was a life that was predestined to be short. It had played its part in being an influence in the lives of the parents, relatives and friends.

The baby or the youth or the husband who dies has completed their part, leaving behind the rest of the cast to carry the play forward. They too, will be affected by the death, and so the baby, youth or husband will be influencing the lives of others even though no longer here.

It may not make the pain any the less to look at it this way, but if the reason for the death is understood, perhaps some of the agonising can be avoided.

It is, however, incidents such as these that affect others indirectly, sometimes favourably and sometimes not.

An observer, having seen a tragedy unfold, may be inspired to take action which later helps others. Grieving parents may be unable to cope with their loss and, as a result, the marriage breaks up.

However, the ripples of multi-million incidents, good and bad, intermesh and bring changes to lives which are unexpected and perhaps unwelcome, but still essential to the development of the Great Play of Life.

Sometimes, when there is death, people attach blame to themselves for some action which they took; they feel it may have led to the death of a loved one or perhaps a stranger. They should not worry.

Sins of omission and commission are all part of the plot. As far as the hereafter is concerned, there can be no retribution for any sins committed on earth. This is not, of course, a carte blanche to engage in an orgy of sin. There may be no punishment in Heaven for earthly sins, but there are man-made laws operating on earth which may bring heavy punishment to the over-enthusiastic sinner.

It must be good news that, whether as a result of carelessness, accident or even deliberate intention, because it was in the storyline, it simply had to happen. It could not 'not happen'.

This thought should take away some of the anxiety which may affect people following an unhappy experience. We are not to blame. All we have been doing is, unwittingly, to speak the lines and follow the directions which are laid down in the script. Whatever it was that someone thought they did, or didn't do, or couldn't do, or even thought they should have done was simply a compliance with the predetermined unfolding of life.

Why does God not reveal Himself to us?

If God did reveal Himself by appearing as a smiling face in the sky, then at least we would be absolutely certain of the truth. A consideration of the consequences of doing so, however, explains why this would be counterproductive.

Every day, thousands of people, young and old, die unexpectedly, tragically, in unforeseen circumstances, quite apart from those whose sad end is predictable because of terminal illness. Those nearest and dearest to the deceased would see the smiling face of God in the sky and resent the complacency. Here was a personal sadness which affected each of them. God would be aware of every individual case, and yet would do nothing to help. Instead of love for God, there would be hatred. An all-knowing God could have foreseen and prevented the illness or the accident or whatever circumstance led to the death. Human nature, programmed as it is, would blame God.

We have, therefore, an unusual situation.

Whilst God remains invisible to us, we bear with fortitude the inequities of life and still love God.

Seeing Him, however, we would be discontented and bitter at His inaction.

On consideration, one is left to conclude that remaining invisible seems the better and wiser option.

But does God need to reveal Himself?

Perhaps a short story might help to illustrate the point.

Some months ago, I had a wasps nest in my loft and after it had been sprayed with insecticide, I took down the nest for examination. The outer shell of the six inch diameter sphere was a protective cover which was made up of microscopically thin wafers of material. Inside there were three structures, rather like mini flying saucers, with the two lower units linked to the one above by a central pillar, perhaps a sixteenth of an inch in diameter. There were four minor pillars towards the perimeter. The honeycomb structure was made up of cells approximately one eighth of an inch wide, and each was a model of precision engineering. This was constructed by the wasps without any architectural plans, in total darkness and without the wasps having had any constructional training whatsoever.

Isn't the little wasp to be admired?

Well, no, not really.

Surely we have to look for a designer who could conceive and then produce such programmed behaviour into each and every teeny wasp brain.

Is not God saying with this and the myriad of quite breathtaking wonders of the world and of life hereon, 'Do I really need to show Myself? Does not the ingeniousness of life and the sheer unbelievability of life together with the logical impossibility of life tell you that there must be a Great Designer – Me?'.

Jesus and the chosen people

Were the Jews the chosen race? If so, in what sense? Were the Jews superior intellectually or were they the medium best suited to transmitting His word to the world? I think the answer is 'yes' to both questions.

I believe that life is programmed to the nth degree.

It follows, therefore, that Jesus and the influence he has had on millions of lives was a part of God's plan.

God's problem – if it is not blasphemous to suggest such a thing – was to introduce Jesus in such a way that he was believed to be the Son of God and that his teachings were believed to be the will of God.

The way chosen was not the obvious one. The most persuasive introduction would have been for Jesus to make a miraculous emergence from Heaven at a time when there could be absolutely no doubt that a Divine spirit had come upon earth. But, as I have argued, miracles do not happen and do not need to happen.

If Jesus had appeared in the 20th century, for example, when there were writers to record his life with accuracy, we would have been in no doubt that Jesus was a Jew who regarded his mission as solely to the Jews. The forces of Light which were to fight on behalf of God were to be the Essene Jews, the 7,000 remnant of Elijah. In these circumstances, his mission would have been recognised as being of no interest to gentiles. The miracles attributed to Jesus, and the virgin birth would have been investigated and would not, on investigation, have supported his claim to be the miracle-working Son of God.

Certain conditions would have to be met if the Jesus legend was to be carried forward to the gentiles, and for it to be an influence on the developing Western civilisation:

1. The life of Jesus needed to be at a time when the written word described religious rather than secular events. Too much 'newspaper style' reporting might have disposed of the myth that later surrounded Jesus and shown him for what he was – a heretical Jewish Rabbi who opposed the establishment and was, as a result, persecuted.

2. It was necessary that he was born among people who were religious to the point of fanaticism. Had they not been religious and keen recorders of the history of their believed association with God, we would not have had the Dead Sea Scrolls, the Bible and the corpus of Rabbinical writings.

3. It was also required that the people were academically and creatively the most outstanding race. To have chosen otherwise – there are some groups that have not, even after 2,000 years, made any significant contributions to civilisation, have not invented writing materials or a script for recording their history – would have meant that there might have been no written record of the life of Jesus.

4. It required the followers of Jesus to write in a veiled, cryptic style which protected them and their beliefs from outsiders. Had the Romans understood that they were likely to be the enemy of the Essenes in the final conflict between the forces of Light and Dark, they may have attacked the Essenes before the fateful rout at Qumran in AD 68, and thus changed the course of history.

5. The secrecy adopted by the Essenes had the further effect of the Scrolls being hidden in caves for safekeeping. The discovery of the Scrolls enabled the truth about the origins of Christianity to be revealed 2,000 years later.

6. The desire for secrecy had another effect; it is obvious that the writers of the New Testament letters attributed to Paul were not particularly well informed about the life of Jesus. Had they been aware that Jesus's mission was intended to be solely to the Jews, the teachings may not have been taken to the gentiles.

If the Jews had not been an academically outstanding race, fanatically religious, inventive, inclined to secrecy and with considerable energy, the Jesus story might never have been recorded; there would have been no Talmud, no Dead Sea Scrolls and no Old and New Testaments. It required a race of outstanding talent to be the medium for delivering God's message to the developing gentile civilisation of the West. In this sense, therefore, I have no doubt that the Jews were the chosen race.

In this way, God's will has been fulfilled. Jesus was accepted by the gentiles as the Son of God who promised that those who committed themselves to him would enjoy forgiveness for their sins and a life in the hereafter.

It was a simple message given by those early Christian fathers who knew only a little of the detailed Essene writings, but encapsulated what they knew into the injunction 'Love thy neighbour'.

The Church which resulted was able to influence Western thinking into taking a more sympathetic attitude to the unfortunates of this world. It has been an immense influence for good. It is possible to point to the pogroms against the Jews, the friction between Protestant and Roman Catholic, between Jew and Arab and, indeed, other non-Christian religions in the world, and berate religion for the cruelties and intolerance which it has bred. In my opinion, these prove only that religion involves fierce passions.

Christianity in particular has motivated men and women to work unselfishly, devoting their lives to caring for others. There can be few people living in Western countries whose lives have not been touched, for the better, either in their physical or mental well-being, by Christian beliefs and a faith in God.

This must continue to be so.

The Church and the future

It might be thought that the Christian Churches, and in particular the Roman Catholic Church, will resist energetically any changes in belief which might be required in the future.

I think not.

I cannot see how the various Churches can do other than accept the evidence in this book and the new light on the origins of Christianity which will be confirmed when the translations of the Dead Sea Scrolls are finally available. When this happens, the Roman Catholic clerics who have had control of the translations will have some explaining to do. In advance of this, we might try to understand their motives for withholding the translations.

They would reason that there must be a God to explain the miraculous Universe we see around us. Their years of study and the words of all past theologians from the Apostolic fathers to the present day have shown Jesus Christ as an essential part of His design. They would conclude, therefore, that if the Dead Sea Scrolls seemed to place Jesus in the 1st century BC and appeared to identify him with the Teacher of Righteousness, then there was something wrong – that somewhere, as yet not revealed, there would be another piece in the jigsaw which would explain this anomaly in a reasonable and sensible way. This missing piece, they would think, would prove that the traditional Christian beliefs about Jesus and the origins of Christianity were absolutely correct. To have published the translations before that vital piece was found would have been to undermine, quite unnecessarily, the beliefs of millions of Christians and throw the Church into confusion.

Unfortunately, there is no missing piece. But you can forgive the thinking. It was well meant. And if I am correct, then there must be sympathy for the almost impossible position which the clerics were (and are) in. They have been criticised for not publishing and would have been censured if they had. Two thousand years of misunderstanding has meant that they simply cannot win. The truth is now revealed, but I do not think there will be resentment from the Churches. Instead, I think there will be relief that the uncertainty is over and that, on reflection, it will be seen as an opportunity to take Christian thinking along a slightly different course.

In a book entitled *The Myth of God Incarnate* which was written by seven leading theologians and deals with some of the problems associated with Christianity, the following statement appears: 'The writers of this book are convinced that another major theological development is called for in this last part of the 20th century'.

Belief in God will continue and be stronger for the emphasis which will be placed on the multiple wonders of the world. Jesus will be recognised as the protégé of God, a man fated to come and give to the developing Western civilisation a new set of standards. Not only should one love God but there should be a recognition of one's duty to one's fellow man and, on the grander scale, a duty of countries to help their neighbours.

The life and teachings of Jesus and the devotion of tens of thousands of Christians who have worked for the Church have influenced the lives of billions of people for the better.

The support which has been built up over 2,000 years must not be lost, but it would be at risk if the Churches mishandle the problems of the immediate future. They could choose to fight the evidence in this book and the translations of the Scrolls when published, and assert their intention to stick to traditional beliefs. If the Churches did so, they would lose not only the respect of the laity but also of many of their own ministers. The evidence is overwhelming. No amount of semantics and clever phraseology will persuade a suspicious and perhaps scornful public that the Churches are right. Very soon they would lose all credibility.

Alternatively, they can accept the new evidence with good grace, even though it throws a new light on the origins of Christianity. They could rightly claim that if there were mistakes, they were errors made on the best evidence available at the time. This will permit the truth to do what the truth has always done – to allow people to make decisions based on fact not fiction. The honesty of the Churches will be respected. And the basic beliefs will remain as before.

Jesus is still Jesus.

Mary, albeit Mary Magdalene, was his mother.

It was an illegitimate birth, but then, it was always suspected as such.

There is a God and Jesus was very much part of His plan.

So, what is new? The perspective has changed rather than the substance.

The old assurance of the Churches that 'Because there was a miracle worker called Jesus, you can believe in God' will now be changed to, 'It is such a wondrous world that you can believe in God – and the evidence clearly tells us that there really was a Jesus who played a vital role in bringing new standards of conduct to the developing Western civilisation'.

The Roman Catholic Church, with its world-wide presence will be influential in bringing the new Christianity to the people. Although generally regarded as the bastion of a traditional and rigidly controlled theology, it is led by men of outstanding ability. They will be able to discard some of the shibboleths which have divided one Church from another. There will be an acceptance that God does not intervene as a result of prayers or in developments which cause problems for those on earth. Gone, too, will be some of the rituals and beliefs which have actually prevented many from joining – and which have possibly influenced many to actually leave – the Church.

As a result, there would be little to separate the various factions within the Christian Churches. This could lead, perhaps, to a unification of the Churches within Christianity. That would be a great step forward. I think we can look forward, in the next 50 years or so, to a Church stronger and more united than ever before. Instead of the Dead Sea Scrolls destroying or weakening the Church, I think they will have the very opposite effect.

The new beliefs will be accepted because they are rational and make sense to people. Prayers will be an accepted way of thanking God for the gift of life, but there will be no prayers for future favours because our lives have already been scripted.

The Church will become more outward looking and develop into an organisation for helping the slow developers, the underdogs of society, and those who live in the poverty-stricken nations. The priests and nuns of various denominations will be invaluable in continuing and broadening the work of bringing physical and spiritual comfort to those in need.

Their work through the various Church agencies and organisations such as the Salvation Army has been exemplary. The Church will become less 'prayer centred' and much more involved in actively helping others.

What better way can there be of loving one's neighbour?
What better way of serving God?